Business Cycles in the Contemporary World

Contributions to Economics

http://www.springer.de/cgi-bin/search_book.pl?series=1262

Georg Bol/Gholamreza Nakhaeizadeh/
Karl-Heinz Vollmer (Eds.)
Risk Measurements, Econometrics and Neural Networks
1998. ISBN 3-7908-1152-1

Joachim Winter
Investment and Exit Decisions at the Plant Level
1998. ISBN 3-7908-1154-8

Bernd Meyer
Intertemporal Asset Pricing
1999. ISBN 3-7908-1159-9

Uwe Walz
Dynamics of Regional Integration
1999. ISBN 3-7908-1185-8

Michael Carlberg
European Monetary Union
1999. ISBN 3-7908-1191-2

Giovanni Galizzi/
Luciano Venturini (Eds.)
Vertical Relationships and Coordination in the Food System
1999. ISBN 3-7908-1192-0

Gustav A. Horn/Wolfgang Scheremet/
Rudolf Zwiener
Wages and the Euro
1999. ISBN 3-7908-1199-8

Dirk Willer
The Development of Equity Capital Markets in Transition Economies
1999. ISBN 3-7908-1198-X

Karl Matthias Weber
Innovation Diffusion and Political Control of Energy Technologies
1999. ISBN 3-7908-1205-6

Heike Link et al.
The Costs of Road Infrastructure and Congestion in Europe
1999. ISBN 3-7908-1201-3

Simon Duindam
Military Conscription
1999. ISBN 3-7908-1203-X

Bruno Jeitziner
Political Economy of the Swiss National Bank
1999. ISBN 3-7908-1209-9

Irene Ring et al. (Eds.)
Regional Sustainability
1999. ISBN 3-7908-1233-1

Katharina Müller/Andreas Ryll/
Hans-Jürgen Wagener (Eds.)
Transformation of Social Security: Pensions in Central-Eastern Europe
1999. ISBN 3-7908-1210-2

Stefan Traub
Framing Effects in Taxation
1999. ISBN 3-7908-1240-4

Pablo Coto-Millán
Utility and Production
1999. ISBN 3-7908-1153-X

Frank Riedel
Imperfect Information and Investor Heterogeneity in the Bond Market
2000. ISBN 3-7908-1247-1

Kirsten Ralf
Business Cycles
2000. ISBN 3-7908-1245-5

Michele Bagella/Leonardo Becchetti (Eds.)
The Competitive Advantage of Industrial Districts
2000. ISBN 3-7908-1254-4

Frank Bohn
Monetary Union and Fiscal Stability
2000. ISBN 3-7908-1266-8

Jaime Behar
Cooperation and Competition in a Common Market
2000. ISBN 3-7908-1280-3

Michael Malakellis
Integrated Macro-Micro-Modelling Under Rational Expectations
2000. ISBN 3-7908-1274-9

Stefan Baumgärtner
Ambivalent Joint Production and the Natural Environment
2000. ISBN 3-7908-1290-0

Henri Capron, Wim Meeusen (Eds.)
The National Innovation System of Belgium
2000. ISBN 3-7908-1308-7

Tobias Miarka
Financial Intermediation and Deregulation
2000. ISBN 3-7908-1307-9

Chisato Yoshida
Illegal Immigration and Economic Welfare
2000. ISBN 3-7908-1315-X

continued on page 166

Bernd Süssmuth

Business Cycles in the Contemporary World

Description, Causes, Aggregation, and Synchronization

With 25 Figures and 17 Tables

Physica-Verlag
A Springer-Verlag Company

Series Editors
Werner A. Müller
Martina Bihn

Author
Dr. Bernd Süssmuth
University of Bamberg
Department of Economics (Economic Policy)
Feldkirchenstraße 21
96045 Bamberg
Germany
bernd.suessmuth@sowi.uni-bamberg.de

ISSN 1431-1933
ISBN 3-7908-1532-2 Physica-Verlag Heidelberg New York

Cataloging-in-Publication Data applied for
A cataolog record for this book is available form the Library of Congress.
Bibliographic information published by Die Deutsche Bibliothek
Die Deutsche Bibliothek lists this publication in the Deutsche Nationalbibliografie; detailed bibliographic data is available in the Internet at <http://dnb.ddb.de>.

Physica-Verlag Heidelberg New York
a member of BertelsmannSpringer Science+Business Media GmbH

Printed in Germany

Softcover Design: Erich Kirchner, Heidelberg

SPIN 10890229 88/3130-5 4 3 2 1 0 – Printed on acid-free and non-aging paper

To Moni, my parents and my grandma († 1990)

Preface

The realization of the research project documented in this study would not have been possible without the kind support and help of several people. I want to take the opportunity to express my gratitude to them. My first and foremost thanks go to my thesis supervisor Claude Hillinger. He steadily supported my work with a host of ideas, criticism and encouragement. He has been influential and inspiring in his comments and criticism on all levels of development of this dissertation. My sincere thanks are due to Ulrich Woitek, teaching me from the very beginning in programming and letting me participate from his expert knowledge in time series analysis. Ulrich Woitek and Michael Reiter kindly provided me with software and encouraged me throughout the whole dissertation project with their comments and in discussions during their stays at Munich and via e-mail. They have helped me to take many hurdles, particularly in the early stages of the project. I am indebted to my co-supervisor Stephan Klasen for his engagement and open-minded interest in my thesis. To make the present work more readable, my friends in the US, Jean Czerlinsky and Radovan Vadovic, made great efforts to correct language and style. I owe a great debt of gratitude to them. I also thank Regina Riphahn and Burkhard Heer for their encouragement and helpful guidance.

Special thanks go to Barbara Dluhosch, Jakob de Haan, Burkhard Heer and Gerhard Illing. As their teaching assistant they all gave me the resources and necessary scope of development for my dissertation project in a stimulating environment at the Economics Department of the University of Munich. I thank Beatrice Dumpert and Brigitte Gebhard for their maternal motivational support and help in administrative matters. Finally, I am indebted to Maximilian Freier for his reliable support and for cross-reading numerous preliminary drafts of the thesis.

I gratefully acknowledge the Bavarian Young Scientists Grant (Promotionsstipendium nach dem Gesetz zur Förderung des bayerischen wissenschaftlichen Nachwuchses) for financial support during the first years of my dissertation project.

Munich, August 2002 *Bernd Süssmuth*

Contents

1. Introduction

Cycles are not like tonsils, separable things that might be treated by themselves, but are, like the beat of the heart, of the essence of the organ that displays them.
J. Schumpeter (1939)

The ultimate cause of cyclical fluctuations must therefore be sought in the investment motives of the business world, or, in other words, in the fluctuating propensity to invest.
L. Metzler (1946)

Perhaps the most important outcome of the acquisition and use of equipment may be what the experience of installing and using capital teaches workers and organizations ... investment is a necessary precondition to launch this process of learning and experience. This view also suggests that good economic policy contains incentives to boost investment in equipment.
J. Bradford De Long and L. H. Summers (1992)

The business cycle: It's still a puzzle. Good fiscal and monetary policy requires a clear understanding of the workings of the economy, especially what drives the business cycle — the periodic ups and downs in economic activity.
L. J. Christiano and T. J. Fitzgerald (1998)

1.1 Business Cycle Research: 21st Century Perspective

To understand the present, we need to know something about the past. This maxim applies also to our understanding of business cycles. Many contemporary economists take the general framework of Real Business Cycle (RBC) theory for granted, cf. Kydland (1995), noting that "[n]eoclassical growth theory has become the dominant theoretical framework in quantitative business cycle theory," p. 132. The RBC paradigm involves a representative agent, who maximizes his consumption stream over an infinite horizon. The resulting equilibrium path is disturbed by technology shocks. This paradigm is now about 20 years old. It has been severely criticized, both for the lack of realism of its assumptions and the continued failure to replicate characteristic features of the data, see for example Mankiw (1989): "In my view, real business cycle theory does not provide an empirically plausible explanation of economic fluctuations. Both its reliance on large technological disturbances as the primary source of economic fluctuations and its reliance on the intertemporal substitution of leisure are fundamental weaknesses ... [R]eal business cycle theory is potentially dangerous. The danger is that those who advise policy-makers might attempt to use it to evaluate the effects of alternative macroeconomic policies or to conclude that macroeconomic policies are unnecessary," p. 79. Similarly Muellbauer (1997) notes: "However empirical evidence ... shows that correcting for cyclical utilization results in shocks which are small and non-persistent. The second issue is empirical methodology. Though the RBC approach was intended as a response to the Lucas critique, by largely assuming away government policy feedback rules, these models are far from policy-relevant," p. 1. Recent criticism from an empirical perspective includes the article by Cochrane (1994), Gregory Mankiw's assessment of the 'important issues in modern macroeconomics,' presented in Snowdon and Vane (1995), p. 465-466, and the articles by Burnside, Eichenbaum and Rebelo (1996) and Hartley, Hoover and Salyer (1997), while Hansen and Heckman (1996), Sims (1996) or Collard (1996) severely criticize the RBC school from a more methodological point of view.[1] For an example, these authors state about the RBC research agenda: "[they] advocate the use of 'well-tested theories' in their essays, they never move beyond this slogan, and they do not justify their claim of fulfilling this criterion in their own research. 'Well tested' must mean more than 'familiar' or 'widely accepted' or 'agreed on by convention,' if it is to mean anything," see Hansen and Heckman (1996), p. 89; an overview of similar criticisms is summarized by Gregory and Smith (1995). A survey of the earlier strong criticisms of RBC theory is given by Stadler (1994).[2]

Prior to the advent of the RBC theory, a different approach dominated for nearly a century. Let us refer to it as the Classic Business Cycle (CBC) school. This approach, which evolved until about 1950, has been nearly forgotten. CBC research was driven by what its proponents regarded as stylized facts, i.e., empirical regularities discovered in the data. Most important was the discovery of *cycles* of characteristic average lengths in the different components of investment. The stylized facts thought to have been discovered by CBC theorists were much stronger and more specific than those assumed within the RBC framework. While the theory which evolved in the CBC tra-

[1] Although Mankiw in Snowdon and Vane (1995), Hartley, Hoover and Salyer (1997) as well as parts of the earlier critics refute the RBC approach on the preponderance of empirical evidence, the debate is partly overshadowed by ideological aspects (*Neo-Keynesian* vs. *Neoclassical* school).

[2] The quoted critiques address primarily the earlier "orthodox" RBC works. This criticisms include, for example, also the fundamental objections stated by Summers (1986) and Mankiw (1989). However, there are some recent research efforts in the RBC tradition ("second generation" RBC) that move away from the sole concentration on productivity shocks to the integration of cyclic investment dynamics. These are discussed in section 1.2.3.

dition to explain these regularities remained somewhat rudimentary, it does have central features which contrast sharply with RBC theory. In CBC theory cycles are generated by an endogenous dynamics involving the investment behavior of firms. Investment flows are adjusted, albeit sluggishly, so as to bring the actual capital stock in line with its desired level. An important role is played by fluctuating and contagious expectations. This feature has some analogy to contemporary work on herding.

The present work is in the CBC tradition in that its primary aim is to establish business cycle stylized facts, reveal their causes, and to unravel and explain what leading contemporary macroeconomists, for example Christiano and Fitzgerald (1998), see as the 'central puzzle' of business cycles: their comovement and synchronized pattern. In contrast to the older tradition, sophisticated statistical tools are employed. These tools for the descriptive analysis of time series have been taken from the contemporary practice of the natural sciences and offer a considerable contrast to current econometric practice with its emphasis on testing. The methodology is well suited to discriminate between the central assumptions of cycles driven primarily by an endogenous dynamics (CBC) or shocks (RBC). The following sections develop more fully the relationship of my work to the CBC and RBC tradition as well as to studies on business cycles at SEMECON, University of Munich, which are the precursors of my investigations.

1.1.1 The Classic View

The Classic view of business cycles originated with the work of Juglar (1889). Before that depressions were viewed as isolated episodes caused by external factors, such as wars or crop failures. Juglar's finding that periods of boom and bust tend to alternate in a roughly periodic fashion led to the coining of the term business cycle.[3] Compared to the modern theory, work on CBC extended over a much longer period and consisted of more scattered and isolated contributions. Nevertheless, there was an evolution, both of factual findings and of theoretical ideas to explain these. The mature CBC school recognized three distinct cycles[4] associated with different components of the capital stock: An inventory cycle of about 4 years (*Kitchin cycle*), an equipment (or fixed investment) cycle of about 8 years (*Juglar cycle*) and a building

[3] It is curious that this term completely replaced the more neutral 'economic fluctuations' both in general use and in the classification system of the American Economic Association (AEA) around the time that economists ceased to believe in the existence of 'cycles.' This is unfortunate, because the distinction between genuinely cyclical and other fluctuations is an important one.

[4] I use the word 'cycle' to describe the type of irregular periodic movement associated with a stochastic process possessing at least one complex root. Hillinger (1992) used the term 'quasi cycle' in this context. However, since no one seriously claims that economic cycles are strictly periodic, it seems better not to multiply terms.

cycle (*Kuznets swing*) of about 20 years.[5] The relative lengths of these cycles were explained by the speed with which the associated capital stock could be adjusted. This speed is greatest for inventories, intermediate for equipment and machinery, longest for building and other structures.

1.1.2 From CBC to RBC School

The transition from CBC to RBC theory involves shifts in several paradigms. The common tendency of these paradigma shifts is a movement away from a fairly direct description of reality, as the first step of the scientific process, towards an approach largely determined by prior theoretical commitments, specifically the neoclassical approach. Intertemporal optimization in the framework of a representative agent model turned attention away from endogenous dynamics and towards the view that fluctuations are essentially driven by random shocks.

Another important factor, motivating the paradigm shift from CBC to RBC, has been the observation of Slutzky (1937) that economic fluctuations look like the summation of a moving average of random shocks. The implication being that any observed periodicity is spurious. Adelman and Adelman (1959) extended this analysis to the case of a highly damped macroeconometric model with random shocks.

1.2 Recent Empirical Findings in Favor of CBC

Recent empirical work, though starting from different premisses, has pointed in the direction of CBC. Immediately following I describe the work of researchers who have looked for the stylized facts of economic fluctuations with a minimum of theoretical preconceptions. The next subsection describes work undertaken at SEMECON, which is more specifically in the CBC tradition in that it establishes the existence of investment cycles in macro-series. Finally, I describe some recent research in the RBC tradition that moves away from productivity shocks to cyclic investment dynamics.

1.2.1 Aggregate Investment Fluctuations and Business Cycles

Several recent studies have found that aggregate investment contributes most of the fluctuations of GDP in many industrialized economies. In his *Macroeconomics* textbook, Barro (1993) notes: "Broadly defined investment accounts for the bulk of the fluctuations in real GNP, 92% on average. Thus, at a first approximation, explaining recessions amounts to explaining the sharp contractions in the investment components," p. 220. Hall (1990) states that the

[5] Cycles of about 50 years, associated with major innovations, variously referred to as 'Kondratieff cycles', or 'long waves' were not a part of the CBC framework.

investment series makes the "greatest procyclical spending variability over business cycles - even adjusted for the smaller magnitude of investment compared to consumption," p. 8. In the same vein Hillinger (1992), p. 33, using data on US business cycles supplied by Gordon and Veitch (1986), calculates that fixed capital investment contributes an average of 51% of pre-war and 41% of post-war cyclical downturns. With regard to the understanding of business cycle dynamics, Courvisanos (1998) notes in his survey: "A rigorous analysis of investment cycles as the dominant feature of the business cycle pattern is a crucial aspect to understanding capital formation and economic progress," p. 4. In a recent empirical study on a comprehensive range of quarterly US post-war macroeconomic time series, Stock and Watson (1998) confirm the strong procyclicality and volatility of investment in equipment, residential and nonresidential structures. In another recent analysis of European business cycle fluctuations based on quarterly data for the period 1960 to 1998, Gallegatti and Gallegatti (2000) find that private total investment for 17 European economies is without exception procyclical and coinciding or slightly lagging to the cycle in GDP. They find the volatility of total investment to be 3 to 5 times that of GDP.

Concerning the causal direction of the equipment investment-cyclical growth nexus, Bradford De Long and Summers (1992) note: "We believe that the most powerful piece of evidence for attributing causal significance to the equipment-[cyclical] growth nexus is the negative association between equipment prices on the one hand and equipment investment and [cyclical] growth on the other. If high rates of investment were a consequence, rather than a cause of [cyclical] growth, one would expect equipment prices to be higher in rapidly growing countries because of strong demand pressing on the limits of supply," p. 176. That the latter is not the case and cyclical growth is "caused" by equipment investment is empirically shown for 31 countries in their so-called 'high-productivity sample'.

1.2.2 The Cyclicality of the Aggregate Investment Series

The business cycle research at SEMECON has attempted to advance the CBC approach both in relation to stylized facts and explanatory models. In this context new statistical methods were developed, specifically continuous time estimation for the explanatory models and Maximum Entropy (ME-) spectral analysis for the determination of stylized facts. The stylized facts reported in the first chapters of part II and III of the monograph were obtained by this method that will be outlined in greater detail in part I. A series of empirical studies analyzed the cyclicality of GDP and its components, most importantly aggregate equipment and inventory investment for several OECD economies. The latest contribution in this series is Woitek (1996), who studied the G7 countries. He detrended the data using both a Hodrick-Prescott (HP) filter, which tends to lengthen the period found in the spectrum, and log differences (logD), which tend to shorten the cycle length. Using the HP filter, a cycle of traditional length is found in gross fixed capital formation (GFCF) of each country, the average length being 8.9 years. As expected the mean cycle length for the logD filter was shorter at 7.6 years and for one country (France) no cycle was found. As is typically the case inventory data are much more volatile. With the HP (logD) filter no cycle was found for France and Japan (Canada), the mean for the remaining countries being 4.2 (3.6) years. For all the results the moduli are quite high, ranging between 0.6 and 0.9.

In another recent contribution to this series of empirical studies, Reiter and Woitek (1999) investigate a test for 'classical business cycles.'[6] In the annual GFCF series (from 1960 to 1993) of 15 OECD economies they find that the long cycle is significant at the ten percentage level in nine cases, at the five percentage level in eight and at the one percentage level in six cases. Given the sample size, the power of the test is rather low. It is noteworthy that in 14 out of 15 cases the spectral bands corresponding to classical business cycles show an increase in mass.

1.2.3 Investment, the RBC View and Disaggregated Dynamics

This subsection deals with some recent developments which move the RBC closer to the CBC approach: first, the work of several authors who focus on the role and dynamics of fixed investment, second, work on sectoral business cycles.

In a simulation study, based on US aggregate data for 1954 to 1990, Greenwood, Hercowitz and Krusell (1998) find that "investment-specific technological change" is the source of at least 30% of output fluctuations. The authors identify that the dynamics stem mainly from investment activities. Nevertheless, they make no effort to explain the cyclic investment dynamics and rather attribute it to "investment-specific technology shocks." This practice makes it an example of the "ad-shockery"-critique brought forward by Cochrane (1994). In contrast to this, the following authors have tried to incorporate investment dynamics into a RBC framework.

Vallés (1997) incorporates adjustment costs and shocks to these costs into a RBC model to reproduce the observed volatility of aggregate investment. He finds that the adjustment cost shock variability needs to strongly offset the productivity shocks, usual in RBC models, to match the data with his model. Wen (1998) develops a neoclassical time-to-build (TTB) model in order to explain a 7 year cycle in the fixed investment to GDP ratio. Asea and Zak (1999) employ mixed difference/differential equations ('delay differential equations'), in the tradition of Tinbergen (1931), to produce intrinsic investment fluctuations in the framework of a neoclassical growth model with TTB technology. Oliner, Rudebusch and Sichel (1999) compare 'new' and 'old' models of business investment. They find that modern approaches based on the estimation of stochastic first order conditions from dynamic models

[6] A modified version of the test proposed by Canova (1996).

derived under rational expectations, are quite restricted by their dynamic structure and unable to capture time lags inherent in the investment process. Their "horse race" test clearly favors the traditional models and shows that Euler-equations produce forecasts of investment spending that are much too volatile.

The lack of a detailed empirical analysis of business cycles based on disaggregated time series has been stressed by Plosser (1991) and Reichlin (1991). A step to remedy this situation was taken by Forni and Reichlin (1998). Based on an earlier version of one of the datasets that will be investigated in the course of the present monograph, they analyze four-digit industrial output and productivity series. These series are the central variables of the RBC models. Their findings imply a need for a more thorough analysis of sectoral series they did not explicitly consider, namely the industrial investment series: "Our results ... suggest a view of the propagation of technological innovations which is quite different from that suggested by a real business-Solow growth model. In that framework, the technological innovation is identified with total factor productivity and it is purely exogenous. On the contrary, a strong positive correlation between technological innovations and the rate of growth of those key sectors [i.e. sectors stemming mainly from the industrial machinery and equipment goods group and in primary and fabricated metals, i.e. from sectors producing investment in capital goods and their inputs] says that since new technology requires new capital goods, it is embodied in capital and it propagates through investment," p. 468-469. An obvious implication of their conclusion is the need to explicitly consider the investment series on the industrial (four-digit) level of disaggregation, as is done in the third part on the sectoral constitution of macroeconomic cycles of the monograph.

Part I

Methodology

2. General Considerations and Historiography

2.1 Methodologies: Econometrics vs. Natural Sciences

Econometrics has evolved into a branch of statistics concerned with the direct testing of models against the data. This is in stark contrast to the natural sciences in which the role of statistical testing has been negligible. Instead, the natural sciences follow a two tier approach. The lower tier involves the determination of empirical regularities, 'stylized facts' in the terminology of economics, directly visible in the data. The upper tier is concerned with the theoretical explanation of the stylized facts. Regarding the stylized facts, the aim is to establish them as robust, i.e. evident in diverse and independently generated data sets. This is the meaning of 'testing' in natural sciences, as opposed to its meaning in statistics and econometrics. The function of theory is then to provide a simple coherent framework for replicating as many of the stylized facts as possible. The past work of SEMECON has dealt with business cycles at both levels and applied the natural science paradigm to their description and explanation. The first chapters of part II and III of the present work concentrate, respectively, on the description of stylized facts. This is also where most of the narrower methodological issues arise. The present section is therefore mainly concerned with descriptive methodologies.

Past efforts at determining the stylized facts of macroeconomic fluctuations exhibit the paradoxical feature that the more sophisticated the mathematical-statistical tool employed became, the more the ability to identify empirical regularities declined. The stylized facts associated with CBC theory had been established by informal, visual inspection of data. During the 1950s and 1960s attempts were made to analyze economic fluctuations by means of 'classical' spectral analysis based on sample autocorrelations. In relation to economic data this was the use of a blunt and unsuitable instrument. A rule of thumb of classical spectral analysis is that a cycle, to be reliably identified, should be present at least 20 times in the data. For a CBC cycle in the 8 to 10 years range, this would require a time series of about 200 years. The spectral analysis of economic time series discovered little beyond the obvious fact that they tend to be correlated at low frequencies.

In contemporary macroeconomics stylized facts are most often mentioned in relation to RBC. This is due less to an intrinsic interest in them, than to the fact that it has not been possible to estimate and test these models by conventional means. The central stylized facts of the RBC approach are low order serial and cross correlations among the data. These correlations do not fully characterize the dynamic processes behind and they do not reveal chracteristic features of the data, particularly the existence of cycles. The following paragraphs describe the methodology, established at SEMECON, which evolved specifically to detect and quantify the types of patterns initially discovered in CBC theory. The representation of time series by means of their (power) spectrum has a long tradition in the natural sciences. The term originally meant the amount of radiation emitted by a glowing body at different frequencies, hence the term 'power spectrum.' With the development of classical spectral analysis, it became the standard method for the empirical computation of the spectrum. Over the past two decades classical spectral analysis was replaced by Maximum Entropy (ME) spectral analysis almost throughout the natural and engineering sciences. The ME approach turns out to be equivalent to the estimation of an AR (VAR) process and the derivation of its (cross-)spectrum. This may seem non-novel to an econometrician. However, both the underlying theory and the pragmatic success of the method are of great relevance for economic applications. The ME approach arose from the classic methods based on a transformation of the empirical autocorrelogram. Implicit in the procedure is the assumption that the unobserved autocorrelations are zero. This assumption is both, very strong and false. It causes the problem of 'aliasing' or the appearance of false peaks, also known as 'side lobes' at both sides of the genuine peak of the spectrum. These can be smoothed out by means of various 'spectral windows,' but only at a further loss of resolution. Poor resolution when the spectrum is estimated from short time series is in any event a major problem associated with the classic approach. It is related to the fact that it is a nonparametric method that imposes no strong prior assumptions on the estimates. The central ideas of ME spectral analysis are due to Burg (1967 and 1968), who was motivated by the search for a spectral estimator suitable for geological research. One commonly used procedure is to set off underground explosions and to analyze the spectra of the resulting shockwaves in order to infer geological features. The burst of a shockwave is extremely brief and thus not suitable for classic spectral analysis. Burg (1967 and 1968) suggested that the unobserved autocorrelations should be assigned in a way, which makes them noninformative regarding the underlying process, given the sample autocorrelations. To operationalize the idea he postulated an underlying Gaussian ARMA process. He then maximized the entropy ($\approx$ negative information) over all autocorrelations, both over those in sample (fixed) and out of sample, to be determined. The basic result is that the derived spectrum equals the one of an AR process. This result motivated an increasing interest in what came to be known ME-spectral estimation in the natural and engineering sciences.[1] The success confirmed the relevance of the new approach in that

[1] Applications are discussed, for example, in Marple (1980).

sharp and accurate spectra could be estimated from limited data. Contrary to what is often the case in econometrics, the method was validated by its prediction. If the inferred geological structure, particularly oil fields, had not be found as predicted, interest in the method would soon have died down.

2.2 The Econometric Approach to Time Series Analysis

The approach to time series analysis was pioneered by Box and Jenkins (1970) and developed further by Clive Granger and his students and associates. The change from classical spectral analysis to the Box/Jenkins/Granger approach may be summarily described as a move from the frequency to the time domain and from description to testing. Box/Jenkins had suggested that the stationary part of an economic time series can be modelled as a Gaussian ARMA process, also known as the general linear model. A central feature of their approach is that, in order to properly model a time series, one needs to test for the order of the AR and MA parts of the process. It turned out that this part of the Box/Jenkins/Granger approach could not be successfully operationalized. The reason is that, given the typical length of an economic time series, the tests that were derived have low power and in addition are biased. An equally fundamental problem which has to be solved before an economic time series can be correctly modelled is the identification and removal of the nonstationary part. For a long time this was done pragmatically by fitting a flexible deterministic trend - most often a polynomial. When it was shown that an inappropriate trend specification may distort the stationary part of the process, the solution was sought in testing between alternative trends. The alternatives considered were a stochastic trend, obtained by integrating the stationary part, or a deterministic linear trend, possibly with a structural break. Again, it turned out that the proposed tests are too weak to allow a reliable discrimination between the alternatives in practice. In contemporary empirical works the unsolved problems are largely ignored. Detrending is routinely done by means of a Hodrick/Prescott (HP) filter, even though it is known that the HP filter tends to accentuate the low frequency part of the spectrum of the residuals. A low order AR or VAR process is then fitted to the residuals. Proceeding in this manner lacks a theoretical rationale. A defect of the currently practiced empirical methodology is that the dynamic properties of the estimated AR or VAR processes are usually not fully explicated. This requires a complete analysis of either the roots or the spectra of the processes. The low order correlations that are usually reported are uninformative in this respect. In the proceeding sections I describe the methodology of the present study that was designed to take the above criticism into account. The basic methodology that will be employed in order to analyze the detrended data is to fit (V)AR processes and to study their dynamics. This is done by investigating both the root(s) of the process and its spectrum. In the course of the present study both is done, depending on what is more convenient in a specific context. The focus is on a complete *description* of the process, particularly the presence of a periodic component corresponding to a CBC. Some test statistics relevant to establishing reliability of the results are also computed. The central two justifications to proceed in this manner are: The first it is essentially pragmatic and related to the use of AR and VAR processes in contemporary econometrics. The second deals with the use of these processes in the natural sciences and the maximum entropy theory on which the application is based on.

3. The Analysis of Cyclical Dynamics

According to the preceding argumentation an important first step in a project to investigate economic fluctuations is the thorough determination of stylized facts. When dealing with business cycles, it seems natural to analyze the time series at stake first by means of a general analysis of variance to quantitatively assess their relative volatility and contribution to the constitution of some aggregate series and second to investigate their cyclical properties in the frequency domain by means of spectral analysis. Given that the latter method seems an ideal tool for studying cyclical phenomena, one might wonder why it has not been used more in economics. In my opinion the answer lies in four problems that spectral analysis faces when confronted with economic data:

First, it can be applied only to stationary time series. Because most of economic variables contain a trend component, this must be effectively removed. Failure to do this leads to the "typical spectral shape," reported by Granger (1966), where most of the mass of the spectrum is skewed in a "hump-shaped" fashion to the low frequency range. The following section suggests adequate strategies as well as recently established detrending technologies to overcome this problem.

The second problem is that many economic series are so short that classical nonparametric methods of spectral analysis cannot be successfully used. Although, this circumstance led to the development of several modified standard methods, like window-smoothing of spectra, they continued to fail to produce reasonable estimates: Both, the standard periodogram and window-smoothed versions of it lack a satisfying degree of resolution in the case of short time series. They usually show many discrete spikes in the estimated spectral densities which often lack a clear shape and make it very difficult, if not impossible, to discriminate between different peaks. These drawbacks can result in misleading interpretations in the sense of spurious cycles.[1] Some authors even claim that this difficulty in interpreting estimates of spectra in an "economically meaningful" way has been the primary obstacle to a wider use of spectral analysis in economics, cf. the argumentation in Zarnowitz

[1] Van den Bos (1971) noted - already thirty years ago: "In the classical approach to calculation of power spectra the sample autocorrelation function is multiplied by some lag window and then transformed. The window is applied to avoid leakage from other parts of the spectrum. On the other hand, the window limits the spectral resolution," p. 493.

(1985 and 1996, chapter 8). For a detailed examination and demonstration of the disadvantages of standard techniques see Woitek (1997, chapter 2). ME-spectral analysis, as developed by Burg (1967 and 1968) and described in the following sections, is extremely well-suited for short time series and overcomes the drawbacks of conventional spectral methods.

A third reason for the relatively slow spread of spectral analytical applications in economics, might be their emphasis on description rather than testing. Though they are recently experiencing a kind of renaissance, reflected in contributions to core journals of the economic mainstream.[2] The request for standard errors and measures of fit of the model is a request with which the business cycle analyst, who applies spectral methods, is not seldomly confronted with. The duality-relationship between the parametric ME approach and AR/VAR processes is a feature that also overcomes this objection. It is demonstrated in the course of the present methodological chapter of the monograph that ascribing standard errors to the central AR spectral estimates is possible without relying on inadequate bootstrapping or similar practices.

Finally, methods from the time domain, like cointegration analysis, still play a predominate role in applied business cycle analysis. However, standard time domain estimates, like cointegration measures, are binary and fail in contrast to multivariate spectral measures to establish different degrees of association. In general, spectral measures are more informative and quantitative in nature in comparison to their corresponding time domain measures. See in the multivariate case (informational content of coherence vs. cointegration measures) Croux, Forni and Reichlin (2001) or in the univariate case (informational content of autocovariance functions vs. spectra) Howrey (1980).

3.1 The Detrending Problem

The raw aggregate and sectoral time series under analysis in the monograph are not stationary and need to be transformed to apply the spectral methods suggested in the following. A large literature on detrending exists which shows that an inappropriate detrending method distorts the spectrum of the residuals and may produce spurious cyclical behavior, see Canova (1994), Harvey and Jaeger (1993), Canova (1998) and more recently Schenk-Hoppé (2000). Much effort has been devoted to developing tests to determine the correct detrending procedure for a given time series. *Inter alia* these unit root (UR) tests imply the Dickey-Fuller, Augmented Dickey-Fuller and Phillips-Perron tests. Unfortunately, these tests are rather weak, cf. the comprehen-

[2] See the recent contributions of Croux, Forni and Reichlin (1999), Forni and Reichlin (1999), Forni et al. (1999) and Forni et al. (2000).

sive outline in Banerjee et al. (1993).[3] An alternative to testing, which has been employed in past SEMECON research is to use several filters, including ones that tend to distort the spectrum in opposite directions, cf. Reiter (1995, Section 2.3), Woitek (1997, Section 4.2 and Appendix A). Features of the spectrum which survive different filtering procedures are considered to be robust. Such a strategy has also been advocated by Canova (1998). The following set of widely used filtering methods is chosen in the present study: first log-differences (logD), i.e. growth rates in a first approximation, the Hodrick-Prescott (HP) filter and a modified version of the Baxter-King (MBK) filter as proposed by Woitek (1998). Their mathematical objectives and determinations are given by the following set of equations:[4]

$$\text{logD:} \qquad \widetilde{y}_t - \widetilde{y}_{t-1} = \ln(y_t) - \ln(y_{t-1}) \approx \frac{y_t - y_{t-1}}{y_{t-1}} \tag{3.1}$$

$$\begin{aligned} \text{HP(100):} \quad & \min_{\{\tau_t\}_t^T} \textstyle\sum_{t=1}^{T} \left(\widetilde{y}_t - \tau_t\right)^2 \quad \text{s.t.} \\ & \textstyle\sum_{t=2}^{T-1} \left[(\tau_{t+1} - \tau_t) - (\tau_t - \tau_{t-1})\right]^2 \leq \mu, \text{ where} \\ & \tau_t \equiv \text{trend}, \ \mu \equiv \text{smoothing} \\ & (\text{Lagrangian} = 100 \text{ for annual data}) \end{aligned} \tag{3.2}$$

$$\begin{aligned} \text{(M)BK:} \quad & \min_{a_j} \textstyle\int_{-\pi}^{\pi} \left|\beta(\omega) - \alpha(\omega)\right|^2 d\omega \quad \text{s.t. } \alpha(0) = 0, \text{ where} \\ & \alpha(\omega) \equiv \text{Fourier transform of } a_j \\ & \beta(\omega) \equiv \text{“ideal” filter gain} \end{aligned} \tag{3.3}$$

---

[3] Another recent reference in the unit root discussion is Diebold and Senhadji (1996) who note: "There is no doubt that unit-root tests do suffer from low power in many situations of interest ... Our results suggest that U.S. aggregate output is not likely to be difference-stationary: the dominant autoregressive root is close to, but less than, unity ... There is simply no substitute for serious, case-by-case, analysis," p. 1297.

[4] In my opinion the most intuitive outline of the HP-filter's logic is given in Prescott (1986). A survey of the statistical justifications of the HP-filter is provided by Reeves et al. (1996). For a detailed specification of the 'digital' or 'bandpass' filters, BK- and MBK-filter, the exact differences in their derivation and their effects on series with different frequencies (i.e. annual, quarterly and monthly), the reader is referred to the thorough presentation and discussion in Woitek (1998). A comparison of unfiltered, HP- and BK-filtered series, having a peak in their spectrum at business cycle frequencies, can be found in Guay and St-Amant (1997).

Fig. 3.1. Spurious cycles' generation comparison

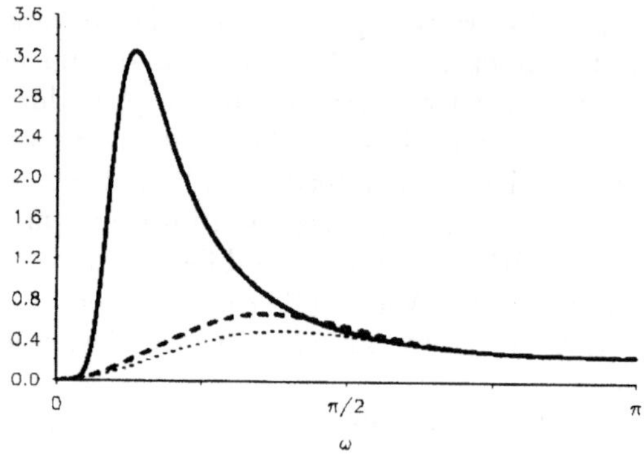

Note: solid: HP-, dashed: BK-, dotted: MBK-filter

According to (3.1) to (3.3) the outcome of log differencing is given by $y_t\,|_{\text{logD}} = \widetilde{y}_t - \widetilde{y}_{t-1} = \ln(y_t) - \ln(y_{t-1})$, of the HP-filtering routine by $y_t\,|_{\text{HP}} = \widetilde{y}_t - \tau_t = \ln(y_t) - \tau_t$, of the MBK-filter by its moving average (MA) representation, i.e. $y_t\,|_{\text{MBK}} = \sum_{j=-K}^{K} a_j L^j y_t$ of order K ($K = 3$ for annual data), respectively.

Figure 3.1 above shows the gain function for different trend filters. It conveys the information which frequencies are on the one hand sustained, on the other hand emphasized in the respective filtering procedure.[5] From the gain functions displayed in Figure 3.1 and the equation and definitions (3.2) it becomes evident why the HP-filter is also called a high pass linear filter: The smoothing parameter of the trend function μ is picked so that the Lagrange multiplier of the constraint in (3.2) equals 100 (if it would take on a zero value, the smooth trend function would be identical to the original series, in its limiting value of $+\infty$, the trend function equals a linear trend). The value of 100 is suggested by Hodrick and Prescott (1997) for data of annual frequency in that it "replicates the curve a business cycle analyst might fit free-hand to the data - [w]ith no better justification than this," see Hartley, Hoover and Salyer (1997), p. 47. Nevertheless, it has become the standard choice for the smoothing parameter in many contemporary work on applied business cycle research. The HP-strategy guarantees the elimination of low periodicities, associated with (growth) trend movements, while high frequencies pass the filter. In contrast, the BK- and MBK-filter are bandpass filters

[5] Obviously, the gain function peaks for the HP(100)-filter in the frequency range corresponding to period lengths of about 15 years. The BK- and MBK-filter's gain functions take on values below or equal to the HP-filter's one and peak at a periodicity of about 7 years. The not displayed gain of the logD-detrending procedure would equal a sigmoid close to linear function peaking at a frequency corresponding to a period length beyond two years, i.e. $> \pi$, see Woitek (1996, Appendix A).

that define a relevant business cycle frequency band $[\omega_1, \omega_2]$, where ω_1 equals the lower cut-off frequency and ensures that (growth) trend movements are not conserved by the filter and ω_2 stands for the upper cut-off frequency ensuring that seasonal patterns are not let through the filter. Figure 3.2 displays the power transfer function (*ptf*) for the BK- and MBK-filter, respectively. Given the full confirmation of a certain frequency, after applying a trend filter, the *ptf* takes on a value of one. Therefore the *ptf* of an ideal filter is rectangular over the relevant business cycle frequency band $[\omega_1, \omega_2]$. As one can see from Figure 3.2, the MBK-filter comes reasonably close to this ideal filter and is superior in both respects, i.e. with regard to the gain as well as the *ptf*, to the conventional BK-filter (see Figures 3.1 and 3.2).[6] In summary, the logD-filter tends to amplify the high frequencies, the HP-filter to amplify the low frequencies and for the MBK-filter the gain function is relatively flat over the relevant business cycle frequencies. As can be seen from equations (3.1) to (3.3), the logD-procedure shortens the time series by one datapoint, the MBK-filter by six (three at the beginning, three at the end of the respective series) and the HP-filter leaves the length of the series unchanged.

Fig. 3.2. Power transfer function (*ptf*) comparison of BK-filters

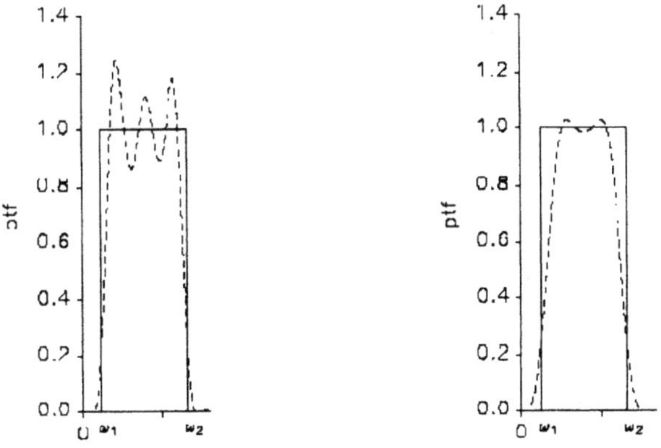

BK-filter by Baxter and King (1995)   MBK-filter by Woitek (1998)

To avoid a cumbersome presentation, for the descriptive spectral analytic investigations I rely primarily on the MBK-filtering procedure, considering the HP- and logD-filter to be for control of findings that might be induced

[6] The fact that the conventional BK-filter does not necessarily prevent the time series analyst from eventually producing spurious cycles has been stressed recently in a simulation study by Schenk-Hoppé (2000). In contrast to this claim, Den Haan and Sumner (2001) show that the BK-filter isolates the desired set of frequencies not only when the series are stationary but also when they are first or second-order integrated processes.

by 'short time series'-features. A further justification of this strategy (and of refraining from UR tests) can be seen in the recent findings of Den Haan and Sumner (2001) who show that band-pass filters like the MBK-filter isolate the desired set of frequencies even in the case when the series are $I(1)$ or $I(2)$, i.e. actually difference stationary. The business cycle band is throughout set to $\left[\omega_1 = 2\pi\frac{1}{8}, \omega_2 = \pi\right]$.

3.2 Volatility and Spectral Analysis

3.2.1 Contribution-to-Variance Analysis

To quantitatively assess the importance and fluctuations of a time series relative to its median trend level value or to the fluctuating properties of a higher-dimensional aggregate series, the following three measures are suggested: relative trend level (RTL), standardized standard deviation (SSD) and contribution to standard deviation (CTS).

The first of these measures is a straightforward method to quantify the relative magnitude or share of the ith constituent series' trend level $\tau_t(y_i)$ to the corresponding aggregate series' trend level $\tau_t\left(\sum_i^N y_i\right)$, where $i = 1, ..., N$. It is calculated according to

$$\text{RTL} = \frac{\tau_t(y_i)}{\tau_t\left(\sum_i^N y_i\right)} \tag{3.4}$$

for all i constituent components at several distinct points of the observation period $t = 1, ..., T$. Actually, as reported in the proceeding chapter, starting point $(t = 1)$, mid point $(t = T_m)$ and end point $(t = T)$ of τ_t are considered.

The standardized standard deviation (SSD), defined as the standard deviation of a detrended series divided by its mid trend level value, provides an adequate measure of the relative volatility:

$$\text{SSD} = \frac{\sigma\left[(y_{i,t} - \tau_t(y_i))\right]}{\tau_{T_m}}. \tag{3.5}$$

This measure is similar, though preferable, to the volatility measure of a variable suggested by Christiano (1988), whose ratio employs the mean of absolute changes of the undetrended time series of a variable in the nominator, the mean of the undetrended series in the denominator, cf. also Fitzgerald (1997).[7] The SSD measure, as given by (3.5), is superior to Christiano's measure, because the latter implies arithmetic means which tend to weight a deviation proportional to the magnitude of the deviation. This undesirable feature is overcome by the SSD measure (3.5).

[7] A survey of similar volatility measures is given by McKenzie (1999).

Consider the aggregate y^a of $i = 1, ..., N$ business cycle components y_i^c, as extracted by an adequate detrending method from the original series. The standard deviation of y^a is then theoretically composed by the following relationship

$$\sigma(y^a) = \sqrt{\sigma^2\left(\sum_i y_i^c\right)} = \left[\sum_i \sigma^2(y_i^c) + 2\sum_i\sum_k \mathrm{cov}(y_i^c, y_k^c)\right]^{\frac{1}{2}},$$

where $i = 1, ..., N$ and $k = i+1, ..., N$. Obviously, the respective variances $\sigma^2(y_i^c)$ contribute positively to $\sigma(y^a)$, but given a constituent y_i^c is mainly correlated negatively with the other constituent series, there might be a damping impact on $\sigma(y^a)$ from including y_i^c in the constitution of y^a. The contribution of the ith component to the aggregate series' standard deviation is

$$\mathrm{CTS} = 1 - \frac{\sigma(y^a - y_i^c)}{\sigma(y^a)} = \frac{\sigma(y^a) - \sigma(y^a - y_i^c)}{\sigma(y^a)}, \tag{3.6}$$

where $\sigma(y^a - y_i^c)$ denotes the reduction in standard deviation of the aggregate, when y_i^c is dropped in the constitution process. It is theoretically given by

$$\sigma(y^a - y_i^c) = \sqrt{\sigma^2(y^a) - \sigma^2(y_i^c) - 2\sum_k \mathrm{cov}(y_i^c, y_k^c)}, \text{ where } k \neq i.$$

Therefore, CTS, as given by (3.6), is the contribution to standard deviation measured in standard deviation terms of the aggregate, i.e. a share of the total aggregate's standard deviation. Following the argumentation above, a CTS-value > 0 characterizes a destabilizing variable, whereas a CTS-value < 0 characterizes a stabilizing constituent variable.

3.2.2 Spectral Analysis: The Univariate Case

The spectral model for discrete-time series. As argued above, the most informative business cycle characteristics of a time series are in terms of its spectral density. The starting point of time series analysis is the (potential) existence of serial correlations in the processes that are observed and recorded. One way to summarize the correlation pattern in a (sample) series is the *autocorrelation* (or *autocovariance*) *function*,[8] defined in the time domain. For a stationary process x_t with mean μ it is defined by

$$\gamma_t(s) = E\left[(x_{t+|s|} - \mu)(x_t - \mu)\right], \text{ where } s = \pm 1, \pm 2, ... \tag{3.7}$$

Given that $\gamma_t(s)$ is summable, its analogue in the frequency domain is its Fourier transform, the power spectrum given by

[8] Besides these conventional terms, Marple (1987) also calls it *autocorrelation sequence*.

$$f(\lambda) = \frac{1}{2\pi} \sum_{t=-\infty}^{\infty} e^{-i\lambda t} \gamma_t, \text{ where } -\pi \leq \lambda \leq \pi \text{ and} \tag{3.8}$$

$e^{-i\lambda t} = \cos(\lambda t) - i \sin(\lambda t)$. The fact that the Fourier transform of the autocorrelation function (the power spectrum) equals the spectral density function defined in the frequency domain links time and frequency domain analysis.

Let me now turn to the spectral model of discrete-time series in a little more detail. For a thorough statistical outline and state of the art spectral analysis of time series, the reader is referred to Koopmans (1995).[9] Forni and Lippi (1997), Woitek (1997) and Sargent (1987, chapter XI) contain expositions of those aspects of spectral analysis that are most relevant for modern business cycle analysis. To avoid a cumbersome presentation and clarify empirical results, I will concentrate on the central formulae defining the spectral parameters and their interpretation.

Given a weakly stationary process with discrete time parameter ξ_t, this process can be written as a superposition of a generally uncountable number of sinusoids with stochastic amplitude. This representation is called the *spectral representation* of ξ_t, defined as

$$\xi_t = \int_{-\pi}^{\pi} e^{i\lambda t} \Phi(d\lambda). \tag{3.9}$$

The *spectral measure* $\Phi(A)$ has the property $\Phi(A + 2\pi) = \Phi(A)$, i.e. the property of being periodic of period 2π. Similarly, the *spectral distribution* $F(d\lambda)$, defined by

$$F(A) = E\left|\Phi(A)\right|^2 \tag{3.10}$$

for every measurable set A, is periodic in the same sense $F(A + 2\pi) = F(A)$. Since $F(A)$ represents the variance that is explained by cycles with a frequency from the set A, the *spectral distribution function* in terms of $F(A)$ is given by the expression

$$F(\lambda) = F((-\pi, \lambda]). \tag{3.11}$$

In analogy to the spectral distribution, the spectral function and density are periodic functions of period 2π. Since periodic functions are completely determined by their values on a single cycle, it suffices to restrict attention to the interval $(-\pi, \pi]$. Assuming that the process ξ_t has a continuous spectrum, the spectral distribution (3.11) has a derivative $\frac{dF(\lambda)}{d\lambda} = f(\lambda)$, which is called the *spectral density function. Nota bene*, it can be shown that a) the spectral density function $f(\lambda)$ equals the Fourier transform of the autocorrelation function γ_t, as displayed in (3.7) and (3.8) above, and b) the integral of $f(\lambda)$ from 0 to π equals the variance of the process. Therefore, the integral of $f(\lambda)$

[9] The argumentation and formulae outlined in the present subsection widely follow Koopmans (1995, section 3.3).

in a certain frequency range $\lambda \in [\omega_1, \omega_2]$ can be interpreted as the part of the variance of the process which is explained by fluctuations having frequencies within this range, see Koopmans (1995, chapter 3) and Reiter (1995, section 3.1). For example white noise, i.e. a totally unstructured process, implies a constant spectral density - no frequency range is prominent.

The ME- (AR-) spectral estimation. As already argued above, the 'short time series'-feature of many macroeconomic series is problematic in the context of spectral analysis. Nonparametric methods like the *periodogram* (sometimes also termed *correlogram*) or (window-)smoothed versions of it offer poor estimates of the spectral density, showing an irregular picture often accompanied by artificial peaks, cf. Marpel (1987, chapter 7) or Woitek (1997). They provide a rather low degree of resolution in the sense of power to discriminate between distinct cycles. A parametric approach is more suitable to extract signal information from a limited number of observations as is usually available in macroeconomics; see Hillinger and Sebold-Bender (1992) and Woitek (1997).

The univariate ME-spectral estimation procedure starts off with the fitting of an AR process to the adequately detrended (and therefore stationary) time series x_t,[10] then calculates the spectral density of the AR model by means of the estimated AR coefficients and finally takes the spectral density of the adjusted AR model as an estimate for the one of the actual series x_t.[11] An AR process of order p, denoted by AR(p), is generally defined as

$$x_t = a_1 x_{t-1} + a_2 x_{t-2} + ... + a_p x_{t-p} + \varepsilon_t = \sum_{j=1}^{p} a_j x_{t-j} + \varepsilon_t, \qquad (3.12)$$

where ε_t follows a white noise process with mean 0 and variance σ^2. Applying the notation of a standard lag operator $a(L)\, x_t = \varepsilon_t$, where $a(L) = 1 - a_1 L - a_2 L^2 - ... - a_p L^p$and $L^n x_t = x_{t-n}$ with $n = 1, 2, ...$, the ε_t can be expressed as the output of a linear filter $a(L)$ applied to the AR process x_t: $\varepsilon_t = a(L)\, x_t$. If the process x_t is a stationary process,e.g. achieved by extraction from the raw series via an adequate detrending procedure, the process x_t can be *vice versa* represented as output of the linear filter $a(L)^{-1}$ applied to the irregular component ε_t: $x_t = a(L)^{-1}\, \varepsilon_t$. The ME-spectral estimation of the true spectral density of the actual series is then formally given by the spectrum of the AR(p) process

[10] Though the matter of choosing the right method of estimation played a decisive role in earlier methodological work on ME- (or AR) spectra conducted at SEMECON, todays computer power allows all forms of estimation methods ranging from OLS to full information maximum likelihood.

[11] In the literature of the engineering sciences AR models are sometimes referred to as *all-pole(s) models*. Therefore the ME-spectral estimation method is sometimes denoted all-pole(s) method; see for example, van den Bos (1971) or more recently, Press et al. (1992, section 13.7).

$$f(\omega) = a(\omega)^{-1}\sigma^2 = \frac{1}{2\pi}\frac{\sigma^2}{\left|1 - \sum_{j=1}^{p}\widehat{a}_j e^{-i\omega j}\right|^2}, \text{ where } -\pi \leq \omega \leq \pi, \quad (3.13)$$

$a(\omega)$ is the Fourier transform of the filter $a(L)$ and $\widehat{a}_j$ denotes the estimated coefficients of the adjusted AR model (3.12) for $j = 1, ..., p$. That the estimate (3.13) of the true spectral density of a series x_t fulfills the *principle of maximum entropy* is outlined in the following subsection that establishes the duality of the AR- and ME-spectral methodology.

The duality of AR- and ME-spectral analysis. In the introductory paragraph of the present section on spectral analysis, we have implicitly omitted the following problematic point: In macroeconometric problems, one is confronted with finite samples representing particular realizations of (potentially) infinitely ongoing processes. Therefore, an economic time series analyst is only able to obtain reliable estimates of a small finite number of autocorrelations for the theoretical functions (3.7) and (3.8). The question then arises regarding what assumption should be made concerning the values of the remaining autocorrelations. Traditional periodogram-based spectral estimation methods either assume this problem away and set these out-of-observation values to zero,[12] or, like the *fast Fourier transformation* (FFT) widespread in engineering, imply a periodic extension of the data and insert periodicities which do not exist in the data; see Smylie et al. (1973), p. 415. In contrast to these methods, the above sketched AR spectral estimation strategy implies an AR autocorrelation sequence's extrapolation scheme. Since estimations of (3.12) imply one or more complex solution(s) and one (or more) corresponding modulus (moduli) of the root(s), generally of value(s) < 1, if the series x_t contains any cyclic component(s), the AR extrapolation pattern gets the more damped the further one considers lags from outside the observation period.[13] Furthermore, the AR spectral estimation strategy maximizes the entropy of the stationary process, i.e. in technical terms, the extrapolation of the autocorrelation function is achieved in such a way that the entropy of the corresponding probability function is maximized in each step of the extrapolation, as originally suggested by Burg (1967 and 1968) and thoroughly investigated in van den Bos (1971), Smylie et al. (1973) and Ulrych and Bishop (1975).

In the remaining part of this subsection, I will try to give the most basic intuition of the ME-principle and the duality between the ME-method and the AR representation of data. For proofs of the details of the outline the reader is referred to the above cited sources. One may ask what *entropy* in

[12] Similarly, Ulrych and Bishop (1975) call these set-to-zero values "data that lie outside of the parameter space," p. 55. This is also the reason why these methods sometimes are termed *direct methods* or *all-zero models*; see Press et al. (1992), p. 573.

[13] An excellent graphical representation of this argument is given in Marple (1987), Figure 7.4, p. 201.

a definable information-theoretic sense actually denotes. An answer is given by Ulrych and Bishop (1975), who define information and entropy (average information per time interval) as additive separable (log-linear) quantities, consisting of probabilities of the occurrence of events. In the context of spectral analysis and the relationship between entropy and the spectral density $f(\lambda)$, Smylie et al. (1973) derive the following entropy rate for an infinite Gaussian (stationary) process[14]

$$E = \frac{1}{4\lambda_N} \int_{-\lambda_N}^{\lambda_N} \log f(\lambda)\, d\lambda, \tag{3.14}$$

where λ_N denotes the Nyquist frequency, which defines the upper limit of measurable frequencies. Rewriting (3.14) in terms of the autocorrelation function $\gamma_t(s)$ of the process, defined by (3.7), and its Fourier transform expression (3.8), gives

$$E = \frac{1}{4\lambda_N} \int_{-\lambda_N}^{\lambda_N} \log \left(\frac{1}{2\pi} \sum_{t=-\infty}^{\infty} e^{-i\lambda t} \gamma_t \right) d\lambda. \tag{3.15}$$

Maximizing (3.15) w.r.t. the unknown γ_t under the constraint that $f(\lambda)$ must also be consistent with the known autocorrelations $\gamma_0, \ldots, \gamma_{T-1}$, where T represents the number of observed realizations of the process x_t, results in the ME-spectral density

$$f(\lambda) = \frac{1}{\pi} \frac{c}{\lambda_N \left| 1 + \sum_{t=1}^{T-1} \varepsilon_t e^{-i\omega j} \right|^2}, \tag{3.16}$$

where c is a constant and the ε_t are prediction errors, both determined from the data. It can be derived via variational analysis as demonstrated in Smylie et al. (1973). This estimate expresses maximum uncertainty w.r.t. the unknown information but is consistent with the known information. According to (3.12) and considering the prediction filter $\varepsilon_t = a(L)\, x_t$, (3.16) is nothing else than the doubled power spectrum, as estimated on the base of an AR(p) model adjusted to the data, given by equation (3.13) above. A straight proof of the one-to-one relationship of AR- and ME-spectral estimation, based on the determinant of the semipositive definite Toeplitz autocovariance matrix of the process x_t (for the ME objective) and correspondingly (for the AR objective) on the determinant of the Yule-Walker equations' matrix of an AR(p) process, can be found in van den Bos (1971) and in a somehow more detailed version in Ulrych and Bishop (1975).

[14] The derivation of the rate is rather complex, implying *inter alia* the Weierstrass approximation theorem and the exploitation of several properties of the Toeplitz matrix, so that it is here just presented. The interested reader is referred to the more thorough outline and derivation in Süssmuth (2002b).

The importance of the AR process analogy for business cycle analysis. With regard to the constitution of macroeconomic time series, Granger and Newbold (1986) note: "Two situations where series are added are of particular interpretational importance. The first is where series are aggregated to form some total, and the second is where the observed series is the sum of the true process plus observational error, corresponding to the classical 'signal plus noise' situation," p. 30. Most macroeconomic series, such as GDP, or in general NIPA aggregates, or the sectoral series analyzed in the third part of the present study, are such aggregated series. In this context, Granger and Newbold (1986) derive a central theorem that implies that "[i]f the observed series is the sum of a 'true' series that is AR(p) plus a white noise observation error, then an ARMA(p,q) series results," p. 31, cf. also Forni and Lippi (1997, chapter 10 and appendix A.7). For ARMA(p,q) models a series x_t is supposed to be generated by[15]

$$x_t = \sum_{j=1}^{p} a_j x_{t-j} + \sum_{j=0}^{q} b_j \varepsilon_{t-j},$$

where ε_t is a zero-mean white noise and $b_0 = 1$. Applying for x_t the lag operator L, leads to

$$a(L)\,x_t = b(L)\,\varepsilon_t$$

so that the corresponding generating function form is

$$a(z)\,x(z) = b(z)\,\varepsilon(z), \text{ where } a(z) = 1 - \sum_{j=1}^{p} a_j z^j \text{ and } b(z) = \sum_{j=0}^{q} b_j z^j.$$

From this Wold representation the following three implications can be proven to hold in general (see Granger and Newbold (1986), p. 25-26):

(i) The ARMA process is stationary if the roots of $a(z) = 0$ all lie outside the unit circle $|z| = 1$;

(ii) if the process is stationary, then there is an equivalent MA(∞) process

$$x_t = \sum_{j=0}^{\infty} c_j \varepsilon_{t-j}, \text{ where } c_0 = 1 \text{ and } c(z) = \sum_{j=0}^{\infty} c_j z^j = \frac{b(z)}{a(z)};$$

(iii) there is an equivalent AR(∞) process

$$x_t = \sum_{j=1}^{\infty} d_j x_{t-j}, \text{ where } d(z) = 1 - \sum_{j=1}^{\infty} d_j z^j = \frac{a(z)}{b(z)},$$

provided the roots of $b(z) = 0$ lie outside the unit circle $|z| = 1$, that is, provided the so-called invertibility condition holds.

[15] The following argumentation summarizes main parts of Granger and Newbold (1986, section 1.5 - 1.7).

From (i) to (iii) it follows that a stationary process "can always be well approximated" by an MA or AR process of sufficiently high order, cf. Granger and Newbold (1986), p. 26. To determine the right order several information criteria are suggested in the literature, including the final prediction error criterion (FPE), Akaike's information criterion (AIC), the Hannan-Quinn criterion (HQ) and the Schwarz criterion (SC), see e.g. Lütkepohl (1991). Recently, several Bayesian information criteria are refined and suggested in the literature. In particular, the BAC criterion by Heintel (1998) has been shown in a series of simulation experiments to be most accurate in determining the order of a (V)AR model. As in the case of choosing the adequate detrending procedure, I follow a serious, case-by-case, strategy. I rely primarily on the BAC, and consider a visual analysis of respective orders and implied spectra for cases in which the standard information criteria FPE, AIC, HQ and SC diverge on the majority from the order suggested by the BAC criterion.

According to the argumentation in the last paragraphs AR spectral analysis provides a most reasonable picture of the processes underlying macroeconomic or industrial time series in that it interprets them as AR processes. Besides this natural justification of the ME spectral approach, it offers a series of additional information provided by its AR interpretation and the underlying estimated AR models. These are outlined in the following section.

3.2.3 The Analysis of Complex Roots

The informational content of complex solutions in the AR interpretation. Since in a general AR(p) model of the form (3.12) ε_t is i.i.d., s.t. $E(\varepsilon_t) = 0$, applying an expectation operator, renders the deterministic part of the process, or in other words, the homogenous part of a difference equation of order p.[16] The deterministic system can always be reformulated in a first order lag form $\mathbf{w}_t = \mathbf{A}\mathbf{w}_{t-1}$, where

$$\mathbf{w}_t = \begin{pmatrix} x_t \\ Lx_t \\ L^2x_t \\ \vdots \\ L^px_t \end{pmatrix}, \quad \mathbf{A} = \begin{pmatrix} a_1 & a_2 & a_3 & \dots & a_p \\ 1 & 0 & 0 & \dots & 0 \\ 0 & 1 & 0 & \dots & 0 \\ \vdots & \ddots & \ddots & \ddots & \vdots \\ 0 & 0 & 0 & 1 & 0 \end{pmatrix}, \text{ and}$$

$$\mathbf{w}_{t-1} = \begin{pmatrix} Lx_t \\ L^2x_t \\ L^3x_t \\ \vdots \\ L^{p+1}x_t \end{pmatrix}.$$

[16] A summary of the elementary mathematics applied in the argumentation of this section, can be found for example in Hamilton (1994, Appendix A).

The eigensystem of the above system is given by $\boldsymbol{\lambda}\mathbf{y} = \mathbf{A}\mathbf{y}$, where $\boldsymbol{\lambda}$ denotes the eigenvalues of the quadratic matrix $\mathbf{A}$ and $\mathbf{y} \neq 0$ expresses the eigenvector of the system. For $\mathbf{y} \neq 0$ the characteristic polynomial is found via $|\mathbf{A} - \boldsymbol{\lambda}\mathbf{I}| = 0$, where $\mathbf{I}$ denotes an identity matrix of order p. Solving the characteristic polynomial renders a real part c_1 and a complex part c_2 for one or more (potentially) complex solutions in terms of the AR coefficients $a_1, ..., a_p$. The (angular) frequency ω for the respective (potentially) complex solution is defined as

$$\omega = \arctan\left(\frac{c_2}{c_1}\right) = \frac{2\pi}{P},$$

where P denotes the period length for a cyclic solution, as given in the case of complex (i.e. negative) roots in the solution of the characteristic polynomial.

The modulus of the respective complex solution is given by

$$\text{mod} = \sqrt{c_1^2 + c_2^2}.$$

A mod-value close to one characterizes the fact that the complex roots are almost undamped and therefore the spectral density function is peaking at the frequency corresponding to an implied period length P of the corresponding cycle. The closer mod approaches a zero value, the more damped is a contained cyclicality of a series. In general, the less damped the roots are, the more regular is (are) the cycle(s) contained in a series under investigation and the higher and sharper is (are) the peak(s) in the spectrum.

Ascribing standard errors: lessons from continuous time econometrics. The above outlined duality-relationship between the parametric ME approach and AR processes allows the assignment of (approximate) standard errors to estimated period lengths and moduli. The method that will be presented in the following is superior to conventional bootstrap strategies since, as Kiefer (1996) notes, "the bootstrap method scrambles the order of the observations," p. 50, by randomly sampling from data and therefore violating the autoregressivity of the series at stake. It stems from an approximation strategy adopted from continuous time econometrics which is called *sensitivity analysis.*

Following Wymer (1993, Section 3.3), the general continuous time model (of sufficient order to imply a complex root) can be written as

$$Dy\,(t) = A\,(\phi)\,y\,(t) + B\,(\phi)\,z\,(t) + u\,(t)\,, \tag{3.17}$$

where $Dy\,(t) = \frac{dy(t)}{dt}$, ϕ is the vector of all parameters to be calculated and the elements of A and B are any differentiable functions of ϕ. The second term on the right-hand side, $B\,(\phi)\,z\,(t)$, can be interpreted as the inhomogeneous part of the differential equation system (3.17) and is for reasons of simplicity left out of the further derivation:

$$Dy\,(t) = A\,(\phi)\,y\,(t) + u\,(t)\,. \tag{3.18}$$

As Wymer (1993) notes, this model can be represented by a stochastically equivalent difference equation system such that its exact discrete model (3.12) will be satisfied by any set of equispaced observations generated by the system of differential equations and can be estimated from a sample of such observations. For any such linear difference equation system the eigensystem is given by

$$\Lambda = H^{-1}AH, \tag{3.19}$$

where, providing that the eigenvalues of A are distinct, H is the matrix of eigenvectors and Λ is a diagonal matrix of eigenvalues λ_i. Complex conjugate eigenvalues of the form $c_1 \pm c_2 i = \nu \pm i\omega$ (where c_1 and c_2 denote real and imaginary values of the complex root, respectively) correspond to a cycle with an amplitude proportional to $e^{\nu t}$, a period of $|2\pi/\omega|$ length and an implied modulus or damping rate $\sqrt{c_1^2 + c_2^2}$; see Wymer (1993, Section 3.4), or Gandolfo (1981, Section 2.2.4). The task of the present subsection is to determine and assign standard errors to periodicities and moduli implied by a discrete analogue of model (3.18), i.e. an AR(p) process of an arbitrary order $p \geqslant 2$; see equation (3.12) above, for which an eigensystem of the form (3.19) can be calculated, given parameter estimates of the model. The applied concept will be the concept of *sensitivity analysis*, as suggested by Gandolfo (1981), Wymer (1993) and Reiter (1995).

At the heart of sensitivity analysis stands the evaluation of the partial derivatives of the eigenvalues λ_i with respect to the elements a_{jk} of the parameter matrix A of the system given in (3.19). These partial derivatives are also called *sensitivity coefficients*. The columns i of the sensitivity coefficient Jacobian matrix with respect to the elements of the difference equation system $J_{A\ i}$ is given by

$$J_{A\ i} = \frac{\partial \lambda_i}{\partial A} = \frac{\partial \lambda_i}{\partial a_{jk}}, \text{ where } A = (a_{jk}) \,. \tag{3.20}$$

And since the elements a_{jk} of A are differentiable functions of the parameters ϕ_p of the system, where p equals the order of the adjusted AR(p) process, the sensitivity coefficient matrix with respect to the estimated AR parameters ϕ_p can be constructed in the following way

$$J_{\phi_p\ i} = \sum_{j,k} \frac{\partial \lambda_i}{\partial a_{jk}} \frac{\partial a_{jk}}{\partial \phi_p} \text{ for all } i, p. \tag{3.21}$$

For a numerically specified system matrix A and estimates of the parameters ϕ_p the calculation of (3.20) is straightforward and can be conducted numerically. Gandolfo (1981) and Wymer (1993) suggest the following general way to obtain J_A and J_{ϕ_p} therefrom via the relationship given in (3.21): Accordingly, J_A can be constructed by letting h_i be the ith column of the matrix of eigenvectors H in (3.19), h_i^* the column vector corresponding to the ith row of the inverse matrix H^{-1}, and λ_i the ith eigenvalue of Λ. Equation (3.20) can then be expressed in terms of h_i and h_i^*:

$$J_{A\,i} = \frac{\partial \lambda_i}{\partial A} = \frac{\partial \lambda_i}{\partial a_{jk}} = h_i^* h_i' \tag{3.22}$$

and J_{ϕ_p} is obtained by (3.21). A formal proof for this procedure is given in Gandolfo (1981), Section 2.2.4.2.

Following Reiter (1995, Section 13.2), the computation of J_{ϕ_p} needs to be computed separately for the real and imaginary parts of Λ (with column elements λ_i^r and λ_i^i, respectively, where superscript "r" and "i" denote real and imaginary parts of the respective column λ_i of matrix Λ). The standard errors of the real c_1 and imaginary parts c_2 of the complex roots of system (3.18) are therefore given as the square roots of the diagonal of the following matrix product, involving the estimated variance-covariance matrix $\widehat{\sum}$ of the regression coefficients ϕ_p (with dimension $p \times p$):

$$\widehat{\sigma}^2_{c_1} = \text{diag}\left[J^r_{\phi_p} \widehat{\sum} \left(J^r_{\phi_p}\right)'\right] \quad \text{and} \tag{3.23}$$

$$\widehat{\sigma}^2_{c_2} = \text{diag}\left[J^i_{\phi_p} \widehat{\sum} \left(J^i_{\phi_p}\right)'\right]. \tag{3.24}$$

Analogously, it is possible to ascribe standard errors to moduli mod_i implied by fully numerically specified systems, where I numerically construct the Jacobian of the moduli with respect to the regression coefficients:

$$J^{\text{mod}}_{\phi_p} = \frac{\partial \, \text{mod}_i}{\partial \phi_p}, \tag{3.25}$$

and apply the analogue strategy as above, in (3.23) and (3.24):

$$\widehat{\sigma}_{\text{mod}} = \text{diag}\left[J^{\text{mod}}_{\phi_p} \widehat{\sum} \left(J^{\text{mod}}_{\phi_p}\right)'\right]^{0.5}. \tag{3.26}$$

I proceed in the same way for the implied period length(s). *Nota bene*: Though the ratio of estimated measure and standard error, determined according to (3.25) and (3.26), can be interpreted in the spirit of a Student's t-value for the mod measures,[17] this interpretation is not possible in the case of estimated period lengths. In the latter case a confidence interval interpretation is quite suggestive, providing an additional piece of information.

[17] The corresponding null would be a mod = 0, implying that the cyclic component plays no role.

3.2.4 Spectral Analysis: The Multivariate Case

Standard time domain estimates, like cointegration measures,[18] are often binary and fail in contrast to multivariate spectral measures to establish different degrees of association. Cross-spectral measures are quite more informative and quantitative in nature in comparison to their (only partly) corresponding time domain measures: Croux, Forni and Reichlin (2001) point out that "two processes are either cointegrated or not, but we can't establish different degrees of association," p. 1. Furthermore, these authors demonstrate that considering only the real part of the cross-spectrum[19] in the construction of a dynamic comovement measure from the frequency domain, leads to a measure[20] that reduces in the bivariate case to (long run) correlation and is related in a simple way to cointegration. The present study's task is to establish different degrees of association and comovement. Therefore I concentrate on traditional bivariate VAR-spectral analysis:

For the general multivariate case, the spectral density matrix $\mathbf{F}(\omega)$ of an n-dimensional stochastic process, in analogy to equation (3.12) and in analogy to equation (3.13) above, is given by the Fourier transform of the covariance function of the process:

$$\mathbf{F}(\omega) = \frac{1}{2\pi} \sum_{\tau=-\infty}^{+\infty} \Gamma(\tau) e^{-i\omega\tau}, \quad -\pi \leq \omega \leq \pi, \tag{3.27}$$

with

$$\Gamma(\omega) = \begin{pmatrix} \gamma_{11}(\omega) & \cdots & \gamma_{1n}(\omega) \\ \vdots & \ddots & \vdots \\ \gamma_{n1}(\omega) & \cdots & \gamma_{nn}(\omega) \end{pmatrix} \text{ and } \mathbf{F}(\omega) = \begin{pmatrix} f_{11}(\omega) & \cdots & f_{1n}(\omega) \\ \vdots & \ddots & \vdots \\ f_{n1}(\omega) & \cdots & f_{nn}(\omega) \end{pmatrix}.$$

Because $\mathbf{F}(\omega)$ is an even function, it is sufficient to examine it in the interval $[0, \pi]$. The diagonal elements $f_{11}(\omega), ..., f_{nn}(\omega)$ are the real-valued *autospectra* or *power spectra* as shown in equation (3.13) above, off-diagonal elements reflect cross spectra $f_{jk}(\omega) = c_{jk}(\omega) - iq_{jk}(\omega)$, consisting of $c_{jk}(\omega)$ cospectra and $q_{jk}(\omega)$ quadrature spectra. Bivariate spectral measures are, in analogy to the univariate case, derived by the estimated parameter matrix $\mathbf{A}$ of a more general VAR(p) process adjusted to a respective pair of series:

$$\mathbf{F}(\omega) = \frac{1}{2\pi} \mathbf{A}(\omega)^{-1} \sum \mathbf{A}(\omega)^{-*}, \tag{3.28}$$

where $\sum$ denotes the error variance-covariance matrix, $\mathbf{A}(\omega)$ the Fourier transform of the matrix lag polynomial $\mathbf{A}(L) = I - A_1 L - \ldots A_1 L^p$ and

[18] See for example Maddala and Kim (1998) for a survey of the recent literature on cointegration.

[19] Namely, the cospectrum, cf. the immediately following presentation.

[20] Which Croux, Forni and Reichlin (2000) entitle "cohesion."

superscript "*" complex conjugate transpose. The off-diagonal elements of (3.27), estimated via (3.28) allow the computation of the phase shift measure by means of the following expression

$$ps(\omega) = \arctan \frac{-q_{jk}(\omega)}{c_{jk}(\omega)}. \tag{3.29}$$

The phase shift (ps) measures the phase lead ($ps > 0$) or lag ($ps < 0$)of a series j over the series k at a certain frequency ω. The ps measure employed here is computed at the maximum of squared coherency sc, i.e. at that frequency $\overline{\omega}$, where the cyclic components contained in the two series at stake show the highest degree of linear relationship, as defined by

$$sc = \kappa_{jk}^2(\omega) = \frac{|f_{jk}(\omega)|^2}{f_{jj}(\omega) f_{kk}(\omega)}. \tag{3.30}$$

The sc measure takes on values between 0 and 1. Precisely, it indicates the proportion of the variance of the component of frequency ω of either series that can be explained by its linear regression on the other series; see Koopmans (1995), p. 142. For example, if the series are statistically independent from each other, sc equals zero; if one process is a linear transformation of the other, sc takes on the value one. Both spectral parameters ps and sc can certainly also be calculated and displayed for a range of different frequencies. These illustrations are called phase and coherence spectrum, respectively. For $sc < 1$, the relationship between the two business cycle components under investigation is not strict, but the phase spectrum can be interpreted as displaying the expected values of respective phase shifts for different frequencies (cf. Koopmans (1995), p. 138).[21]

[21] Reiter (1995) accurately summarizes: "The bivariate spectral parameters are ideal tools for investigating the comovements of series over the business cycle. For example, a good leading indicator is a series having a positive lead relative to the reference series, which can be seen from the phase spectrum, and a high coherency," p. 25.

Part II

National, Supra- and International Cycles

4. The G7 and Euro15 Economies: 1960 - 2000

The American experience indicates that the major business cycle has had an average duration of a little over eight years ... Since one to two minor peaks regularly occur between the major peaks, it is clear that the minor cycle is something less than half of the duration of the major cycle.

P. A. Samuelson (1961)

On the heels of the U.S. growth crunch, the world has gone from boom to bust in less than a year ... the global economy is probably already in a recession. Sort of what Bruce Springsteen's "Born in the U.S.A." would sound like if the lyrics had been written by an economist.

S. Roach (Morgan Stanley) in *Wall Street Journal Europe* (July 6-7, 2001)

4.1 Data and Strategy

The central data source for the analysis of the present chapter is the national income and productivity accounts (NIPA) annual statistics database maintained by EUROSTAT, statistical office of the European Commission. As supplementary sources the OECD Statistical Compendium (on CD-ROM) and the International Financial Statistics (IFS on CD-ROM) provided by the IMF are considered.[1] The series are annual for the period 1960 to 2000, making a total of 40 observations. Throughout, they are provided in deflated form on the base year 1990.[2] Furthermore, the NIPA classification scheme of the US Bureau of Economic Analysis (BEA) is widely adopted. Accordingly, the quantities add to GDP as displayed in the following:

[1] This reverting to OECD and IMF data sources concerns in detail: the private consumption (CON) series for Canada for the years from 1961 to 1963 and the observation for 2000. The GDP series for Canada from 1961 to 1964, the total private investment (TPI) series for Canada for the years 1961 to 1963, 1993, 1994 and 1997 to 2000, as well as for the US from 1996 to 2000. The data for gross fixed capital formation (GFCF) and inventory investment (II) series stem for all analyzed economies from OECD databases.

[2] The quantities are throughout billion US$ in prices and exchange rates from 1990.

Gross Domestic Product (GDP)
1. Personal consumption expenditures (Private consumption: CON)[3]
2. Gross private domestic investment (Total private investment: TPI)
    2a. Fixed investment (Gross fixed capital formation: GFCF)
    2b. Change in private inventories (Inventory investment: II)
3. Net exports of goods and services (Primary current account: PCA)
    3a. Exports (EXP)
    3b. Imports (IM)
4. Government consumption and gross investment (Gov. spending: GOV)

By considering explicitly the two investment components, GFCF and II, the present study places in the tradition of CBC and SEMECON research special emphasis on these two variables. By means of the instruments described in detail in the preceding methodological chapter of the monograph, I essentially address the following questions:

1. How volatile is a series and how much does it, as a constituting component, contribute in magnitude and volatility terms to a respective aggregate of higher statistical dimension?
2. Are there regular cycles in the series? What are the period lengths of these cycles?
3. Is the cyclical structure significant and how prominent is it in the overall dynamics, i.e. how strongly and significantly is it damped?
4. If the series show profound and significant cyclical structure, how many cycles can be identified?
5. How important are they, i.e. how large is the part of the variance explained by one or more complex roots?
6. How robust are the results for different detrending procedures?
7. What can be said about the lead-lag relationship between the constituting cycles and the respective national and supranational aggregate?

The following paragraphs give a short overview of the central calculated volatility and spectral measures of the present chapter's analysis, including how to quickly interpret them.

Relative trend level (RTL), *standardized standard deviation* (SSD) & *contribution to standard deviation* (CTS):
The relative trend level quantifies the relative magnitude or share of the constituent series' trend level to the corresponding aggregate series trend level; see equation (3.4) above. The SSD assesses the relative volatility of a variable. It is defined as the standard deviation of the detrended series of a variable at stake standardized on its mid trend level value; see equation (3.5) above.

[3] In parentheses are the (eventually) more familiar notations, mainly, though not uniformly, used by the central databases of EUROSTAT, OECD and IMF.

CTS gives the contribution to standard deviation measured in standard deviation terms of the respective aggregate, i.e. in percent of the total aggregate's standard deviation; see equation (3.6) above. A positive CTS-value identifies a destabilizing constituent component, a negative CTS-value identifies a stabilizing constituent component.

Period length (per.) & *modulus* (mod.):
Period denotes the period length (in years) of the contained cyclic structure in the series according to the ME-spectral estimate. For the multivariate estimates it denotes the period length (in years) at maximum of squared coherency (*sc*). The modulus measures the damping rate of a cyclicality contained in a series. For a starting amplitude-value Θ, a modulus of 0.5 implies that the cyclic component of the series has a remaining amplitude-value of $\frac{1}{2}\Theta$ after one year, $(0.5)^2\,\Theta$ after two years, etc.

Squared coherency (sc) & *phase shift* (ps):
Suppose that the spectra of two series exhibit peaks at a certain frequency ω^*. *sc* then measures the extent of the linear relationship between the cycles in the two series. It can be interpreted similarly to a correlation coefficient. Phase measures the lead-lag relationship between two cyclicalities of the same frequency ω^* in the two series at stake, i.e. the distance between the turning points of contained cyclicalities with the same frequency. A value of phase > 0 indicates a phase lead (in years), a value < 0 a phase lag (in years), see equations (3.29) and (3.30) above.

4.2 National Uni- and Bivariate Stylized Facts

The results of the analysis of volatility, relative magnitude and contribution to aggregate volatility are presented in Table 4.1. The univariate spectral estimates are displayed in Tables 4.2 to 4.4 for the above outlined three detrending procedures and Figures 4.1 to 4.3 for the MBK-filtered series over the eight NIPA aggregates GDP, CON, TPI, GFCF, II, EXP, IM and GOV. It should be noted that in the case of two contained periodicities in the national series, the respectively longer cycles and corresponding moduli are displayed throughout in the first row of the respective NIPA aggregate's column, the respectively shorter cycle lengths and corresponding moduli in the second row. The reported period lengths are given in years and the adjusted R^2s are taken from the corresponding AR model estimates. A visual inspection of the raw inventory investment series leads to the conclusion that most of these series show stationary behavior. Log-differencing these series leads to a destruction of any potentially contained cyclic dynamics. Therefore, I display the estimation results for the unfiltered inventory investment series in Table 4.4.

The results of the first set of bivariate spectral estimates, i.e. every NIPA aggregate relative to its respective national GDP aggregate, are presented in Tables 4.5 to 4.7. Again, in the case of the two complex roots implied by the adjusted VAR system, the respectively longer cycles and corresponding bivariate measures are displayed first.

4.2.1 General Salient Facts

All of the following spectral estimates have to be seen in the light of the relative shares of contribution of the analyzed aggregates to the respective national GDP. This needs to be taken into account in both respects, first with regard to their relative trend levels (NIPA constituent series to national GDP) and relative standard deviation (of NIPA constituent series to mid trend level value of the constituent series), see equations (3.4) and (3.5) above. This information is summarized in Table 4.1.

The first measure, constituent trend level value relative to respective GDP trend level value, is given at three distinct points of the estimated MBK-trend functions: a) at the starting point, i.e. corresponding to the year 1963,[4] b) at the mid point, i.e. corresponding to the year 1980, and finally c) at the end point, i.e. corresponding to the year 1997. There are several things to note, regarding the results given in Table 4.1: For all economies the majority of results shows quite constant shares of their NIPA constituents to national GDP over the three selected points of observation - with inventory investment generally showing the smallest, private consumption the largest fraction. The exception is given by the two PCA constituents that display the least stable fractions over time, ranging from 4 to 5% for the US at the starting point up to equal or close to 40% for Canada at the mid point of the observation's horizon.

Concerning the SSD measures, changes in private inventories, i.e. the II series, show throughout the highest volatility for all NIPA constituent series. This volatility of inventory dynamics is, in comparison to the volatility of the respective national GDP data, the highest for Germany, the U.K. and especially Canada (making up to about 50-times the volatility of Canadian GDP), the lowest it is for the Japanese economy (making up a little less than 5-times the volatility of Japanese GDP). This suggests the interpretation that the extensive implementation of innovative inventory management systems like just-in-time production, the Kanban-system, etc. during the last decades has led to a remarkable reduction of the volatility in the II series of the Japanese economy in an international comparison. Nevertheless, Japan shows the highest relative variance in GDP. A fact that might at least partially be induced by the recent and severe breakdown of the financial system in Japan. With the exception of the Japanese economy, the second most volatile series

[4] Remember the MBK-filter shortens the series by three datapoints at the beginning and end of the series, respectively.

for all other G7 economies are the two remaining investment series under investigation, namely TPI and GFCF. Furthermore, the US economy shows a most distinct characteristics: The high SSD measures of TPI and GFCF, compared to the US GDP series,[5] can be seen as an indication that the United States play the role of an "investment dynamics dominated" economy. An indication which is further underscored in the course of this chapter, as well as in part III of the monograph. Throughout the G7 economies the least volatile series are the EXP and CON series, while IM and GOV series seem to be intermediary volatile.

Let us turn to the remaining CTS measures, presented in Table 4.1. As argued above, a CTS-value > 0 characterizes a destabilizing component, a CTS-value < 0 a stabilizing constituent variable; see equation (3.6). As widely agreed on, the calculated figures of Table 4.1 classify for all G7 countries the IM series as a stabilizing variable. Technically, it should be noted that for a substractively contributing variable, like IM (since GDP = CON + TPI + GOV + PCA, where PCA is defined as EXP − IM), the construction of the CTS-measure is modified in that the nominator of equation (3.6) becomes $\sigma(y^a) - \sigma(y^a + y_i^c)$. There are three more negatively valued CTS measures displayed in Table 4.1, but their negligible absolute sizes suggest that these series hardly contribute to the respective GDP series' standard deviation at all. While for all other G7 economies, the pattern is such that the CON series contributes about double the value (on average 57% of standard deviation terms of the aggregate) to the respective national product in contrast to the investment components TPI, GFCF and II (for example TPI on average 24%), the US stand out: For the US economy the TPI series contributes 57% to the standard deviation in US GDP and furthermore it shows, in comparison to the CON series, a close to 1.6-times higher CTS value (37% vs. 57%). Even the isolated GFCF series still contributes 39%, and therefore more than US CON, to the standard deviation of the US GDP series. This is a further evidence pointing in the direction that the US product's business cycle component extracted by means of the MBK-filter is dominated by its constituting investment variables, cf. section 1.2 of the present study.[6]

It should be noted that RTL is given in separate rows at starting, mid, and end point of series. The SSD measures for the respective national GDP series are: Canada: 0.03, France: 0.06, Germany: 0.08, Italy: 0.07, Japan: 0.14, U.K.: 0.06, US: 0.01.

[5] Even outnumbering the SSD measure of US GDP by taking on a value more than 5- to 6-times that of GDP.

[6] The question of indications for 'automatic stabilizers' (i.e. stabilization through GOV) on the basis of these and the following findings is discussed in Süssmuth (2002c).

Table 4.1. *G7 Economies*: RTL, CTS and SSD measures (MBK-filter)

	CON	TPI	GFCF	II	EXP	IM	GOV
Canada							
	0.61	0.23	0.22	0.01	0.18	0.18	0.14
RTL	0.59	0.18	0.18	0.01	0.40	0.38	0.33
	0.55	0.23	0.23	0.01	0.26	0.25	0.33
CTS	0.43	0.27	0.27	0.01	0.11	-.23	0.27
SSD	0.02	0.06	0.05	1.44	0.04	0.04	0.04
France							
	0.61	0.24	0.23	0.01	0.13	0.12	0.13
RTL	0.60	0.17	0.18	0.01	0.25	0.22	0.19
	0.58	0.23	0.22	0.01	0.21	0.21	0.17
CTS	0.57	0.24	0.23	0.02	0.18	-.19	0.16
SSD	0.06	0.08	0.07	0.55	0.06	0.07	0.06
Germany							
	0.59	0.27	0.25	0.01	0.17	0.16	0.15
RTL	0.65	0.21	0.21	0.01	0.25	0.24	0.11
	0.62	0.21	0.21	0.01	0.25	0.24	0.14
CTS	0.61	0.24	0.18	0.04	0.17	-.22	0.13
SSD	0.08	0.11	0.09	2.19	0.09	0.09	0.08
Italy							
	0.62	0.23	0.27	0.01	0.14	0.14	0.13
RTL	0.61	0.17	0.18	0.01	0.26	0.22	0.16
	0.60	0.25	0.23	0.01	0.23	0.23	0.14
CTS	0.59	0.25	0.24	0.02	0.17	-.22	0.13
SSD	0.07	0.10	0.08	0.66	0.05	0.07	0.07
Japan							
	0.58	0.34	0.31	0.02	0.09	0.09	0.08
RTL	0.60	0.28	0.28	0.01	0.10	0.08	0.09
	0.58	0.31	0.30	0.01	0.12	0.12	0.09
CTS	0.60	0.26	0.26	0.00	0.04	-.02	0.10
SSD	0.14	0.13	0.13	0.67	0.06	0.11	0.15
U.K.							
	0.65	0.18	0.17	0.01	0.19	0.20	0.17
RTL	0.64	0.16	0.17	0.01	0.28	0.29	0.18
	0.59	0.18	0.17	0.01	0.27	0.26	0.21
CTS	0.62	0.18	0.19	-.01	0.19	-.24	0.18
SSD	0.07	0.10	0.09	3.23	0.05	0.08	0.06
USA							
	0.62	0.19	0.13	0.06	0.05	0.04	0.17
RTL	0.70	0.18	0.18	0.01	0.11	0.13	0.15
	0.63	0.20	0.14	0.06	0.09	0.09	0.16
CTS	0.37	0.57	0.39	0.16	-.01	-.22	-.02
SSD	0.01	0.05	0.06	0.07	0.05	0.04	0.01

General salient facts, regarding the spectral estimation results reported in Tables 4.2 to 4.4 and the spectra in Figures 4.1 to 4.3 are: As discussed earlier, the HP(100)-filter is most obviously biased in favor of the lower frequencies, i.e. higher period cyclicalities. Furthermore, as is the case for several national series, the HP-filter does not sustain potential second periodicities. As expected the logD-filter destroys a lot of contained periodicity and is biased towards relatively short cyclicalities, cf. the results for the Japanese economy in Table 4.4.

The graphics of the spectral densities displayed in Figures 4.1 to 4.3 are inspired by Sargent (1987, chapter XI, section 10). The central features that should become obvious are a) the shape of the spectrum and b) its position (left or right) towards the median peak frequency (below or above) of the G7 economies, as indicated by the parallel straight line to the ordinate. Concerning a) on the one hand it is interesting whether one or more periodicities are contained in the series, i.e. whether the power spectra are single or double peaked. Secondly, the sharpness of the spectrum is relevant, i.e. the less damped the roots are, the more regular are the cycles in the series, and the higher and sharper is the peak in the spectrum, cf. the remarkably low bandwidth of the spectral density for the Japanese GDP series, for example in comparison to the relatively flat spectrum of the Canadian TPI series. Concerning b) the median period length is matched for GDP and CON by Italy, for TPI, GFCF and II by Japan, for EXP and GOV by the US and finally for the IM series by the U.K. economy. A final feature of the spectral graphics displayed in Figures 4.1 to 4.3 is the dashed line that represents the integrated spectrum. The closer this line is to an imaginary 45 degree line, the more the dynamics of the series are driven by noise. The integrated spectrum of a white noise process would exactly equal the 45 degree line.[7]

Disregarding the two primary current account (PCA) components, the clearest double peaking spectral density is given by the German economy. Except for the two private investment components the peak in the higher frequency range dominates the long cycle in the German case. For the German investment components (GFCF and II, as well as TPI, i.e. the sum of both,) both cycles concentrate a reasonable amount of spectral power, while the longer cycle bears about 20 to 50% more spectral mass.

Another important and interesting piece of information is given by the median values of estimated univariate spectral measures. These are displayed in the respective last row of Table 4.2 to 4.4. As a technical remark, note that only in cases where ≥ 2 periodicities and corresponding measures are estimated over the 7 economies a median value is calculated. Furthermore, in

[7] Note, there exist several tests that avail this feature of the integrated spectrum to test on cyclicality. These include the Fisher Test, Bartlett's Test, the Durbin-Test and the Kolmogorov-Smirnov-Test, see for example Brockwell and Davis (1991, § 10.2). Unfortunately, they are throughout of weak power and based on the (nonparametric) periodogram method and therefore unsuited for the short time series under analysis in the present study.

cases when the underlying distribution over the G7 economies is of an even number of results, the median values are 'artificial' figures corresponding to the averages of the two middle-valued estimation results. This is the case for the variables CON, GFCF and II in Table 4.2, for GDP and IM in Table 4.4. Comparing these median values for the different detrending filters (Table 4.2 to 4.4) it becomes obvious that in general the highest importance, in the sense of explaining variance of the detrended series (adjusted R^2 values), of the contained cyclicalities is estimated for the HP-, followed by the MBK-filter. In both cases the cycles explain from about one third to more than 60% of the variance of the respective series (in median terms). For the MBK-filter results, the most variance is explained in median terms by the cycle in GFCF, followed by the one contained in the GDP and GOV series, respectively. For the HP-filter results the corresponding top three important cycles are to be found in CON, GDP and GFCF - throughout explaining more than half of the variance contained in the respective series. For the logD-filter these are II, CON and TPI. Concerning the prominence of the cycles, as expressed by the median values of the moduli, the following patterns are striking: For the MBK-filtered series, the cyclicalities of the TPI, II and GFCF series are the most prominent, showing reasonably high moduli > 0.85. Similarly, for the HP-filtered series, the cycles contained in the CON, GFCF, GDP, II and GOV series imply moduli > 0.8. Finally, for the logD-detrending procedure, the inherent cycles in CON, TPI and II, though over all rather weakly significant (in median R^2 terms), still show moduli > 0.65. Nearly all median values of estimated period lengths (in years) lie in the frequency range of classical (Juglar) business cycles with periodicities ranging from about 5-6 years up to approximately 9 years. The only exception, in the sense of an outlier, is given for the logD-filtered GDP series' result (12.42 years). As expected the median values of period lengths for the II series reflect the shortest cyclicalities over the 8 analyzed aggregates, taking on values from about 3 to 6 years. Broadly interpreted, this is (weak) evidence for a Kitchin periodicity in the G7 II series.

4.2.2 Robust Univariate Stylized Facts: National Cycles

Germany most clearly shows a "two cycle"- or "M/W-cyclical" dynamic structure over all NIPA aggregates. With the exception of the two PCA series this M/W-shape is confirmed over all three detrending procedures and might therefore be seen as a robust stylized fact. As indicated by the relatively higher moduli and lower standard errors, the shorter cyclic pattern dominates the German economy, cf. also the argumentation above and the spectra in Figures 4.1 to 4.3. As we will see this fact will be confirmed by the national and supranational bivariate spectral estimations, too. In contrast to this finding, for the French economy, only in the case of series detrended by the MBK-filter, the GFCF and II series show a long as well as a short business cycle periodicity at the classical frequencies. Japan shows a remarkably prominent long cycle of about 7 years length in its NIPA aggregates. Taking the results for the HP- and logD-filter into account, Japan's TPI and GFCF series seem to also bear this period length, while Japanese inventory investment series show a weakly estimated and more strongly damped classical Kitchin periodicity of about 4 to 5 years length. The latter seems to hold also for the U.K. economy. Although the shorter and more strongly damped cycle seems to stem from an aliasing[8] of a double-cycle inventory dynamics. In line with earlier findings, cf. Woitek (1996), the United States seem (in contrast to the other G7 economies) be predominated by a periodicity of an intermediary length of about 5 to 6.5 years length in GDP and TPI. This can clearly be seen also from Figure 4.1, where the US spectra nearly throughout peak right from, i.e. at a higher frequency than the median G7 frequency, as indicated by the parallel line to the ordinate. The exceptions are the US government spending and export series that match the G7 median frequencies.

4.2.3 Robust Bivariate Stylized Facts: National Cycles

In this subsection I will first describe and interpret the bivariate spectral findings country by country (for all three filters) and then illuminate the salient bivariate features of the NIPA business cycle components in general by means of the mean bivariate spectra (for the MBK-filter), as displayed, constituent by constituent, in Figure 4.4:

Canada: The Canadian exports series contribute about 5 to 10% to the standard deviation of Canadian GDP and lag the Canadian GDP cycle, according to the MBK- and HP-filter results of Table 4.5 and 4.6, by 1 to 2 years. Most probably this also holds for the Canadian imports (a stabilizer, reducing GDP volatility by about 20%), though by slightly less time, i.e. by about 0.5 to 1 year. Both PCA components fluctuate less coherent with Canadian GDP than the other NIPA constituents that behave remarkably coherent. According to the MBK- and logD-filter results, the cycle in Canadian inventories obviously lags the national product cycle by approximately 2.5 to 3 years, though contributing negligibly to the variance of the Canadian product cycle.

France: One can not make any robust statement on the bivariate dynamics of the French NIPA series with its GDP cycle. Nevertheless, it can be stated that: Firstly the French PCA components seem to move quite coherent with the French GDP cycle at a single periodicity of about 6.5 to 10 years period length. And secondly, according to the logD- and HP-filtered series' results, the inventory cycle potentially bears an unconventionally long period length of about 9 to 10 years length and lags the GDP cycle by about one year.

[8] Aliasing in the context of spectral analysis denotes the case when two frequencies close in value "fuse" due to their closeness to one single frequency in the spectrum; see, for example, Marple (1987, section 2.6).

Germany: All German constituent series are highly coherent with the national GDP cycle, while in growth rates (logD-filter) only CON and the two investment components (GFCF and II) show coherent cyclic dynamics with regard to the German GDP cycle. Most of the German constituent NIPA aggregate cycles also fluctuate quite in phase with the cyclic pattern in GDP. Comparing the MBK- and HP-filter results, it remains unclear whether German exports lead or lag the GDP cycle by about one year.

Italy: According to the national GDP bivariate estimation results, the Italian economy is especially characterized by a traditional and approximately in GDP cycle phase TPI cycle with a traditional length of about 7.5 to 10 years, see Table 4.5 and 4.6. Furthermore, Italy seems to bear a robust (i.e. over all filtering methods consistently estimated) inventory cycle in the constitution of its national GDP with a rather unconventional length of about 6 to 10 years. This inconvenient II cycle fluctuates, as in the case of the French economy, only weakly coherent to the GDP cycle and lags it by up to about a half year.

Japan: The Japanese economy is robustly characterized by its highly GDP coherent investment (including inventory investment) cycle dynamics and the cyclicalities inherent in its import series. The former[9] reflects the "central role" that "investment has played ... in both the growth and fluctuations in the Japanese economy." This feature as well as the questions why "business cycles in Japan were basically investment-led" and "why Japanese firms invest so much," are extensively outlined in a historical perspective of the Japanese post world war II economy by Yoshikawa (1995), chapter 7, p. 244-291. For the Japanese inventory series, the in GDP cycle phase periodicity shows the classical short cycle period length of 4 to 5 years, although it is certainly estimated less coherent and contributing marginally in standard deviation terms (for the aforementioned reasons) to the longer Japanese GDP cycle periodicity, cf. Figure 4.1. The GFCF series contributes about 27% to the product series' standard deviation. It shows its highest coherency with the GDP cycle at period lengths of about 11 to 12 and 7 years. These periodicities might be aliased to a single periodicity of 10.75 years length at the maximum of squared coherency in the HP-filter case. A further indication for an aliasing problem in this context is that for both logD- and MBK-filter results, the one cycle slightly leads, the other slightly lags the GDP cycle. Similarly, the two periodicities (of about 12 and 2 to 7 years length) at maximum of squared coherency for logD- and HP-filtered TPI series might be aliased to a single period length of 6.5 years, shared with the GDP cycle, in the case of the MBK-filtered TPI series. On the contrary, there is a robust double period coherency pattern for the Japanese import series, though stabilizing the Japanese GDP cycle only marginally ($< 10\%$). Most robustly, the Japanese imports fluctuate a) quite regularly, cf. the narrow bandwidth of the spectrum displayed in

[9] Contributing roughly 30% to the standard deviation of the Japanese GDP cycle component.

Figure 4.2, b) highly and the most coherent with the Japanese GDP cycle at a period length of about 7 to 7.5 years[10], and c) with a phase lead of approximately 1.5 years relative to the national GDP cycle.

United Kingdom: As expected on the basis of the univariate spectral estimates and since the U.K. shows the longest of all G7 GDP cycles, see Figure 4.1, the highest coherency of U.K. NIPA constituents with the national GDP cycle is estimated at a period length of, on average, 8 years. Especially the TPI and GOV series show a high coherency at a traditional long cycle frequency corresponding to 8 to 9 years and a relatively lower coherent classical short cycle at a period length of approximately 3 to 4 years. Robustly, the TPI cycles slightly lag, while the GOV cycles slightly lead the cyclicalities contained in the U.K. GDP series. Concerning the TPI cycle the long one most probably stems from a traditional long and GDP coherent common cycle in the GFCF series ($<$ 8 years) in combination with an approximately 8 years cycle, contained in the II component and lagging the GDP cycle by about 2 years. The short lagging cycle, also inherent in the TPI series, may be constituted from the short cyclicality of about 4 years contained as well in the II series. This is at least indicated for the MBK- and logD-filtered series' results. Furthermore, it should be noted that the CON series of the U.K. fluctuates robustly both strongly coherent to and in phase with the national GDP series at a somehow shorter than the univariate GDP cycle length of about 7 to 8 years.

United States: As can be seen from the CTV measures in Table 4.5, the US TPI and GFCF series highly contribute to the standard deviation of the MBK-filtered GDP series (in both cases even more than does the MBK-filtered private consumption series). It is noteworthy that, as in the case of the Japanese economy, the US economy is robustly characterized by its highly GDP coherent investment (including inventory investment) cycle dynamics[11] and the cyclicalities inherent in both national PCA components. There is a small but growing body of empirical literature that investigates the business cycle nexus between Japan and the United States as well as generally on international business cycle interdependencies. It is surveyed, for example, in Selover (1997), Artis and Zhang (1999) and Imbs (1999). Selover (1997) also finds that despite the popular saying in Japan that 'if the United States sneezes, Japan catches a cold', "the US does not 'drive' the Japanese economy, rather it transmit shocks which partially synchronize the two economies, perhaps through the 'mode-lock' phenomenon," p. 385. For a thorough discussion of the 'mode-lock' hypothesis in the context of international business cycles' synchronization the reader is referred to chapter 5 of the present part of the monograph. Besides its cyclic dynamic analogy

[10] Although there is another shorter period cycle of about 3 to 4 years length that less coherently fluctuates in line with the Japanese GDP cycle.

[11] These, although sometimes showing two periodicities at their respective maximum of squared coherency, are dominated by a 5 to 5.5 years cycle that manifests itself and is reflected in the US GDP cycle - at least for the MBK-filtering routine.

to the Japanese economy, the US exports quite robustly fluctuate the most coherent with national GDP at a periodicity of 6.5 to 8 years length and lag the GDP cycle by about 1.5 to 2 years. On the contrary, US imports slightly lead the GDP cycle and show an intermediate strength of coherency at a period length of approximately 6 to 6.5 years.

Let me now turn to document the salient bivariate features of the NIPA business cycle components in general, i.e. constituent by constituent series. I will do so on the base of the mean bivariate spectra (for the MBK-filter), namely the mean densities of the respective coherence spectra, see equation (3.30), and phase spectra, see equation (3.29). The idea to construct mean bivariate spectral densities over a population of units of investigation (in the present case economies) is adopted from Forni and Lippi (1997, Fig. 14.4) and Forni and Reichlin (1998, Fig. 7). These authors proceed similarly in constructing the sum of cospectra[12] over sectoral estimation results. The essential findings can be summarized in the following: The respective CON series fluctuates on average highly coherent to the respective GDP series of the G7 economies. Both bivariate spectra show a clear and smooth shape. The phase spectrum suggests that the fluctuations contained in the CON series, on average, represent a leading indicator for the GDP cycles with a phase lead of about one year, as measured at the maximum of *sc*. The TPI cycles fluctuate also highly coherent to the GDP cyclicalities - maximally at frequencies corresponding to periodicities of approximately 9 and 4.5 years. It should be noted that the first peak of the coherence spectrum is rather broad, suggesting that for the first periodicity high coherence values are also obtained for classical cyclicalities with period lengths starting from 6 up to 9 years. These first shared cyclicalities nearly coincide with the GDP cyclicalities, while the second shorter ones obviously lead it by about two years. The GFCF cycles are on average as well estimated strongly coherent to the GDP cyclicalities, the strongest at a period length of 7.6 years with a marginal phase lag. On the other hand, the II series fluctuate on average less coherent to the GDP cycles, reflected in a maximum peak of the mean coherence spectrum at a *sc*-value of about 0.6. The mean phase spectral density has a quite jagged shape and indicates a coincidence relationship to the GDP cycle at a period length of about 6 to 7 years. Both PCA components show on average a quite high *sc* with GDP cycles, taking on a maximal value at the classical frequencies, corresponding to period lengths of about 7.5 to 7.8 years. Both represent rather coinciding GDP indicators. Finally, the coherence spectra of the GOV series show on average their highest coherence with GDP cycles at a periodicity of about 10 years, though the peak is, as in the case of TPI quite broad, implying also periodicities with higher frequencies (shorter period cycles) to stand in a relatively high coherence relation to the GDP cycles.

---

[12] I.e. the real parts of the cross-spectra, implied in squared absolute expressions in the nominator of the coherence spectrum's definition, see equation (3.30) above.

4.3 Supranational Bivariate Stylized Facts

The implied central message in the introductory citations to this monograph by J. Bradford de Long and L. Summers, Secretary of the Treasury during the Clinton Presidency in the United States, as well as the one by L. J. Christiano and T. J. Fitzgerald, is that (investment) cycle dynamics have far reaching implications for economic policy, see also the discussion in Courvisanos (1996, chapter 8). According to Christiano and Fitzgerald (1998) "good fiscal and monetary policy requires a clear understanding of the workings of the economy, especially what drives the business cycle ... Since at least the late 1800s, a full swing from the start of an economic expansion to a recession and back to the start of another expansion has generally taken between two to eight years. Every citizen is keenly aware of the state of the economy, whether it is in prosperity or in recession," p. 56.[13] To my opinion this is especially important with regard to the recent early stages of implementation of the EMU and the impending second 'Delors Stage' of the Maastricht Treaty. Only a clear understanding of the national business cycle dynamics in relation to a 'supranational' economy like the EMU, based on a thorough and sophisticated descriptive analysis, will show the potential effectiveness, range of coverage and limits of a concerted fiscal and monetary policy.[14] The following paragraphs and estimations, reported in Table 4.8 and Figure 4.5, undertake a step in this direction. Related studies are, among others, the ones based on time domain analysis by Artis and Zhang (1999), Duecker and Wesche (1999) and Gallegatti and Gallegatti (2000) and, based on time and frequency domain analysis, the ones by Croux, Forni and Reichlin (2001), Forni and Reichlin (1999), Forni et al. (1999) and Forni et al. (2001).

Hitherto our investigations have shown that the MBK-filter provides reasonably intermediary results concerning the spectral estimation results of all three applied filtering procedures. Furthermore, it is the latest detrending technology and in several respects superior to the conventional BK band-pass filter, see Woitek (1998). I therefore decided to concentrate on spectral estimation results based on MBK-filtered series. In Figure 4.5, the univariate GDP cycle estimates for the (artificial) supranational economies G7 and the so-called Euro15-zone (EURO 15), including the economies of Austria, Belgium, Denmark, Finland, France, Germany, Greece, Ireland, Italy, Luxembourg, Netherlands, Portugal, Spain, Sweden and Great Britain, are dis-

[13] In a similar vein, though quite more pessimistic, K. Hasset (American Enterprise Institute) states on the recent situation of the US economy in *Wall Street Journal Europe* (article: *Rx for the Economy*, May 7, 2001): "Christina and David Romer found that fiscal measures generally have failed to push the economy out of recession because they have been too small to have much of an effect. Indeed, large fiscal stimulus packages have generally not been passed near cyclical troughs. Instead, they have historically emerged only because of slow recoveries, as was the case with the 1964 tax cut."

[14] Cf. also the discussion in Muellbauer (1997), whether Great Britain really should participate in Delors II from a strategic (business cycle) policy point of view.

played. Both show a double peaking ME spectrum at approximately similar periodicities of about 8 and 4 years. In contrast to the G7 GDP cycle, the EURO15 GDP cycle is characterized by a quite stronger prominence of its contained shorter classical cycle. In analogy to the bivariate stylized facts of national cycles, I will first make some brief general statements and then go through (only) the most salient supranational bivariate stylized facts country by country.
In general it can be noted that, for the above discussed reasons, Japan contributes the most in standard deviation terms to the total G7 GDP fluctuations, followed by the German, French and U.K. economy. The Canadian and US economy contribute the least. The CON series contribute the most, followed by the investment components (with the exception of II, contributing at maximum 1% in CTS terms), while both PCA components contribute throughout marginally to the amplitudes in supranational product series. Regarding the signs of CTS-values, the IM series play the role of a stabilizer. Germany, Italy and France contribute more or less in equal shares of about 18% to EURO15 GDP in standard deviation terms. In contrast, the U.K. contributes a relatively smaller figure of about 12%. *Prima facie*, the German economy seems to be responsible for the profound short cycle in the EURO15 GDP series and maybe also for the rather less profound one in the G7 GDP series. Most national GDP cycles coincide closely with the respective supranational ones. The period lengths at maximum of *sc* throughout match with classical frequencies, for Germany mainly with a short Kitchin periodicity of about 4 years, for the other 6 economies mainly with a traditional Juglar frequency of about 6.5 to 8 years length.

Canada: For Canada only the cyclicality inherent in the GFCF and CON series fluctuates - at a period length of slightly more than 7 years - profoundly coherent with and leads the G7 cycle by about 1.5 and 2 years, respectively.

France: Obviously, the French economy contributes to the classic long investment cycle of about 6 to 9 years found in both supranational GDP cycles. French inventory investments clearly lag the supranational product cycles and fluctuate only weakly coherent to and in phase with the short cycle frequency contained in both of them, cf. Figure 4.5. The most in phase with a supranational GDP cycle is French TPI, namely with the EURO 15 GDP cycle.

Germany: Looking at the period lengths that a VAR system with German NIPA and supranational GDP series bears, it becomes quickly obvious that, despite the German GFCF series and partly also the German EXP series, all other German NIPA series at stake contribute clearly and, as reflected in relatively high *sc* values, profoundly to the secondary short periodic regularity found in both analyzed supranational series. Most constituent series, as well as the German GDP aggregate, are at this frequency quite in phase with both supranational series. Only the German GFCF series seems to slightly lag the supranational cycles and German exports lead the G7 product cycle by about one year.[15] It is noteworthy that the German economy shows the highest CTS to the EURO 15 GDP values with regard to the other European economies.[16]

Italy: The Italian NIPA series share an "in between"-frequency with the G7 product cycle, i.e. in between of the two frequencies found in the G7 GDP series. This might be due to the fact that the spectra for Italian series are mainly one-time peaking, see Figures 4.1 to 4.3. The Italian series seem to be closely related to the short European GDP periodicity, indicated by the shared period lengths, relatively high *sc* values (with the exception of the fluctuations in the II series) and a phase position quite in phase (< 1 year) with both supranational product cycles. This may be interpreted as an indication in favor of the hypothesis put forward by Artis and Zhang (1999). Accordingly, the Italian cycle had a "strong idiosyncratic element" in the pre-1975 period, while for the post-1975 period EU countries in general had become "more synchronized with the German cycle," p. 120-122.

Japan: The outstanding volatility of the Japanese business activity is reflected in the highest destabilizing CTS measures of all analyzed economies. This fact is, as already mentioned, not that surprising if one considers the development of the Japanese economy in the last 15 years. For example Kiyotaki and West (1996) note: "In the last decade, the Japanese economy has gone through both its strongest expansion of the last twenty years and its most severe recession of the last forty years. During this decade, business fixed investment was unusually volatile, and ... seemed to be a dominant factor in both the recent 1986-1991 boom and the post-1991 bust," p. 277. As in the Italian case, Japanese NIPA series are characterized by sharing "in between"-frequencies with the G7 product cycle. With the exception of the Japanese inventory fluctuations, they move quite coherent and, with the exception of the bivariate VAR for Japanese imports and supranational product series, quite in phase with the G7 GDP cycle.

United Kingdom: In contrast to German macro aggregates, the ones of the U.K. behave first and foremostly in line with the long traditional cycle, found in both supranational GDP series. The constituent and national GDP series move quite coherent and in phase with the supranational product cycles. The obvious exception, as in the case of the French economy, is the II series that shares an intermediary periodicity in combination with a weak coherence with and a phase lag relationship to the supranational product cycles.

United States: As already stated above and indicated in the results displayed in Table 4.1, the US economy's cyclical structure is coined by investment cycle dynamics. A fact that is also reflected in the bivariate spectral

[15] Regarding the national stylized facts above, the reader may be warned that the latter result may be dependent on the applied detrending procedure.

[16] A recent related figure by Stephen Roach (Morgan Stanley) was cited in *Wall Street Journal Europe* (article: *Global Economic Contagion Spreading Gloom*, July 6-7, 2001): "In aggregate, the U.S., Japan, and Germany account for 34% of the world's GDP (based on International Monetary Fund data)."

estimations for its investment components and the G7 GDP series. In contrast to the other US NIPA series, there is a strong coherency between the G7 GDP cycle and the US investment NIPA series, TPI and GFCF. It is estimated at a classical business cycle frequency corresponding to an approximate period length of 7.5 to 8 years. The US TPI and GFCF cycles are lagging the G7 GDP cycle by a little less than one year. On the contrary, US private consumption and exports are clearly leading indicators for the G7 GDP cycle with a phase lead of 2.1 and 1.2 years, respectively.

Table 4.2. *G7 Economies*: Univariate spectral estimates (MBK filter)

Canada

	GDP	CON	TPI	GFCF	II	EXP	IM	GOV
per.	7.206	7.923	5.025	7.447	4.787	5.608	5.614	5.253
	(0.102)	(0.170)	(0.202)	(0.087)	(0.014)	(0.324)	(0.050)	(0.057)
mod.	0.777	0.760	0.436	0.812	0.812	0.822	0.760	0.721
	(0.002)	(0.002)	(0.006)	(0.001)	(0.001)	(0.001)	(0.002)	(0.002)
R^2	0.305	0.316	0.018	0.398	0.199	0.324	0.158	0.166
ord.	3	3	2	3	3	3	3	2

France

	GDP	CON	TPI	GFCF	II	EXP	IM	GOV
per.	6.202	6.073	8.381	6.499	6.839	6.305	6.120	5.190
	(0.062)	(0.059)	(3.843)	(0.069)	(0.043)	(0.054)	(0.056)	(0.084)
			3.864		3.218			
			(0.850)		(0.003)			
mod.	0.767	0.770	0.872	0.782	0.947	0.798	0.781	0.541
	(0.002)	(0.002)	(0.003)	(0.002)	(0.001)	(0.001)	(0.002)	(0.003)
			0.809		0.869			
			(0.023)		(0.002)			
R^2	0.167	0.166	0.245	0.224	0.180	0.294	0.239	0.097
ord.	3	3	5	3	5	3	3	2

Germany

	GDP	CON	TPI	GFCF	II	EXP	IM	GOV
per.	9.683	9.933	9.200	8.282	5.664	5.919	4.942	9.268
	(2.222)	(2.457)	(1.703)	(2.660)	(1.878)	(0.037)	(0.016)	(2.237)
	4.113	4.180	3.887	3.797	3.031			4.124
	(0.313)	(0.303)	(0.383)	(1.258)	(2.162)			(0.371)
mod.	0.820	0.839	0.838	0.859	0.899	0.791	0.774	0.838
	(0.009)	(0.013)	(0.038)	(0.072)	(0.001)	(0.001)	(0.001)	(0.028)
	0.953	0.981	0.925	0.876	0.857			0.954
	(0.009)	(0.010)	(0.001)	(0.001)	(0.001)			(0.007)
R^2	0.408	0.520	0.413	0.268	0.436	0.133	0.359	0.485
ord.	5	5	5	5	5	3	2	5

Italy

	GDP	CON	TPI	GFCF	II	EXP	IM	GOV
per.	6.389	6.313	8.064	8.064	7.279	5.685	6.026	8.141
	(0.054)	(0.048)	(2.568)	(2.568)	(7.698)	(0.045)	(0.035)	(2.541)
			3.676		3.324			3.989
			(0.508)		(0.573)			(0.769)
mod.	0.789	0.793	0.871	0.807	0.775	0.703	0.817	0.889
	(0.001)	(0.001)	(0.001)	(0.001)	(0.023)	(0.001)	(0.001)	(0.007)
			0.824		0.875			0.769
			(0.029)		(0.007)			(0.009)
R^2	0.234	0.225	0.190	0.327	0.230	0.327	0.303	0.330
ord.	3	3	5	3	5	2	3	5

Table 4.2 (continued).

Japan

	GDP	CON	TPI	GFCF	II	EXP	IM	GOV
per.	7.069 (0.028)	7.156 (0.019)	6.517 (0.043)	6.645 (0.034)	5.350 (0.028)	7.845 (0.156)	6.689 (0.025)	7.131 (0.020)
	2.515 (0.024)	3.418 (0.058)			2.772 (0.004)	3.289 (0.016)	3.208 (0.009)	3.304 (0.022)
mod.	0.991 (0.001)	0.990 (0.001)	0.895 (0.002)	0.939 (0.001)	0.872 (0.001)	0.990 (0.003)	0.994 (0.001)	0.993 (0.001)
	0.537 (0.007)	0.531 (0.004)			0.641 (0.004)	0.865 (0.014)	0.561 (0.005)	0.605 (0.001)
R^2	0.446	0.510	0.309	0.383	0.197	0.252	0.700	0.502
ord.	4	3	2	3	4	5	4	5

U.K.

	GDP	CON	TPI	GFCF	II	EXP	IM	GOV
per.	7.861 (0.988)	7.876 (1.152)	8.381 (3.843)	8.237 (2.671)	5.655 (0.037)	6.821 (0.050)	5.971 (0.031)	7.331 (0.990)
	3.606 (0.704)	3.651 (0.794)	3.864 (0.850)	4.294 (1.824)	2.988 (0.005)	2.945 (0.005)		3.745 (0.691)
mod.	0.951 (0.002)	0.955 (0.010)	0.872 (0.003)	0.900 (0.016)	0.867 (0.001)	0.880 (0.001)	0.832 (0.001)	0.913 (0.001)
	0.762 (0.050)	0.751 (0.034)	0.809 (0.023)	0.746 (0.009)	0.867 (0.001)	0.614 (0.004)		0.780 (0.033)
R^2	0.483	0.505	0.245	0.486	0.365	0.351	0.341	0.377
ord.	5	5	5	5	4	4	3	5

USA

	GDP	CON	TPI	GFCF	II	EXP	IM	GOV
per.	5.229 (0.025)	5.385 (0.191)	6.171 (0.037)	5.438 (0.014)	6.197 (3.809)	6.174 (0.040)	4.739 (0.044)	5.583 (0.067)
			2.895 (0.004)		2.824 (3.809)			
mod.	0.737 (0.009)	0.704 (0.002)	0.853 (0.001)	0.918 (0.001)	0.787 (0.002)	0.828 (0.001)	0.547 (0.003)	0.625 (0.002)
			0.656 (0.003)		0.810 (0.001)			
R^2	0.334	0.191	0.261	0.439	0.128	0.520	0.062	0.233
ord.	2	2	4	4	4	2	2	2

median

	GDP	CON	TPI	GFCF	II	EXP	IM	GOV
per.	7.069	7.256	8.064	6.517	5.664	6.174	5.971	7.131
	3.606	3.651	3.864		3.103			3.867
mod.	0.789	0.793	0.871	0.859	0.867	0.822	0.781	0.838
	0.762	0.751	0.809		0.862			0.774
R^2	0.334	0.316	0.245	0.383	0.199	0.324	0.303	0.330

Table 4.3. *G7 Economies*: Univariate spectral estimates (HP-filter)

	GDP	CON	TPI	GFCF	II	EXP	IM	GOV
Canada								
per.	10.09 (0.29)	11.40 (0.327)	9.140 (0.293)	9.747 (0.142)	6.053 (0.043)	6.181 (0.126)	8.020 (0.170)	7.316 (0.446)
mod.	0.823 (0.001)	0.871 (0.001)	0.762 (0.001)	0.901 (0.001)	0.836 (0.001)	0.611 (0.002)	0.747 (0.002)	0.607 (0.002)
R^2	0.629	0.724	0.402	0.694	0.162	0.285	0.297	0.397
ord.	3	3	3	3	3	2	3	2
France								
per.	9.337 (1.837)	9.096 (1.381)	8.620 (1.518)	8.941 (3.025)	–	8.733 (0.913)	8.230 (0.947)	10.66 (–)
mod.	0.559 (0.002)	0.554 (0.003)	0.621 (0.002)	0.602 (0.002)	–	0.669 (0.001)	0.625 (0.002)	0.504 (0.069)
R^2	0.457	0.438	0.502	0.498	–	0.541	0.476	0.434
ord.	2	2	2	2	–	2	2	2
Germany								
per.	12.70 (3.92)	12.96 (4.486)	12.18 (1.63)	10.78 (2.14)	5.766 (3.312)	7.934 (0.137)	10.76 (2.204)	12.35 (8.59)
	3.966 (0.628)	4.006 (0.620)	3.832 (0.003)	3.248 (2.47)	2.910 (0.067)		3.995 (0.663)	3.949 (0.012)
mod.	0.888 (0.038)	0.910 (0.063)	0.879 (0.012)	0.849 (0.001)	0.623 (0.005)	0.768 (0.008)	0.814 (0.038)	0.873 (0.023)
	0.940 (0.001)	0.956 (0.001)	0.917 (0.003)	0.797 (0.001)	0.868 (0.003)		0.880 (0.001)	0.922 (0.013)
R^2	0.568	0.635	0.606	0.463	0.225	0.309	0.477	0.629
ord.	5	5	5	4	5	3	5	5
Italy								
per.	8.951 (0.217)	8.845 (0.215)	7.777 (1.383)	7.940 (0.339)	–	8.718 (0.635)	7.565 (0.371)	8.753 (0.126)
mod.	0.787 (0.002)	0.780 (0.002)	0.565 (0.002)	0.682 (0.001)	–	0.693 (0.001)	0.643 (0.002)	0.830 (0.001)
R^2	0.514	0.474	0.387	0.529	–	0.579	0.453	0.523
ord.	3	3	2	2	–	2	2	3

Table 4.3 (continued).

Japan

	GDP	CON	TPI	GFCF	II	EXP	IM	GOV
per.	7.052 (0.047)	6.969 (0.035)	7.574 (0.102)	7.701 (0.143)	4.257 (0.019)	7.030 (0.109)	7.119 (0.037)	7.337 (0.027)
mod.	0.906 (0.001)	0.918 (0.001)	0.723 (0.001)	0.753 (0.001)	0.558 (0.002)	0.848 (0.001)	0.877 (0.001)	0.919 (0.001)
R^2	0.603	0.624	0.544	0.590	0.051	0.302	0.555	0.568
ord.	4	4	2	2	2	3	3	3

U.K.

	GDP	CON	TPI	GFCF	II	EXP	IM	GOV
per.	7.931 (0.037)	7.999 (0.037)	7.870 (0.078)	8.348 (0.064)	6.534 (0.063)	6.969 (0.109)	6.899 (0.119)	7.261 (0.052)
					3.019 (0.003)			
mod.	0.905 (0.001)	0.908 (0.001)	0.833 (0.001)	0.884 (0.001)	0.841 (0.001)	0.713 (0.001)	0.694 (0.001)	0.837 (0.001)
					0.670 (0.003)			
R^2	0.623	0.640	0.543	0.647	0.251	0.485	0.458	0.460
ord.	3	3	3	3	4	2	2	3

USA

	GDP	CON	TPI	GFCF	II	EXP	IM	GOV
per.	6.679 (0.086)	10.59 (1.09)	6.006 (0.102)	10.52 (3.07)	8.874 (0.169)	7.918 (0.114)	7.089 (7.118)	8.908 (2.410)
		4.071 (1.221)		4.724 (0.193)	2.857 (0.001)			
mod.	0.715 (0.001)	0.953 (0.002)	0.610 (0.002)	0.829 (0.002)	0.804 (0.001)	0.806 (0.001)	0.456 (0.005)	0.615 (0.002)
		0.802 (0.018)		0.894 (0.035)	0.810 (0.001)			
R^2	0.466	0.597	0.272	0.498	0.125	0.654	0.218	0.512
ord.	2	5	2	5	4	2	2	2

median

	GDP	CON	TPI	GFCF	II	EXP	IM	GOV
per.	8.951	9.069	7.870	8.941	6.053	7.934	7.565	8.753
					2.910			
mod.	0.823	0.908	0.723	0.829	0.804	0.713	0.694	0.830
					0.810			
R^2	0.568	0.624	0.502	0.529	0.162	0.485	0.458	0.512

Table 4.4. *G7 Economies*: Univariate spectral estimates (logD-filter)

Canada

	GDP	CON	TPI	GFCF	II	EXP	IM	GOV
per.	–	–	–	–	5.309 (0.045)	–	–	–
mod.	–	–	–	–	0.814 (0.002)	–	–	–
R^2	–	–	–	–	0.160	–	–	–
ord.	–	–	–	–	4	–	–	–

France

	GDP	CON	TPI	GFCF	II	EXP	IM	GOV
per.	–	–	8.708 (–)	16.37 (–)	–	–	–	–
mod.	–	–	0.279 (0.021)	0.233 (0.017)	–	–	–	–
R^2	–	–	0.100	0.100	–	–	–	–
ord.	–	–	2	2	–	–	–	–

Germany

	GDP	CON	TPI	GFCF	II	EXP	IM	GOV
per.	17.77 (8.57)	19.53 (8.80)	11.95 (9.35)	11.68 (8.51)	6.045 (8.997)	–	9.805 (–)	4.026 (0.010)
	4.012 (0.334)	4.109 (0.309)	3.798 (0.374)	3.654 (0.704)	2.929 (0.075)			
mod.	0.725 (0.001)	0.736 (0.001)	0.790 (0.010)	0.753 (0.010)	0.774 (0.008)	–	0.409 (0.045)	0.688 (0.001)
	0.834 (0.005)	0.856 (0.006)	0.852 (0.001)	0.757 (0.001)	0.848 (0.008)			
R^2	0.117	0.214	0.163	0.006	0.212	–	0.059	0.222
ord.	5	5	5	5	5	–	2	3

Italy

	GDP	CON	TPI	GFCF	II	EXP	IM	GOV
per.	16.64 (–)	–	7.026 (0.144)	–	12.51 (12.14)	–	7.599 (–)	–
					3.387 (0.521)			
mod.	0.198 (0.014)	–	0.671 (0.003)	–	0.831 (0.005)	–	0.380 (0.039)	–
					0.835 (0.005)			
R^2	0.077	–	0.058	–	0.370	–	0.048	–
ord.	2	–	3	–	5	–	2	–

Table 4.4 (continued).

	GDP	CON	TPI	GFCF	II	EXP	IM	GOV
Japan								
per.	2.761 (0.747)	2.690 (1.023)	5.834 (–)	6.694 (–)	–	–	8.385 (–)	–
mod.	0.401 (0.002)	0.218 (0.021)	0.290 (0.023)	0.290 (0.023)	–	–	0.238 (0.016)	–
R^2	0.001	0.001	0.017	0.054	–	–	0.052	–
ord.	4	4	2	2	–	–	2	–
U.K.								
per.	8.208 (0.135) 3.304 (0.042)	8.201 (0.142) 3.378 (0.051)	8.539 (0.257) 3.393 (0.054)	8.949 (2.839) 3.691 (0.633)	7.671 (1.620)	5.842 (1.121)	5.428 (0.221)	6.124 (0.054)
mod.	0.902 (0.001) 0.634 (0.014)	0.907 (0.001) 0.612 (0.017)	0.879 (0.002) 0.681 (0.015)	0.908 (0.001) 0.705 (0.007)	0.581 (0.003)	0.427 (0.005)	0.468 (0.004)	0.727 (0.002)
R^2	0.001	0.271	0.177	0.306	0.365	0.051	0.054	0.081
ord.	5	5	5	5	2	2	2	3
USA								
per.	–	–	–	7.793 (6.708)	2.924 (0.002)	11.53 (–)	–	–
mod.	–	–	–	0.540 (0.025)	0.757 (0.001)	0.446 (0.053)	–	–
R^2	–	–	–	0.001	0.804	0.069	–	–
ord.	–	–	–	3	4	2	–	–
median								
per.	12.42	8.201	8.539	8.949	6.045		7.992	
mod.	0.563	0.736	0.671	0.540	0.774		0.395	
R^2	0.039	0.214	0.100	0.054	0.365		0.050	

Fig. 4.1. Univariate spectral densities (*G7 Economies*)

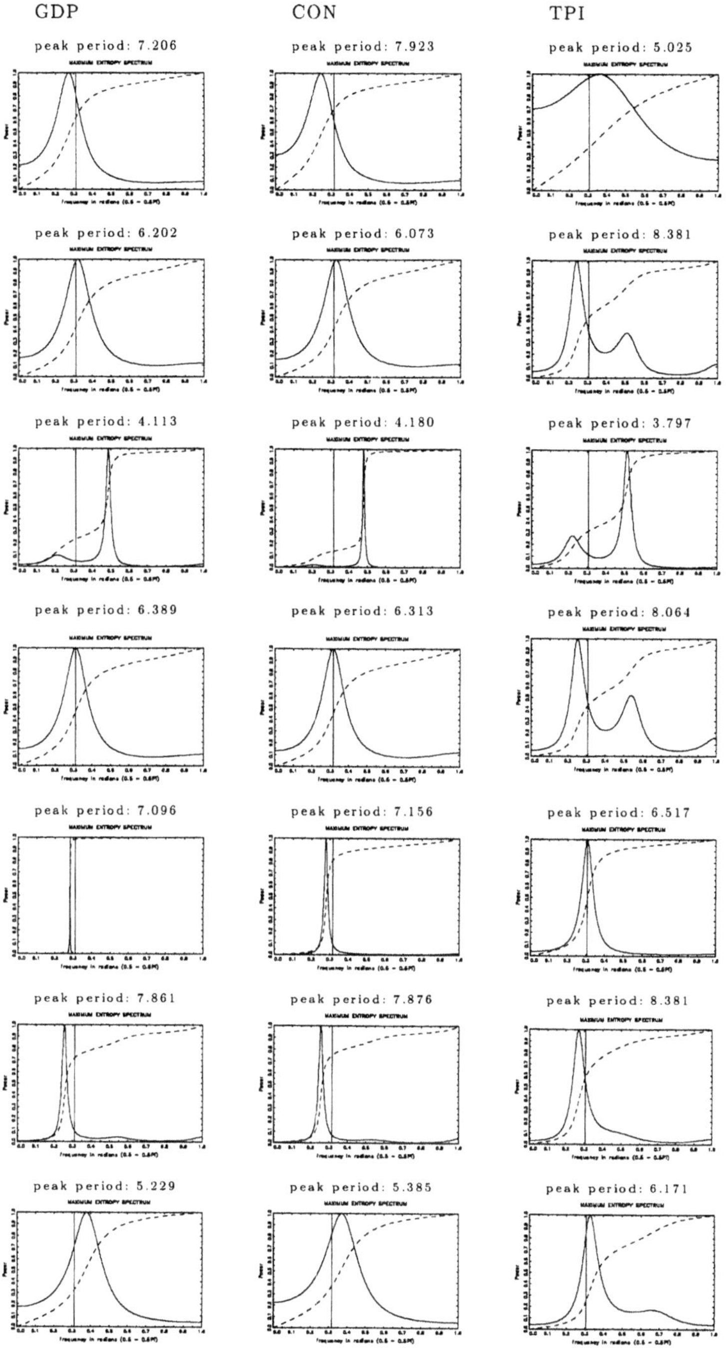

Note: rows (top down): Canada, France, Germany, Italy, Japan, U.K., USA

Fig. 4.2. Univariate spectral densities (*G7 Economies*)

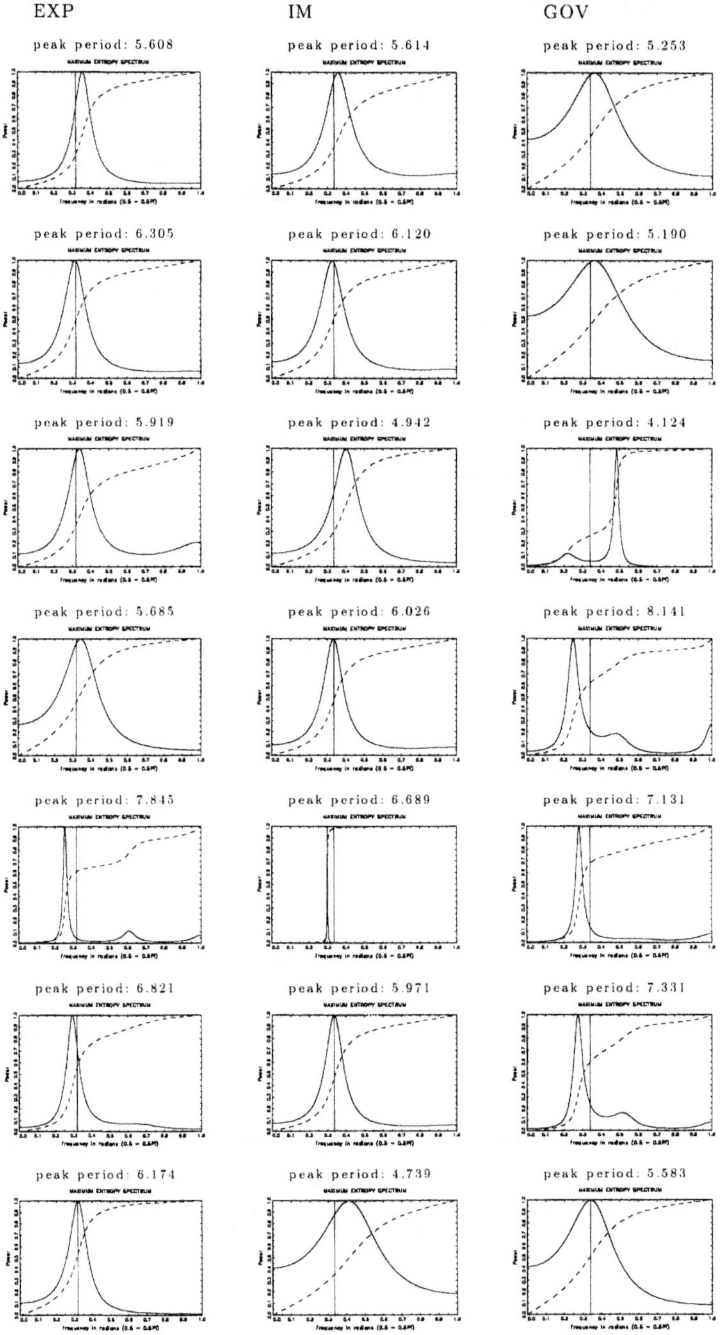

Note: rows (top down): Canada, France, Germany, Italy, Japan, U.K., USA

Fig. 4.3. Univariate spectral densities (*G7 Economies*)

GFCF II

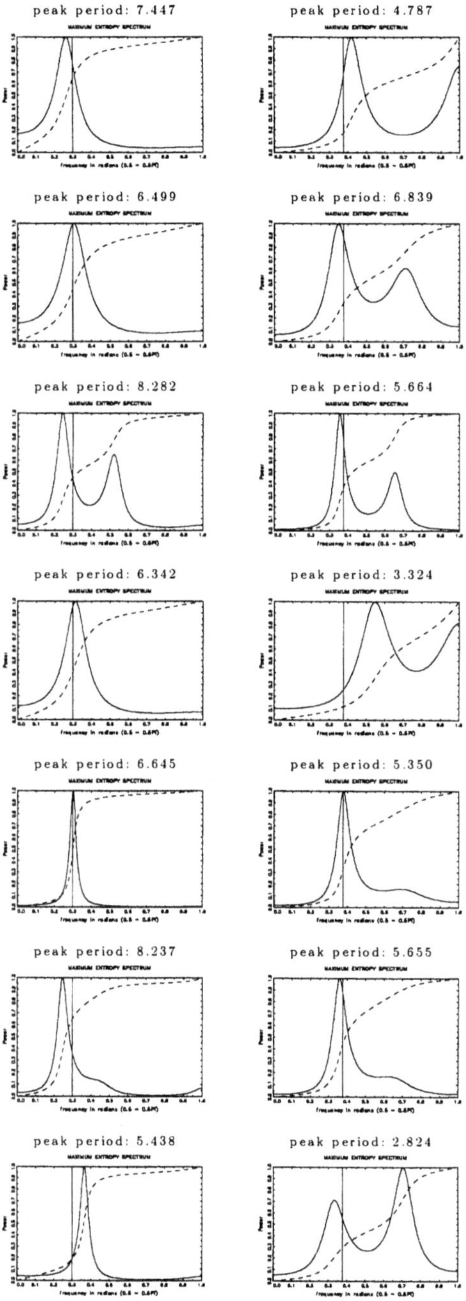

Note: rows (top down): Canada, France, Germany, Italy, Japan, U.K., USA

Table 4.5. *G7 Economies*: National GDP-bivariate measures (MBK-filter)

Y to	CON	TPI	GFCF	II	EXP	IM	GOV
Canada							
CTS	0.434	0.275	0.278	0.004	0.113	-.237	0.275
per.	8.62/3.06	8.62/3.23	8.85/3.04	8.62/2.31	8.57/3.67	8.26/3.27	9.00
sc	0.98/0.82	0.90/0.73	0.93/0.60	0.95/0.85	0.75/0.67	0.64/0.67	0.95
ps	0.29/-.18	-.47/0.18	-.29/0.11	-3.2/0.20	-1.4/0.28	-1.1/0.25	0.40
ord.	2	3	3	2	2	2	5
France							
CTS	0.578	0.248	0.232	0.026	0.182	-.199	0.166
per.	6.15	—	—	—	7.09	6.36	—
sc	0.99	—	—	—	0.93	0.93	—
ps	0.07	—	—	—	0.15	0.33	—
ord.	2	—	—	—	2	2	—
Germany							
CTS	0.612	0.242	0.188	0.043	0.179	-.225	0.130
per.	10.9/4.23	12.5/4.14	9.34/4.44	4.21/2.89	7.51/4.29	6.53/3.98	7.40/4.23
sc	0.99/0.99	0.97/0.99	0.99/0.99	0.99/0.97	0.97/0.99	0.71/0.88	0.99/0.99
ps	0.22/0.09	0.33/0.02	0.16/-.30	0.30/-.73	1.03/-.40	0.53/-.14	-.23/0.13
ord.	5	5	5	5	5	2	5
Italy							
CTS	0.596	0.258	0.242	0.020	0.152	-.217	0.157
per.	9.80/4.36	7.51	7.56	6.32/2.75	19.6	6.32	—
sc	0.99/0.99	0.93	0.96	0.40/0.08	0.83	0.89	—
ps	0.06/0.06	0.06	0.21	-.38/0.93	-.42	0.28	—
ord.	5	2	3	2	1	2	—
Japan							
CTS	0.602	0.262	0.267	-.003	0.043	-.026	0.102
per.	6.53	6.53	11.4/7.44	6.75/4.08	7.04	7.57/3.57	6.75/2.35
sc	0.99	0.96	0.95/0.99	0.95/0.64	0.99	0.99/0.79	0.99/0.99
ps	-.01	0.32	-.14/0.20	2.18/0.10	0.67	1.52/0.63	-.06/0.02
ord.	3	1	4	4	3	4	4
U.K.							
CTS	0.627	0.183	0.198	-.011	0.190	-.245	0.188
per.	7.24	8.00/3.98	7.81/3.23	8.00/4.92	8.13/3.96	8.00/4.23	7.46/4.85
sc	0.99	0.98/0.65	0.98/0.87	0.91/0.58	0.98/0.75	0.95/0.68	0.98/0.90
ps	0.06	-.16/-.27	0.07/0.20	-2.0/-1.6	-.30/-.13	-.04/-.31	0.37/0.25
ord.	3	5	5	5	5	5	3
USA							
CTS	0.375	0.571	0.399	0.169	-.015	-.225	-.020
per.	5.68	5.34/2.84	7.51/5.05	5.52	6.41/3.33	5.65	5.49/2.81
sc	0.87	0.99/0.85	0.87/0.99	0.67	0.85/0.23	0.80	0.68/0.67
ps	-.21	-.02/0.09	-.65/0.21	-.20	1.57/-.27	0.38	2.27/1.27
ord.	2	4	4	2	2	2	5

Table 4.6. *G7 Economies*: National GDP-bivariate measures (HP-filter)

Y to	CON	TPI	GFCF	II	EXP	IM	GOV
Canada							
CTS	0.526	0.313	0.322	-.021	0.046	-.203	0.267
per.	14.4/8.47	11.3/2.36	9.17/2.47	4.76/2.25	9.52/3.10	10.5	10.5
sc	0.99/0.98	0.93/0.74	0.93/0.60	0.95/0.90	0.49/0.51	0.64	0.78
ps	-.01/0.37	-.30/0.14	-.37/0.16	1.53/0.30	-2.1/0.01	-.54	0.54
ord.	5	3	3	5	2	3	2
France							
CTS	0.572	0.250	0.227	0.023	0.195	-.204	0.172
per.	15.3	13.6/8.33	8.85/13.5	9.52	10.6	9.90	14.0/4.40
sc	0.99	0.98/0.97	0.99/0.99	0.59	0.97	0.96	0.99/0.98
ps	0.12	-.54/0.36	0.47/-.44	-.73	0.28	0.44	0.41/0.12
ord.	1	5	5	2	2	2	5
Germany							
CTS	0.612	0.245	0.205	0.035	0.158	-.208	0.130
per.	13.6/4.13	13.1/4.08	13.5/4.18	13.5/2.82	14.2/8.26	13.1/4.03	13.6/4.11
sc	0.99/0.99	0.99/0.98	0.99/0.98	0.99/0.98	0.99/0.99	0.99/0.98	0.99/0.99
ps	0.27/0.08	0.10/-.01	0.21/-.27	-.50/-.85	-1.2/0.81	0.09/0.01	0.24/0.13
ord.	5	5	5	5	5	5	5
Italy							
CTS	0.589	0.278	0.245	0.036	0.152	-.212	0.157
per.	—	10.8	—	10.0	6.94/15.1	9.00	10.7
sc	—	0.93	—	0.48	0.95/0.88	0.93	0.96
ps	—	0.07	—	-.41	-.37/1.48	0.50	0.16
ord.	—	2	—	2	4	2	2
Japan							
CTS	0.577	0.287	0.284	0.005	0.048	-.040	0.096
per.	7.63	12.6/6.99	12.1/7.09	11.1/5.29	7.57	7.14/4.40	6.94
sc	0.99	0.97/0.99	0.98/0.99	0.62/0.76	0.98	0.99/0.91	0.99
ps	0.03	-.36/0.23	-.33/0.17	-.2.2/0.87	0.55	1.56/0.43	-.07
ord.	3	4	4	4	2	5	3
U.K.							
CTS	0.627	0.206	0.219	-.013	0.181	-.239	0.176
per.	7.93	9.17/4.40	11.7/7.69	7.81	7.93	8.00	8.19/3.95
sc	0.99	0.97/0.62	0.97/0.99	0.64	0.95	0.88	0.98/0.83
ps	0.04	-.45/-.57	-.95/0.29	-2.2	-.23	-.12	0.37/0.11
ord.	3	5	5	3	3	3	3
USA							
CTS	0.468	0.397	0.317	0.173	-.032	-.248	0.040
per.	7.93	11.9/5.98	7.40/4.60	9.25/2.81	7.93	6.71	11.3/4.29
sc	0.87	0.95/0.98	0.92/0.99	0.73/0.90	0.54	0.76	0.45/0.18
ps	-.08	-2.1/-.08	-.21/-.10	0.42/0.08	1.91	0.15	0.32/1.89
ord.	2	4	5	5	2	2	2

Table 4.7. *G7 Economies*: National GDP-bivariate measures (logD-filter)

Y to	CON	TPI	GFCF	II[a]	EXP	IM	GOV
Canada							
CTS	0.572	-.619	-.210	-.010	-.213	-1.27	-1.47
per.	—	—	—	8.13	—	—	—
sc	—	—	—	0.39	—	—	—
ps	—	—	—	-2.5	—	—	—
ord.	—	—	—	2	—	—	—
France							
CTS	0.879	0.461	0.643	0.025	0.498	-.935	0.746
per.	—	—	—	10.3	—	—	—
sc	—	—	—	0.27	—	—	—
ps	—	—	—	-1.2	—	—	—
ord.	1	—	—	1	—	—	—
Germany							
CTS	0.825	0.418	0.526	0.055	0.363	-.899	0.726
per.	8.19	—	12.0/3.95	4.16/2.80	—	—	—
sc	0.98	—	0.96/0.95	0.99/0.98	—	—	—
ps	0.14	—	0.17/-.05	0.25/-.75	—	—	—
ord.	1	—	5	5	—	—	—
Italy							
CTS	0.874	0.262	0.517	0.024	0.451	-1.00	0.661
per.	—	—	—	5.95	—	—	—
sc	—	—	—	0.21	—	—	—
ps	—	—	—	-.05	—	—	—
ord.	—	—	—	2	—	—	—
Japan							
CTS	0.826	0.539	0.645	-.005	0.085	-.734	0.671
per.	—	12.1/2.35	10.75	7.14/3.96	—	6.71/2.77	—
sc	—	0.95/0.95	0.95	0.91/0.36	—	0.96/0.66	—
ps	—	-.11/0.01	0.18	3.29/0.09	—	1.45/0.91	—
ord.	—	4	1	4	—	5	—
U.K.							
CTS	0.712	0.132	0.320	-.014	0.358	-.936	0.588
per.	6.99	8.69/3.62	—	8.00/4.71	—	—	8.06/2.43
sc	0.99	0.96/0.65	—	0.88/0.53	—	—	0.98/0.94
ps	0.04	-.26/-.07	—	-2.0/-1.3	—	—	0.34/0.01
ord.	3	5	—	5	—	—	4
USA							
CTS	0.432	-2.14	-2.06	-.195	-2.46	-3.17	-.549
per.	—	5.12/2.44	4.71	5.49/2.84	6.49	5.71	—
sc	—	0.98/0.88	0.88	0.79/0.84	0.54	0.51	—
ps	—	-.03/0.13	-.02	-.25/0.09	1.40	0.59	—
ord.	—	5	2	4	1	1	—

Fig. 4.4. *G7 Economies*: Mean bivariate spectra (filter: MBK)

Mean G7 Coherence Spectra (w/ GDP)	Mean G7 Phase Spectra (w/ GDP)

CON

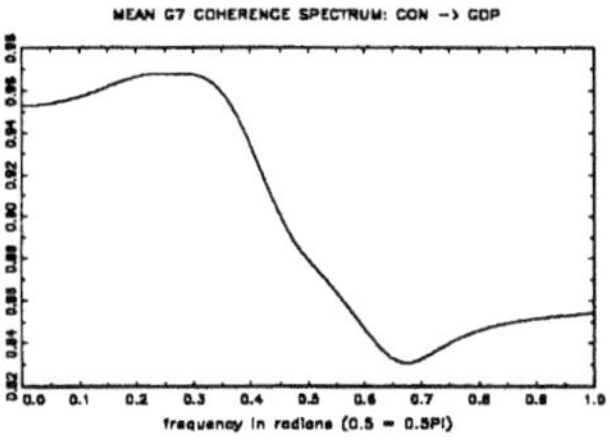

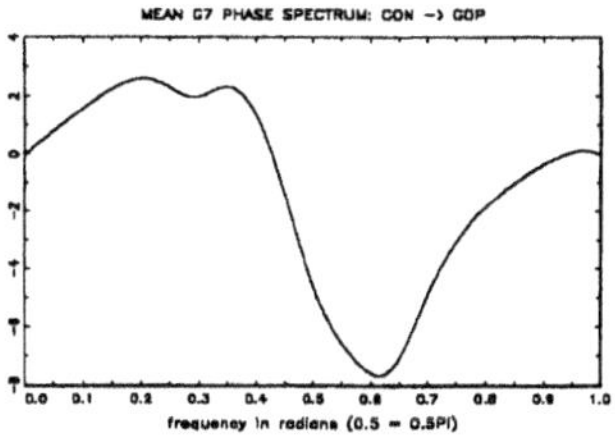

max. at period (yrs.): 6.99 — *ps* at max. of *sc* (yrs.): 1.01

TPI

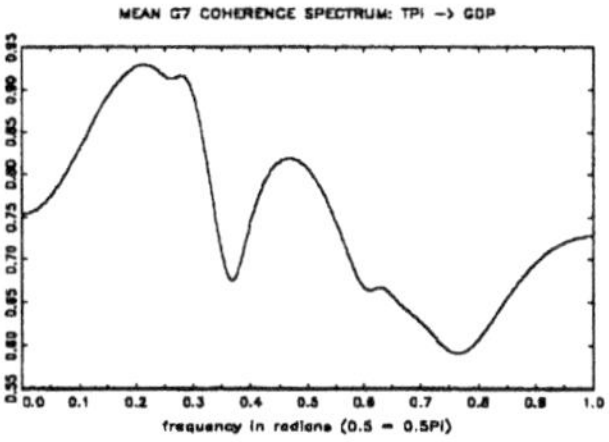

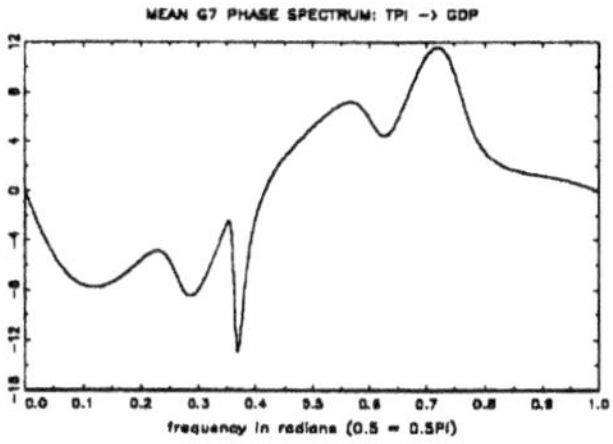

max. at period (yrs.): 9.25 4.44 — *ps* at max. of *sc* (yrs.): -.39 1.95

GFCF

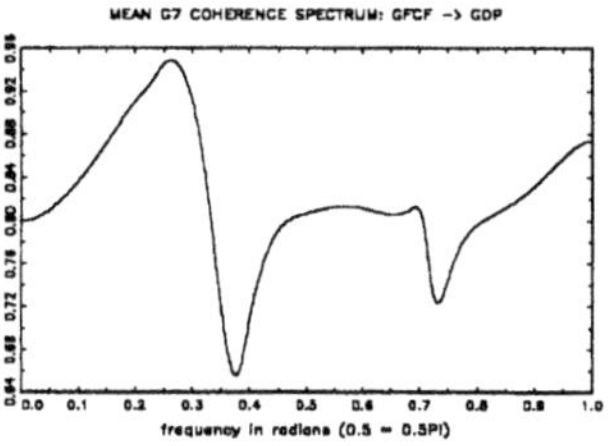

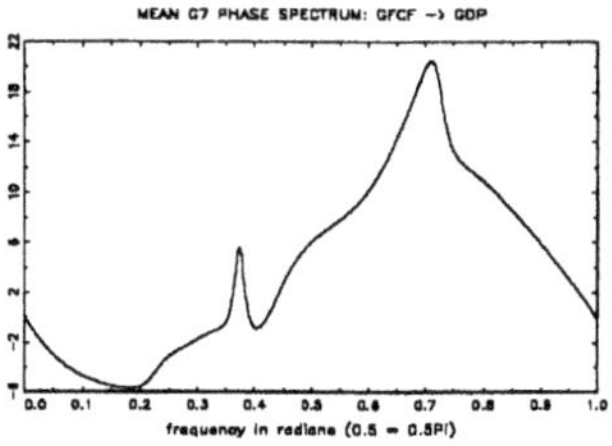

max. at period (yrs.): 7.63 — *ps* at max. of *sc* (yrs.): -.74

II

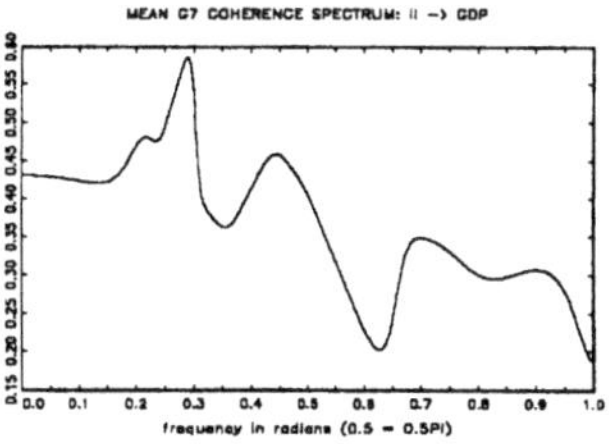

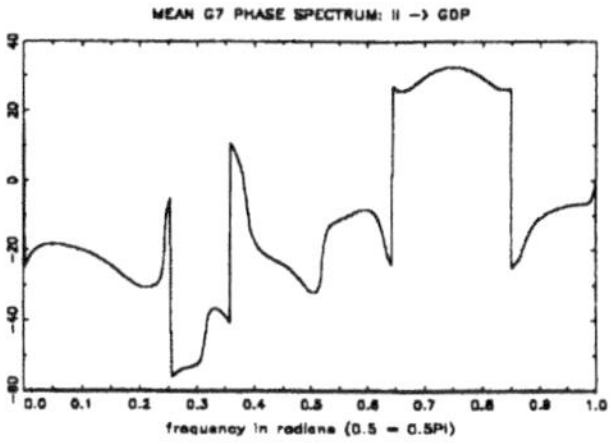

max. at period (yrs.): 6.89 4.54 — *ps* at max. of *sc* (yrs.): -.03 - 10

Table 4.8. *G7 Economies*: Supranational bivariate measures (filter: MBK)

GDP	CON	TPI	GFCF	II	EXP	IM	GOV
Canada							
$CTS_{(G7\text{-}Y)}$							
0.003	0.001	0.002	0.002	0.001	0.006	-.004	0.001
$per._{(G7\text{-}Y)}{}^{a}$							
7.576	7.246	6.667	7.299	8.197	6.494	7.752	7.194
$sc_{(G7\text{-}Y)}$							
0.672	0.980	0.535	0.987	0.491	0.843	0.563	0.944
$ps_{(G7\text{-}Y)}{}^{a}$							
1.705	2.471	1.040	1.489	-1.28	0.323	0.461	2.170
ord.							
1	5	2	5	2	3	2	1
France							
$CTS_{(G7\text{-}Y)}$							
0.163	0.094	0.044	0.038	0.007	0.030	-.030	0.027
$CTS_{(EU\text{-}Y)}$							
0.179	0.103	0.048	0.043	0.007	0.035	-.037	0.030
$per._{(G7\text{-}Y)}{}^{a}$							
6.667	6.623	6.849	6.579	5.780	8.403	6.579	6.667
$per._{(EU\text{-}Y)}{}^{a}$							
5.814	—	7.692	7.874	7.874	8.621	6.369	4.219
$sc_{(G7\text{-}Y)}$							
0.930	0.923	0.901	0.871	0.452	0.980	0.900	0.890
$sc_{(EU\text{-}Y)}$							
0.967	—	0.984	0.974	0.429	0.989	0.920	0.987
$ps_{(G7\text{-}Y)}{}^{a}$							
0.239	0.280	0.354	0.371	-.376	0.350	0.649	0.219
$ps_{(EU\text{-}Y)}{}^{a}$							
-.073	—	0.040	0.164	-1.20	0.139	0.267	0.098
$ord._{(G7)}$							
2	2	2	2	2	5	2	2
$ord._{(EU)}$							
2	—	3	3	1	5	2	5

Table 4.8 (continued).

Germany	CON	TPI	GFCF	II	EXP	IM	GOV
$CTS_{(G7-Y)}$							
0.173	0.105	0.043	0.041	0.005	0.038	-.036	0.023
$CTS_{(EU-Y)}$							
0.184	0.113	0.047	0.038	0.011	0.046	-.046	0.024
per.$_{(G7-Y)}$[a]							
4.202	4.255	4.032	6.803	3.953	7.042	4.049	4.255
per.$_{(EU-Y)}$[a]							
4.098	4.149	4.000	6.897	4.132	4.367	4.975	4.132
$sc_{(G7-Y)}$							
0.998	0.999	0.990	0.976	0.924	0.999	0.978	0.997
$sc_{(EU-Y)}$							
0.996	0.996	0.990	0.999	0.922	0.980	0.839	0.999
$ps_{(G7-Y)}$[a]							
0.045	0.128	0.039	-.407	0.209	0.950	0.044	0.127
$ps_{(EU-Y)}$[a]							
-.018	0.034	0.029	-.429	0.265	-.385	0.070	0.101
ord.$_{(G7\ /\ EU)}$							
5 / 5	5 / 5	5 / 5	5 / 5	5 / 5	5 / 5	5 / 2	5 / 5
Italy							
$CTS_{(G7-Y)}$							
0.141	0.086	0.040	0.036	0.007	0.029	-.033	0.023
$CTS_{(EU-Y)}$							
0.183	0.112	0.051	0.046	0.008	0.033	-.041	0.029
per.$_{(G7-Y)}$[a]							
6.757	6.667	6.061	4.049	5.882	6.667	6.329	2.222
per.$_{(EU-Y)}$[a]							
4.065	4.115	—	2.128	5.952	6.250	6.289	4.202
$sc_{(G7-Y)}$							
0.988	0.993	0.686	0.945	0.195	0.876	0.839	0.969
$sc_{(EU-Y)}$							
0.997	0.998	—	0.966	0.195	0.937	0.882	0.949
$ps_{(G7-Y)}$[a]							
0.673	0.799	0.426	0.112	0.049	0.289	0.642	-.305
$ps_{(EU-Y)}$[a]							
0.039	0.079	—	-.070	-.305	-.157	0.259	0.037
ord.$_{(G7\ /\ EU)}$							
3 / 5	3 / 5	3 / —	5 / 5	2 / 2	2 / 2	2 / 2	5 / 5

Table 4.8 (continued).

Japan	CON	TPI	GFCF	II	EXP	IM	GOV
$CTS_{(G7-Y)}$							
0.267	0.172	0.103	0.101	0.003	0.015	-.019	0.031
$per._{(G7-Y)}$[a]							
6.757	2.212	6.579	6.623	5.319	2.217	8.333	2.208
$sc_{(G7-Y)}$							
0.996	0.966	0.952	0.997	0.267	0.940	0.991	0.971
$ps_{(G7-Y)}$[a]							
-.311	0.331	-.090	-.203	0.717	0.340	1.230	0.349
ord.							
3	3	3	3	2	5	5	5
U.K.							
$CTS_{(G7-Y)}$							
0.108	0.067	0.026	0.024	0.003	0.025	-.030	0.020
$CTS_{(EU-Y)}$							
0.125	0.076	0.024	0.025	0.001	-.001	-.032	0.026
$per._{(G7-Y)}$[a]							
8.000	8.065	7.353	6.897	6.711	6.494	6.289	8.197
$per._{(EU-Y)}$[a]							
7.813	7.874	—	7.194	6.329	7.246	7.246	7.407
$sc_{(G7-Y)}$							
0.995	0.999	0.659	0.928	0.393	0.893	0.820	0.965
$sc_{(EU-Y)}$							
0.979	0.982	—	0.888	0.492	0.875	0.711	0.984
$ps_{(G7-Y)}$[a]							
0.637	0.745	0.477	0.438	-1.27	0.493	0.572	0.832
$ps_{(EU-Y)}$[a]							
0.152	0.175	—	0.059	-1.70	-.011	0.075	0.448
$ord._{(G7)}$							
5	5	2	3	2	2	2	5
$ord._{(EU)}$							
4	5	—	3	2	2	2	5

Table 4.8 (continued).

USA	CON	TPI	GFCF	II	EXP	IM	GOV
CTS(G7-Y)							
0.043	0.009	0.018	0.024	-.039	0.017	-.022	0.001
per.(G7-Y)[a]							
6.803	4.292	7.576	7.752	—	5.988	6.711	2.299
sc(G7-Y)							
0.640	0.822	0.955	0.952	—	0.969	0.531	0.896
ps(G7-Y)[a]							
-.875	2.100	-.892	-.923	—	1.212	-.131	-.595
ord.							
2	2	2	5	—	2	2	5

Note: a.Throughout only measures for contained cyclicality with highest sc-value displayed. First column refers to respective national GDP (Y).

Fig. 4.5. Supranational GDP series' spectra (filter: MBK)

G7 GDP-Cycle (filter: MBK)

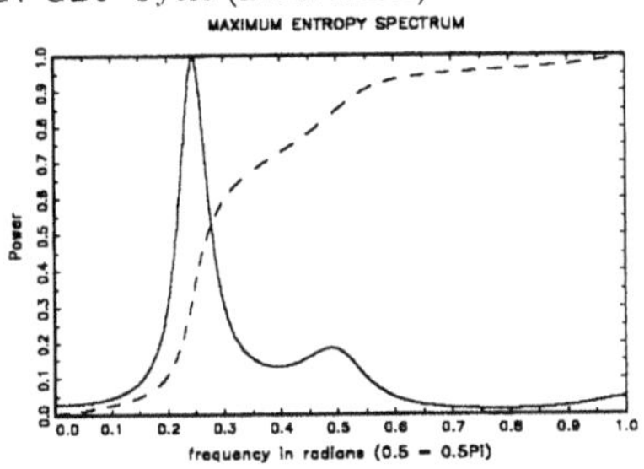

per.[a]	mod.[a]	adj. R^2	ord.
8.206	0.906	0.389	5
(3.203)	(0.001)		
3.963	0.804		
(1.084)	(0.027)		

EURO15 GDP-Cycle (filter: MBK)

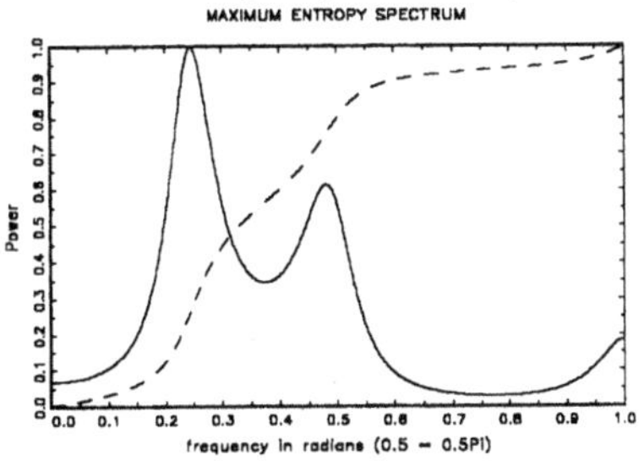

per.[a]	mod.[a]	adj. R^2	ord.
8.324	0.854	0.307	5
(1.048)	(0.012)		
4.076	0.833		
(1.259)	(0.014)		

Note: a. standard errors in brackets

5. Mode-Locking and the Global Cycle

Even though comovement is a defining characteristics of the business cycle, in recent decades macroeconomists have tended to focus on understanding the persistence in the ups and downs of aggregate economic activity. They have generally been less concerned with understanding this synchronized pattern.
L. J. Christiano and T. J. Fitzgerald (1998)

An idea about the global cycle: it is an example of 'phase-locking'.
P. Krugman (1996)

Recent empirical evidence suggests that national business cycles got and get synchronized *over time*. For example Duecker and Wesche (1999) note: "National business-cycle indices from France, Germany, Italy are consistent with the claim that the European economies are becoming more harmonized over time," p. II. Similar results are documented by Artis and Zhang (1999), Imbs (1999) and Selover and Jensen (1999). On the other hand novel evidence on the determinants of the synchronization of business cycles by Imbs (1999) suggests that trade, as well as geographic considerations have no systematic or surprisingly small quantitative effects on the synchronization of business cycles. Although openness to trade is by far the most frequently cited culprit for this apparent 'globalization' of cycies,[1] Imbs (1999) notes: "Within the academic profession, however, few economists would agree that this is the sole - or even most important - mechanism. There are two reasons to this restraint. First openness as measured for instance by the share of exports to GDP rarely reaches levels compatible with promoting trade as the sole responsible for co-fluctuations ... Second, economic theory offers no definite answer to the question of what drives the international business cycles," p. 2.

This chapter first reexamines an article that tried to give an answer on this question, namely the article *'Mode-locking' and international business*

[1] An example of the public opinion, is given by Stephen Roach, chief economist at Morgan Stanley, in *Wall Street Journal Europe* (article: *Global Economic Contagion Spreading Gloom*, July 6-7, 2001), cf. the citation at the beginning of the present part of the thesis: In his opinion the actual global economic contagion is primarily transmitted through the channels of 1) cross-border trade ('trade fluctuations spill over'), 2) global supply chains, and 3) multinational corporations.

cycle transmission by David Selover and Roderick Jensen, published in a recent volume (23, 1999) of the *Journal of Economic Dynamics and Control* (*JEDC*). It gives a general formalization of economic cycles' synchronization through mode lock modelling. Furthermore, a simple model based on the interactive economic behavior of globally operating firms, is briefly outlined, calibrated and simulated on the basis of empirical data for six of the G7 countries and the Netherlands. Incorporating positive information externalities, it combines the endogenous generation of genuine cycles *and* coupling, resulting in the observed comovement of national business cycles and a robust global business cyclic pattern.

5.1 Introduction and Motivation of the Discussion

In the introduction to their paper Selover and Jensen (1999) note: "The paper presents a new theory of world business cycle formation based upon a nonlinear process known as 'mode-locking'," p. 592. They conclude their article with regard to the tendency for business cycles of different national economies to synchronize and create what is called a 'world business cycle': "In this study we suggested a new explanation, a new mechanism behind the formation of this synchronization - a nonlinear phenomenon called 'mode-lock', which is capable of reproducing many features of the empirical data," p. 614.

The idea of 'mode-locking' as the theoretical base model to explain the synchronization of national business cycles resulting in an observed robust and periodic aggregate global business cycle, is not as "new" as Selover and Jensen might have had in mind at the time of their contribution to the *JEDC*. In fact Hillinger and Weser (1988a and 1988b) - although in a quiet brief outline and under keywords like 'parametric resonance' and the 'aggregation problem of modelling economic cycles' - but nevertheless also in the same journal (*JEDC*, vol. 12, 1988a), as well as Weser (1992) suggested 'mode-locking' as a general explanatory approach for the synchronization of the cyclic dynamics of disaggregated economic units. To my knowledge, the first author who conjectured mode-locking "across national boundaries" is Forrester (1977) noting that "a capital-sector fluctuation ... would have similar causes and a tendency toward the same range of periodicities in all of the market-directed economies of the developed countries. A small amount of coupling, even much less than that provided by international trade and financial flows," p.538, could be responsible for the synchronization of different national modes into a robust cyclic global motion. Another more recent source is Krugman (1996) who noted as an "idea about the global business cycle: it is an example of 'phase locking'," p. 72, where *phase locking* is just a synonym of *mode locking* as are other expressions like *phase coordination*, *nonlinear entrainment*, *resonant stimulation*, *frequency pulling* or *synchronization of interacting oscillators* that are also frequently used to describe the same phenomenon.[2] He verbally outlined the implementation of a mode-lock mechanism into an international version of the Hicks-Goodwin and Scheinkman-Woodford business cycle models. Another recent model of international business cycle co-movements, based on phase locking and remarkably close to the one of Selover and Jensen, is the model of Brenner, Weidlich and Witt (1998). Compared to the one of Selover and Jensen, it does not have an empirical motivation, is not simulated and is more complicated due to its structure, based on time variant probabilities developing according to the master equation. Although the motivation and the underpinning argumentation may differ, the central synchronization mechanism is identical.

In contrast to the highly stylized or idealized mathematical mode-lock model of Selover and Jensen, the model of Weser (1992) is based on a production/inventory-accelerator model of Metzlerian type. This model can be derived from convex adjustment cost optimization of globally operating firms, whose operations make up a significant part of world market's activity. Furthermore, it is able to induce mode-locking, leading to a meaningful, endogenous model structure. The implementation of the coupling can be based on a micro-theoretical argumentation as Selover and Jensen suggest in "form of information and fads," more precisely by basing it on - what in the literature on social learning is known as - 'endogenously-timed herding'. To stress this point once more, Selover and Jensen note that their "coupling mechanism is set up to demonstrate the intuition behind mode-locking," p. 599, as already done in Hillinger and Weser (1988a and 1988b), but here, as well as in Weser (1992), the argumentation is embedded in an economic model endogenously generating cycles *and* coupling. In contrast to the Selover/Jensen-model these models are not derived from the assumption of an exogenous sinusoidal driving function. Another shortcoming of their abstract modelling of the deterministic components of the national cyclicalities via simple sinusoidal functions, is that thereby the empirically observed heterogeneous damping of these components is not taken into account. It is shown that in the context of parametric (autoregressive) spectral analysis, cf. part I of the monograph, this damping is reflected in the respective moduli of the conjugate complex roots of the AR processes adjusted to the data.

[2] See for example the numerous publications of the research group around John Sterman and Erik Mosekilde: Larsen et al. (1992), Mosekilde et al. (1992), Mosekilde et al. (1993), Kampmann et al. (1994), Sterman and Mosekilde (1994) and Haxholdt et al. (1995), as well as the ones of Brenner, Weidlich and Witt (1998) and Focardi and Marchesi (2000).
A more distinct analysis of these concepts of cycles' synchronization and recent developments and insights, especially from statistical physics, are given in the last two chapters of part III of the dissertation.

In the course of this chapter, I will demonstrate that the Selover/Jensen-model[3] is part of a wider class of mode-lock models. A mathematical generalization of economic cycles' mode-lock modelling based on this demonstration is given in the following section. In the remaining parts of the chapter an endogenous mode-locking model of national business cycle synchronization induced by the economic behavior of (only) nationally representative firms, operating on the world market, is outlined, calibrated, enriched with exogenous shocks and simulated on the basis of empirical data and findings for six of the G7 countries and the Netherlands.[4]

5.2 Generalizing Economic Cycles' Mode-Lock Modelling

This section tries to demonstrate that the Selover/Jensen-model is closely related to the second order accelerator models suggested by Hillinger and Weser (1988a and 1988b) and is part of a wider class of models to explain the synchronization of firm-level, sectoral and national business cycle phenomena. In the terminology of mechanical physics this class of models is subsumed under the header of 'parametric resonance models.'

Consider first the basic two economies (denoted by x and y) case of Selover and Jensen (1999). Accordingly, the industrial production of countries x and y follows a sinusoidal law of motion ("idealized business cycles with sinusoidal waveforms," p. 598) associated with a certain frequency θ_x, θ_y, respectively:

$$x = \sin(\theta_x), \tag{5.1}$$

$$y = \sin(\theta_y). \tag{5.2}$$

Let us call these base frequencies "outer" frequencies of the system and denote them out_x, out_y, respectively: $out_x = f(\theta_x)$, $out_y = f(\theta_y)$. We will return to the explanation of this notation later. But before going on, let us bring the basic system in an "accelerator-representation" by constructing the second temporal derivatives of (5.1) and (5.2) using $\frac{d\theta_x}{dt} = (\theta_x)' = \omega_x^u$ and $\frac{d\theta_y}{dt} = (\theta_y)' = \omega_y^u$, where ω_i^u, $i = x, y$, stands for the respective "uncoupled" frequency, see Selover and Jensen (1999), p. 598:

$$x'(t) = \cos(\theta_x)\,\omega_x^u \Rightarrow x''(t) = -\sin(\theta_x)\,(\omega_x^u)^2,$$

$$y'(t) = \cos(\theta_y)\,\omega_y^u \Rightarrow y''(t) = -\sin(\theta_y)\,(\omega_y^u)^2.$$

Simplifying, according to (5.1) and (5.2), we get:

---

[3] As are the interaction model of long-wave, Kuznets-swings and business cycles of the Sterman/Mosekilde-team, the models by Hillinger/Weser, and the recent models by Brenner, Weidlich, Witt (1998) and Focardi and Marchesi (1998).

[4] This selection of economies corresponds to the one chosen in the 'empirical evidence'-section of Selover and Jensen (1999).

$$x''(t) = -x(t)\left(\omega_x^u\right)^2, \tag{5.3}$$

$$y''(t) = -y(t)\left(\omega_y^u\right)^2. \tag{5.4}$$

To develop the mode-lock system, Selover and Jensen now introduce coupling by replacing ω_x^u, ω_y^u with ω_x^c, ω_y^c, where superscript "c" stands for "coupled," and $\omega_x^c = \omega_x + k_x \sin(\theta_x - \theta_y)$, $\omega_y^c = \omega_y + k_y \sin(\theta_y - \theta_x)$, i.e. they add to the respective base frequency $k_x \sin(\theta_x - \theta_y)$ and $k_y \sin(\theta_y - \theta_x)$. In quadratic terms, see (5.3) and (5.4), this implies analogously adding $k_x\left[\frac{1}{2} - \frac{1}{2}\cos(2\theta_x - 2\theta_y)\right]$, $k_y\left[\frac{1}{2} - \frac{1}{2}\cos(2\theta_y - 2\theta_x)\right]$, respectively:

$$x''(t) = \left\{\omega_x^2 + k_x\left[\frac{1}{2} - \frac{1}{2}\cos(2\theta_x - 2\theta_y)\right]\right\} x(t), \tag{5.5}$$

$$y''(t) = \left\{\omega_y^2 + k_y\left[\frac{1}{2} - \frac{1}{2}\cos(2\theta_y - 2\theta_x)\right]\right\} y(t). \tag{5.6}$$

As can be seen from these equations, the inner frequencies in_x, in_y are functions of the doubled values of θ_i, $i = x, y$: $in_x = f(2\theta_x)$, $in_y = f(2\theta_y)$.

The system of equations (5.5) and (5.6) consists in two equations of the so called *Mathieu type*, as e.g. defined in Arnol'd (1983): "Equations or systems with constant coefficients in the leading term and with coefficients in the form of trigonometric polynomials in the lower-order terms have special properties, and can be called equations of *Mathieu type*," p. 216. The central special property of such an equation or system lies in its potential to resonantly stimulate different phases (*parametric resonance phenomenon*) and periodically entrain them. This means, as resonance occurs, one - or in the case of more than two cyclic behaving economies - some of the cycles get excited (eventually start to grow exponentially). The most rapidly excited one pulls the phases of the other cycles towards itself. This effect depends on what is usually called forcing amplitude or depth of modulation, corresponding to the coupling parameters k_i, in the notation of Selover and Jensen used above, i.e. the strength of interdependence 'due to trade and capital flows' of the modeled economies. As Selover and Jensen correctly note, the general restriction is $|k_i| < 1$, see p. 601. This is one mathematical condition for parametric resonance to occur and to guarantee one mode-lock frequency as attractor, as well as to avoid chaotic behavior of the system. The other *conditio sine qua non* is a certain constellation of outer to inner frequency (*in* is sometimes also called perturbation or frequency of driving signal): If many such constellations for different values of k_i exist, these zones of parametric resonance or periodic entrainment are usually visualized in so called *Arnol'd tongues*, see Arnol'd (1983, 1989) and Norris (1993) in general and the publications of Sterman/Mosekilde et al. for applied examples of the *Arnol'd tongue* concept. For systems of Mathieu type, by far the largest zone of periodic entrainment lies for a depth of modulation $|k_i| \in (0,1)$ at the constellation of

$$\frac{out}{in} \approx \frac{1}{2},$$

see Arnol'd (1983). The approximate equality comes about, since this large area of parametric resonance also captures many constellations of *out* to *in* that only roughly equal 0.5.[5] As can be seen from equations (5.1), (5.2) and (5.3), (5.4) and following the above argumentation: this 1 : 2 relationship is intrinsic or in-built in the model of Selover and Jensen and opens the synchronization potential via parametric resonance.

What do we learn from scrutinizing the Selover/Jensen-model in the light of parametric resonance theory? What does theory tell us about implications of such a model design before running any simulations? We can summarize in the following statement:
Parametric resonance leading to synchronization will *not* occur, as

Corollary 5.2.1. *of* $|k_i| \in (0, 1)$ *being too small, i.e. too close to* 0 *and/or*

Corollary 5.2.2. *of* $\theta_x = \theta_y \Rightarrow f(\theta_x) = f(\theta_y) \Rightarrow \omega_x = \omega_y$ *and/or*

Corollary 5.2.3. *of* $\omega_x \wedge \omega_y$ *being too apart from each other.*

On the cause of corollary 1, the concrete critical values of $|k_i|$ can directly be found in the respective Arnol'd Tongue diagram for different constellations of *out* to *in*, for basic Mathieu equation systems, see e.g. Arnol'd (1983). The reasoning of the cause of corollary 2, can directly be seen from equations (5.5) and (5.6): Equal frequencies, corresponding to equal parameters $\theta_x = \theta_y$, of the two national production cycles leads to a situation, where the argument of the respective cos- function would equal 0. And therefore, there would be no inner oscillation of the system at all and thereby no mathematical base for parametric resonance or mode-locking. The justification for corollary 3 is based on the same equations. The case of the two national frequencies drifting too far apart from each other, due to a cancelling out, no longer guarantees the double-valued inner frequency of the system, i.e. the resonance condition to be fulfilled. Nevertheless, we can rigorously abstract from such a situation regarding the empirical fact that although the spectral analytically estimated frequencies of national production series are heterogeneous, this heterogeneity is restricted to a quite narrow range, at least for the main industrialized economies, see Selover and Jensen and section 5.3.3 of the present chapter.

All three above points of corollary 1 to 3, are reflected in Table 3: "Sensitivity tests for mode-locking simulations"of the Selover/Jensen-paper, p. 610. As has been shown in this section, many parts of their findings, could have been already obtained by analytic considerations applying the theoretical concept of parametric resonance or considering novel insights of statistical physics.

[5] For a detailed mathematical intuition of parametric resonance, formal derivations of the conditions for its occurence, as well as novel insights and recent findings from modern (statistical) physics, see Hillinger and Weser (1988b), Weser (1992), and Süssmuth (2002a).

5.3 A Model Incorporating Information Externalities

Let us consider $j = 1, ..., N$ producing firms of N different industrialized economies, operating on the world market. We will start our outline in a world without any information externalities with the medium and long run objective of the respective firm, before going over to integrate the consequences of global herding phenomena in the model.

5.3.1 The Model without Information Externalities

The derivation and development of the model follows Hillinger, Reiter and Weser (1992). The central assumptions underlying the model are the following quite standard assumptions of production smoothing models that are formalized and specified in greater detail in the course of this subsection: First, as regards their operating field, the global market, the model's firms have price and demand expectations, produce with a given convex technology, and hold inventories, which have a buffer function between their sales and production. The firms decide directly about production and thereby control inflows of inventories, whereas the outflows are determined by sales on the world market. Second, based on these expectations and the technology, some desired paths of inventory stock and production are predetermined. For reasons of unforeseeable fluctuations of international demand, these paths cannot be realized precisely. Third, the internationally operating, nationally representative firms face convex costs, assumed quadratic, in deviation terms of their inventory stocks, production streams, and changes of the latter, from their respective predetermined desired paths. Finally, the relevant planning horizon for adjustment processes is limited by the time horizon of a precise forecast of the world market's demand. This time span is typically short in comparison to a national inventory cycle of about three to five years length, cf. the spectral estimation results of the preceding chapter.

Production Q_j may be split into sales Z_j and inventory investment $\frac{d}{dt}K_j$:

$$Q_j = \frac{d}{dt}K_j + Z_j \tag{5.7}$$

For the moment, price and demand expectations are assumed to be exogenously given. Assuming profit-maximization behavior and a strictly convex technology, they imply uniquely determined optimal values for production Q_j^* and inventories K_j^* as well as global market's sales expectations Z_j^* of a firm j. This holds also true for the time derivatives of the respective optimal inventory stock K_j^*. I will weaken this assumption when it comes to simulate the model. But now, as K_j^* and Q_j^* are assumed to be derived from medium-term profit-maximization, the further analysis may be limited to the question of optimal control of differences $k_j = (K_j - K_j^*)$ and $q_j = (Q_j - Q_j^*)$ in order to minimize costs due to deviations from K_j^* and Q_j^*, depending on $z_j = \left(Z_j - Z_j^*\right)$. These costs will be approximated by a sum of contributions, each quadratic in k_j, $q_j = k_j^{'} + z_j = \frac{d}{dt}\left(K_j - K_j^*\right) + \left(Z_j - Z_j^*\right)$, and $q_j^{'} = k_j^{''} + z_j^{'} = \frac{d}{dt}\left[\frac{d}{dt}\left(K_j - K_j^*\right)\right] + \frac{d}{dt}\left(Z_j - Z_j^*\right)$:

Assumption 5.3.2. *Costs arise due to national deficit or excess inventories: $k_j > 0$ expresses excess inventories of a representative national firm j leading to inflexibility, inefficient storing costs, enhanced depreciation, etc. $k_j < 0$ stands for an suboptimal low level of inventories of a firm in economy j, leading to less sales and profits than possible (penalty costs).*

Assumption 5.3.2. *Costs arise due to national production deficits: $q_j > 0$ and $q_j < 0$. Given some optimal production plan Q_j^*, suitable capacities (equipment capital) have to be provided. In case of over- or undershooting this optimal production level costs arise that are approximated as quadratic in $q_j = \left(Q_j - Q_j^*\right)$.*

Assumption 5.3.3. *Costs arise due to changes of the national strategy of production: $q_j^{'} > 0$ and $q_j^{'} < 0$. This contribution corresponds to the well-known 'adjustment costs' caused by the fact that changes of production strategies imply changing (or subefficient) use of factor inputs (e.g. training or lay-off costs for changes in labor input).*

Taking all the components expressed in these assumptions into account we can formulate the following cost function for an internationally active firm in economy j:

$$C_j\left(k_j, q_j, q_j^{'}\right) = \alpha_j k_j^2 + \beta_j q_j^2 + \gamma_j \left(q_j^{'}\right)^2 . \tag{5.8}$$

Every firm determines the time paths of future production in such a way that the present value of all potential medium-term cost components, i.e. (5.8) discounted with an appropriate discount rate, is minimized. Since we are concerned with a medium-term objective, we are confronted with a situation of imperfect foresight. Hence, the relevant discount factor for an intertemporal optimization calculus is the medium-term discount rate ρ^m, where naturally $\rho^m > \rho^l$, i.e., the long-term discount rate ρ^l (as reflected in the world market discount rate) usually takes on lower values than ρ^m:

$$\min_{k_j(t),\, q_j(t)} \int_{t_0}^{\infty} \left[\alpha_j k_j^2 + \beta_j q_j^2 + \gamma_j \left(q_j^{'}\right)^2\right] e^{\rho^m (t_0 - t)} dt. \tag{5.9}$$

Given the initial values for the respective national inventory stock and level of production, $k_j(t_0)$ and $q_j(t_0)$, the relevant transversality conditions are:

$$\begin{aligned}\lim_{t\to\infty} q_j e^{\rho^m(t_0-t)} &= k_j' e^{\rho^m(t_0-t)} = 0,\\ \lim_{t\to\infty} q_j' e^{\rho^m(t_0-t)} &= k_j'' e^{\rho^m(t_0-t)} = 0,\\ \lim_{t\to\infty} q_j'' e^{\rho^m(t_0-t)} &= k_j''' e^{\rho^m(t_0-t)} = 0.\end{aligned} \tag{5.10}$$

These conditions ensure that changes in production and its time derivatives do not take place faster than firms discount the future medium-term time horizon.

Considering equation (5.7) and the argumentation following it, we can state the identity

$$k_j' = q_j - z_j. \tag{5.11}$$

As firms can control production but not sales on the international market, the latter equation yields

$$\Delta q_j = \Delta\left(k_j'\right) = \frac{d}{dt}\left(\Delta k_j\right), \tag{5.12}$$

Using (5.12), we are able to derive the following Euler equation for $k_j(t)$ and $q_j(t)$ by means of standard techniques of variational analysis:

$$\alpha_j k_j + \beta_j\left(\rho^m - \frac{d}{dt}\right) q_j + \gamma_j\left(\rho^m - \frac{d}{dt}\right)^2 q_j' = 0. \tag{5.13}$$

Differentiating (5.13) and remembering (5.11) yields

$$\alpha_j q_j + \beta_j\left(\rho^m - \frac{d}{dt}\right) q_j' + \gamma_j\left(\rho^m - \frac{d}{dt}\right)^2 q_j'' = \alpha_j z_j. \tag{5.14}$$

We find the characteristic polynomial of the homogenous part of this fourth order differential equation in q_j to be:

$$P(x) = \alpha_j + \beta_j\left(\rho^m - x\right)x + \gamma_j\left(\rho^m - x\right)^2 x^2. \tag{5.15}$$

$P(x)$ is obviously quadratic in $y = (\rho^m - x)\,x$, so that applying the quadratic formula, we get the following two solutions for (5.15) in terms of y:

$$y_{1,2} = \frac{1}{2\gamma_j}\left(-\beta_j \pm \sqrt{\beta_j^2 - 4\alpha_j\gamma_j}\right). \tag{5.16}$$

Solving $y = (\rho^m - x)\,x = \rho^m x - x^2$ for x and substituting (5.16) in, leads us to the following potential solutions of (5.15) that fulfill the transversality conditions:

$$\begin{aligned}x_{1,2} &= \frac{\rho^m}{2} - \sqrt{\frac{(\rho^m)^2}{4} + \frac{1}{2\gamma_j}\left(\beta_j \pm \sqrt{\beta_j^2 - 4\alpha_j\gamma_j}\right)}\\ &= \frac{\rho^m}{2}\left[1 - \sqrt{1 + \frac{2}{\gamma_j(\rho^m)^2}\left(\beta_j \pm \sqrt{\beta_j^2 - 4\alpha_j\gamma_j}\right)}\right]\end{aligned} \tag{5.17}$$

Obviously, the solutions are oscillatory for $\beta_j^2 < 4\alpha_j\gamma_j$, i.e., sufficiently large values of the cost parameters associated with discrepancies in the national stock of inventories and with changes in the production strategy. Approximately, we can simplify equation (5.17) as:[6]

$$x_{1,2} \approx \frac{\rho^m}{2}\left[1 - 1 + \frac{1}{\gamma_j\left(\rho^m\right)^2}\left(\beta_j \pm \sqrt{\beta_j^2 - 4\alpha_j\gamma_j}\right)\right]$$
$$\approx \frac{1}{2\gamma_j\rho^m}\left(\beta_j \pm \sqrt{\beta_j^2 - 4\alpha_j\gamma_j}\right). \tag{5.18}$$

The values of $x_{1,2}$ given by (5.18) are the roots of the following polynomial:

$$\alpha_j + \beta_j\rho^m x + \gamma_j\left(\rho^m\right)^2 x^2, \tag{5.19}$$

which can be regarded as the characteristic polynomial of the differential equation

$$\alpha_j k_j + \beta_j\rho^m q_j + \gamma_j\left(\rho^m\right)^2 q_j^{'} = 0. \tag{5.20}$$

Finally, substitution of the relationship $k_j = \left(K_j - K_j^*\right)$ leads by setting $(K_j^*)' = (K_j^*)'' = 0$, according to our assumption about long run variables, to:

$$Q_j^{'} = K_j^{''} = \frac{\alpha_j}{\gamma_j\left(\rho^m\right)^2}\left(K_j - K_j^*\right) - \frac{\beta_j}{\gamma_j\rho^m}K_j^{'} = a_j\left(K_j - K_j^*\right) - b_jK_j^{'}, \tag{5.21}$$

$$\text{where } a_j = \frac{\alpha_j}{\gamma_j\left(\rho^m\right)^2} \text{ and } b_j = \frac{\beta_j}{\gamma_j\rho^m}.$$

In conclusion, the second order accelerator equation (5.21) reflects the production smoothing process due to national institutional medium-term frictions. It expresses the acceleration $K_j^{''}$ of the respective nationally representative firm j's inventory stock K_j or, in other words, the rate of change of production behavior $Q_j^{'}$ by the respective firm j in the medium run. Accordingly, parameter a_j is mainly responsible for the rate at which individual investment is adjusted. While parameter a_j is mainly responsible for the period length of the cyclic series described by equation (5.18), parameter b_j determines the rate of damping.

Imbs (1999) argues on the base of the findings of his comprehensive empirical study on international business cycles that pairs of industrialized economies with similar high aggregate income level experience synchronized business cycles, largely because they have similar production patterns.[7] In the context of our model this would mean that in the case where parameters a_j

[6] Actually, we apply $\sqrt{1+x} \approx 1 + \frac{x}{2}$ assuming sufficiently small values of x.

[7] Furthermore, he finds that trade has surprisingly small quantitative effects and geographic considerations do *not* matter systematically.

and b_j would take on similar values, due to similar institutional, sectoral, etc. national production environments, the national cyclicalities would synchronize to a robust global cycle, given by $\sum_j^N Q_j'$ of the behavioral equations (5.21). In the simulations of section 5.3.3, we will see that a_j and b_j are similar for the G7 countries at stake, but taking this into account does not necessarily lead to a synchronization of national business cycles. Therefore, I argue that similar production patterns as reflected in the national cost parameters a_j and b_j of the model are only a necessary, in the sense of corollary 3 above, but not a sufficient condition for the synchronization of national production cycles. This point will be outlined in greater detail in the following paragraphs.

5.3.2 Introducing Information Externalities

According to leading contemporary professionals in the field of business cycles the central 'puzzle' about business cycles is their comovement and synchronized nature: "Even though comovement is a defining characteristic of the business cycle, in recent decades macroeconomists have tended to focus on understanding the persistence in the ups and downs of aggregate economic activity. They have generally been less concerned with understanding this synchronized pattern...," see Christiano and Fitzgerald (1998). These authors, like Selover and Jensen (1999), suggest *herd behavior* as described for example by Banerjee (1992) as situations, where "everyone doing what everyone else is doing, even when their private information suggests doing something quite different," p. 798, as a potential candidate for the explanation of business cycle comovement. They note that "[i]t hardly needs to be stated that herd behavior sounds like comovement," p. 68.

The early and mid 1990s have seen a growing interest of the economic community in herding phenomena. Pioneered by the works of Scharfstein and Stein (1990), Banerjee (1992) and Bikhchandani, Hirshleifer and Welch (1992), where herd externalities depended on the ordering or queuing of players, the latest contributions focus on endogenous timing and information revelation in herding models of investment, see e.g. Chamley and Gale (1994), Gul and Lundholm (1995) or Sgroi (1999). A survey of these models is given in Gale (1996a). This recent body of literature leads to the suggestion that the rate a_i at which an individual changes production or inventory investment behavior for strategic reasons is not constant and is affected by the overall or global production behavior. Informational cascades can cause longer lasting strategic delay of inventory stock building or reducing able to affect the medium-term production behavior and eventually also lead to aggregate fluctuations. The few existing models in this vein that build the bridge to aggregate cycles are the ones by Gale (1996b) and Chalkley and Lee (1998). These authors focus on coordination failures among agents either based on production or information externalities leading to the generation of genuine business cycles. Besides they both put a lot of emphasis on the explanation of potential asymmetry in business cycle time series caused by strategic delay. Their models relate to some extent to the approach that is adopted here, but none of them explicitly applies it to explain the synchronization of different individual cycles (national production cycles) underlying the aggregate series (global cycle). In general, the crucial reasoning behind endogenously-timed herding is that the short run timing of an individual investment decision is not independent of the overall investment behavior of the other agents in the respective sector or economy. This channel of aggregate influence arises due to uncertainty about the profitability of future projects: The individual strategy consists in weighing up the option value of waiting and thereby gaining information by observing others' actions with the costs of this delay.

A more thorough outline of herding behavior in the context of the synchronization of sectoral investment behaviors is given in chapter 8. Let me here just state the central result and refer to the central sources of the relevant strand of literature on endogenously-timed herding for a detailed elaboration and proofs of the argument.

The central result of an endogenously-timed herding scenario with $N \in \mathbb{N}_{++}$ nationally representative producers might be summarized in the following proposition:

Proposition 5.3.1. *Additional*[8] *collective action, i.e., inventory stock building or reduction, can take place if and only if some or at least one global market's producer acted observably and obviously more or differently than required by an ordinary production smoothing objective one myopic point in time earlier than the other firms. A single period of no additional action parallely by all producers at one moment of the time array will trigger the opposite, namely additional collective inactivity.*

Proof. See Gale (1996a) or Sgroi (1999).[9]

How can we implement this result in the non-interactive models described by equation (5.21)? Obviously, it is a matter of signs of a) the individual national producer's and b) the observed aggregate production activity on the world market. If individual inventory stock deficit or excess, $k_j = \left(K_j - K_j^*\right)$, i.e. the individual incentive to produce or not to produce, and aggregate production activity $\sum_j^N Q_j$ are of equal signs, then there is an additional

[8] Production activities additional to the non-interactive behaviour required by national economy specific medium-term production smoothing (see equation (5.21) above) is meant.

[9] For an empirical underpinning and evidence for endogenously-timed herding phenomena, the reader is referred to the documentation and interpretation of a *herding experiment in endogenous time*, recently conducted at Nuffield College, University of Oxford, by Sgroi (2000).

positive effect on the rate of adjustment of production a_j in the respective firm's equation. On the other hand are the signs of these two quantities of opposite sign, there is an additional negative effect (first part of the above bullet point). And finally, if one quantity equals zero, the other would do straightforwardly, too (second part of the above bullet point). The latter cascade would coincide with the case of a long run steady state equilibrium which is assumed not to be reached in the medium run by this disequilibrium production cycle model.

Formally, we achieve the synthesis by modifying our model of equation (5.21) in the following way:

$$Q_j^{'} = K_j^{''} = a_j \left\{ 1 + \chi_j \cdot \Psi \left[(K_j - K_j^*) \sum_j Q_j \right] \right\} (K_j - K_j^*) - b_j K_j^{'}, \text{ where} \tag{5.22}$$

Ψ is defined as a transform function of the simple form:

$$\Psi [x] = \begin{cases} +1 \text{ for } x > 0 \\ \ \ 0 \text{ for } x = 0 \\ -1 \text{ for } x < 0 \end{cases} \text{ and} \tag{5.23}$$

parameter $\chi_j \in (0, 1]$ is assumed to be strictly positive, allowing it being interpreted as the *strength of* individual (or national) *interaction* with the aggregate (or global) behavior. Obviously, the equation system described by (5.22) and (5.23) is of *Mathieu type* , as are (5.5) and (5.6) above, and bears the potential to synchronize national in such a manner that co-fluctuations, resulting in a robust world business cycle pattern, are generated. A demonstration based on calibrating and simulating the equation system (5.22) and (5.23) is given in the following subsection.

5.3.3 Calibration of the Model and Some Simulations

The complementary parts of the differential equations (5.21) imply the following roots

$$\lambda_{j,\ 1,2} = \frac{1}{2} \left(-b_j \pm \sqrt{(b_j)^2 - 4a_j} \right). \tag{5.24}$$

For $a_j > 0.25b_j$ the discriminant is negative, the Eigenvalues are conjugate complex and the solution of (5.21) takes the form of a damped cycle[10]

[10] Most evidently, this is a quite more realistic and economically meaningful implication in contrast to the sinusoidal waveform-shaped business cycle 'dummies' of the Selover/Jensen model. Cf. also the fact that moduli implied by AR spectral estimations of real world economic time series generally take on values < 1. For an interpretation of the relationship between damping rates and moduli, see the immediately following paragraph.

$$Q_j(t) = A_{1j} e^{\rho_j t} \cos(\omega_j t - \phi_{1j}) \qquad (5.25)$$
$$K_j(t) = A_{2j} e^{\rho_j t} \cos(\omega j t - \phi_{2j}).$$

The damping rate ρ, frequency ω and period P are given by

$$\rho_j = -b_j/2, \qquad (5.26)$$
$$\omega_j = \frac{1}{2}\sqrt{4a_j - b_j},$$
$$P_j = 2\pi/\omega_j.$$

In reality we do not observe production behaviors, as described by equations (5.21), in continuous time. Therefore to calibrate the model, i.e. to find empirically consistent parameter values a_j and b_j, we need to rely on the discrete analogue of (5.21) and this is a set of AR(2) equations. By means of AR spectral analysis we are able to obtain estimates $\widehat{P_j}$ for $j = 1, ..., N$ different national production series. Furthermore, the modulus mod$_j$ of the complex root of the respectively adjusted AR(2) model has the following interpretation: Starting for example in period zero with an amplitude of $A = 1$, a mod-value of 0.5 means, that the process has a remaining amplitude value of 0.5 in period one, $(0.5)^2$ in period two, etc. Therefore we are able to define an estimator for ρ_j.

Definition 5.3.1. *Since* mod$_j^t$ *corresponds to* $e^{\ln(\text{mod}_j)t}$, $\ln(\text{mod}_j) = \widehat{\rho}_j$.

From this definition estimations of b_j are directly derivable by substituting the latter relationship into the first expression of (5.26):

$$\widehat{b}_j = -2\widehat{\rho}_j = -2\ln(\text{mod}_j) \qquad (5.27)$$

Using this estimate and the definitions of ω_j and P_j from (5.26), we obtain an empirical measure for a_j, too:

$$\widehat{a}_j = \frac{1}{4}\left[\left(\frac{4\pi}{\widehat{P_j}}\right)^2 + \widehat{b}_j\right]. \qquad (5.28)$$

Given a) estimates of $\widehat{P_j}$ and mod$_j$, see Table 5.1 below, b) initial values for end of period national inventory stocks K_j and changes in end of period national inventory stocks K_j', and c) a law of motion for K_j^*,[11] we are now ready to simulate equations (5.21) and the equation system (5.22) and (5.23) for the case $\chi_j = 0$. The latter remains the only 'free' parameter according to which we will be able to achieve an agreement between model and data.

It should be noted that such a calibration strategy would neatly meet virtually all requirements stated by Cooley (1997) in his *rules for calibration*

[11] We will assume for simplicity that the desired inventory capital K_j^* will be a share of global demand Z.

(of course, originally stated for equilibrium models): i) it does not justify parameter choices by referring to prior studies, we rather rely on the following appropriate spectral estimations using one of the latest detrending technology in form of the MBK-filter, ii) a framework is defined that one can use to study questions about the behavior of economies, iii) the measurements are matched to the model, iv) the model is matched to the measurement. As we will see more clearly in the course of the following simulations ii) to iv) are met for the present study.

In the following Figure 5.1 the business cycle components (MBK-filtered) of the industrial production series for 7 major economies, in prices of 1990, for the period 1952 to 1997, are displayed. From left to right, these are Canada, France, Germany, Japan, Netherlands, the United Kingdom, and the US. They fluctuate with such an homogenous pattern that they can hardly be discriminated via a simple visual inspection, cf. also Figure 1 in Selover and Jensen (1999), p. 594. The following Table 5.1 summarizes the spectral features period length (in years), i.e. $\widehat{P_j}$, and the implied moduli (mod_j) of the AR models, the corresponding roots, the signal-to-noise ratio that measures the variance of the signal relative to the variance of the noise in the series, and some goodness of fit measures of the underlying AR models, as well as the estimated AR coefficients and their t values.

On the basis of these estimates and initial values for K_j and $K_j^{'}$, taken from the IFS International Financial Statistics Series (source: International Monetary Fund, IMF) for the years 1952 and 1953, I calibrate the model as described above and simulate the equation system (5.22) and (5.23) for 40 periods:

(i) setting $K_j^* = 0$ and $\chi_j = 0$, i.e. the *case of no interaction* corresponding to model (5.21) above: *dashed* lines in Figure 5.2,
(ii) setting $K_j^* = 0$ and $\chi_j = 0.65$, i.e. the *case of interaction* with the aggregate productive activity. It demonstrates the synchronization potential of the model based on resonance and the obvious mode-locking of the national cycles to form a robust deterministic cyclic world pattern: *solid* lines in Figure 5.2. In order to highlight the 'drawing-together' of phases dashed parallels of the ordinate are displayed in the subdiagrams of the respective country's production series simulation.

Finally, a simulation is run, where I assume that demand on the world market Z follows pseudo-Brownian motion:

$$Z(t) = \varepsilon\sqrt{t}, \text{ where } \varepsilon \text{ is i.i.d. and } \sim N(0,1), \tag{5.29}$$

and

$$K_j^*(t) = \vartheta Z(t), \tag{5.30}$$

where $\vartheta = 0.01$. The output of an exemplary simulation's run is displayed in Figure 5.3, where I set $\chi_j = \chi = 0.65$ equally for all $j = 1, ..., N$. Obviously, the mode-locking mechanism works, as Selover and Jensen also showed, as well in such a stochastic environment and the model matches the data very well: The standard deviation of the empirical global cycle is 0.036, for the simulated global cycle it is 0.038. The computation of some performance statistics gives a similar picture: Mean squared error (MSE) = 0.003, root MSE (RMSE) = 0.05, mean absolute deviation (MAD) = 0.04, Theil's U = 0.97 - needless to mention that the spectral properties of the two series are very close.

Fig. 5.1. Industrial production of 7 major industrialized economies

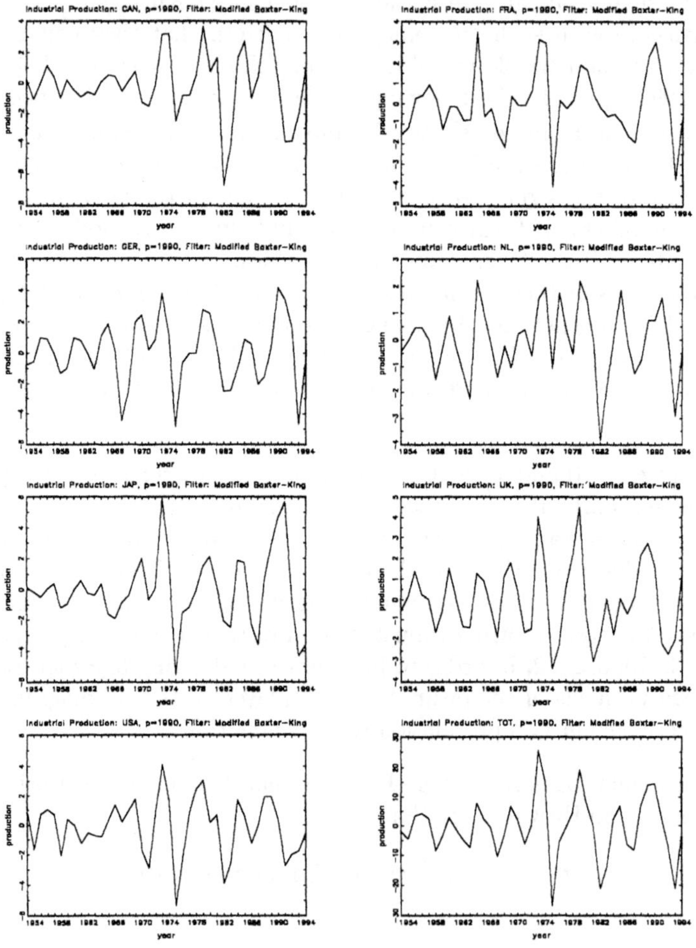

Data source: IMF International Financial Statistics (1952-1997: annual frequency); Detrending: MBK-filter.

Table 5.1. Classical spectral estimation results for 2 subperiods (logD-filter)

Country	Phase (radians)		Period length (months)	
	Early per.[a]	Late per.[b]	Early per.	Late per.
Canada	+ 3.12	− 1.46	31.5	64.0
France	− 1.51	− 1.40	31.5	48.0
Germany	+ 1.44	− 0.57	47.0	48.0
Japan	+ 2.13	− 0.98	63.0	48.0
Netherlands	+ 1.68	− 0.65	47.0	48.0
U.K.	− 1.87	− 2.26	37.8	48.0
US	− 3.01	− 1.54	31.5	48.0

Source: Selover and Jensen (1999), p. 606

Data: Industrial production in monthly frequency

Data source: IMF International Financial Statistics

Note: a. defined as 1958:01 - 1973:09, n=189, b. defined as 1980:01 - 1995:12, n=192

Table 5.2. Univariate ME-spectral features, 1952-97 (modified BK-filter)

country	per.	roots	mod	R^2	logL	SNR	coefficients*)	
Canada	5.08	0.23±0.65i	0.69	0.25	-80	0.4	0.45 (3.14)	-.47 (-3.24)
France	4.75	0.11±0.45i	0.46	0.03	-74	0.1	0.22 (1.43)	-.21 (-1.27)
Germany	4.91	0.22±0.74i	0.77	0.32	-77	0.6	0.44 (3.25)	-.58 (-4.04)
Japan	5.27	0.28±0.71i	0.77	0.37	-80	0.7	0.57 (4.15)	-.59 (-4.13)
NL	4.48	0.11±0.64i	0.65	0.32	-77	0.2	0.44 (3.25)	-.59 (-4.04)
UK	4.90	0.23±0.76i	0.79	0.39	-70	0.7	0.45 (3.46)	-.63 (-4.75)
U.S.	4.84	0.20±0.71i	0.74	0.32	-73	0.5	0.40 (3.01)	-.55 (-4.05)
sum over	per.	roots	mod	R^2	logL	SNR	coefficients*)	
→ World	4.91	0.22±0.73i	0.76	0.32	-144	0.6	0.43 (3.22)	-.58 (-4.06)

Note: Values in parentheses are t-values; SNR = signal-to-noise ratio, see Woitek (1997)

The results given in the above Table 5.2. make the base of calibration of models for the following presentation of simulation results. The calculation of the structural parameters of models (5.22) in combination with (5.23) is done routinely according to (5.27) and (5.28) in the text. Since the exact discrete analogue of the model given in (5.21), or in terms of the language of statistical physics, the approximate representation of a "second-order continuous AR process" generally written as $k_2 \frac{d^2 x(t)}{dt^2} + k_1 \frac{dx(t)}{dt} + x(t) = a(t)$, cf. Ulrych and Bishop (1975), p. 56, is given by an AR(2) process, the adjusted AR order is throughout of dimension 2. For the following numerical simulations of the differential equation system (5.22) in combination with (5.23)

I programmed and applied standard Euler-methods as adequate numerical simulation devices, see for example Judd (1998), part III, chapter 10.

Fig. 5.2. Simulation of equation system (5.22) and (5.23), see (i), (ii) above

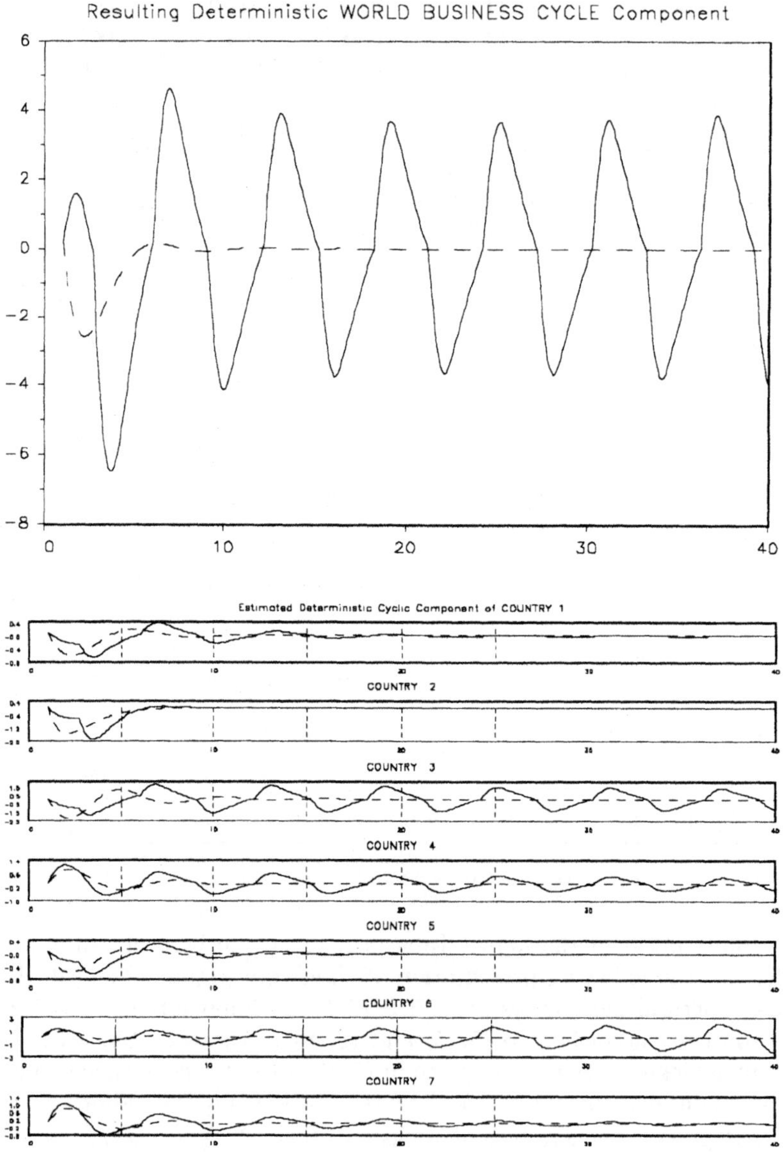

Note: solid line: $\chi = 0.65$, dashed line: $\chi = 0$

Country codes: 1 Canada, 2 France, 3 Germany, 4 Japan, 5 Netherlands, 6 U.K., 7 US

Fig. 5.3. Sample simulation run of model (5.22) and (5.23), where $\chi = .65$ and Z follows pseudo-Brownian motion

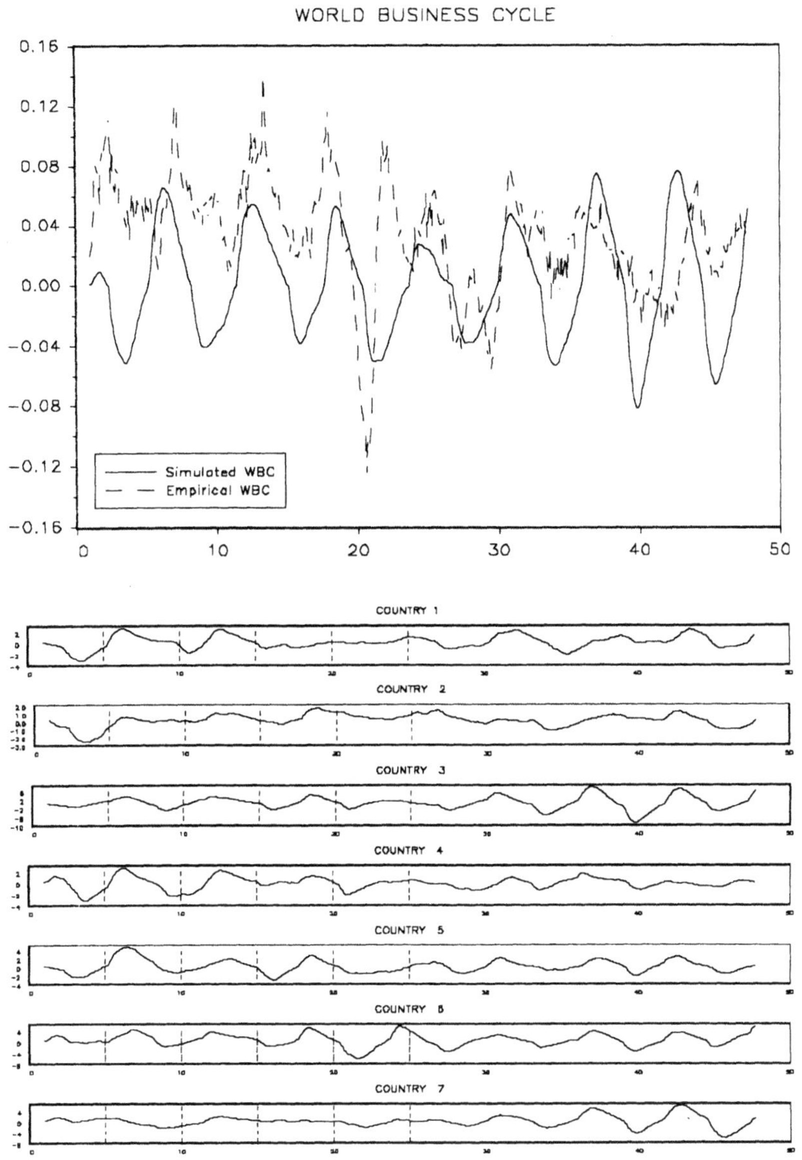

Note: Empirical world business cycle is displayed in monthly growth rates, source: IMF
Country codes: 1 Canada, 2 France, 3 Germany, 4 Japan, 5 Netherlands, 6 U.K., 7 US

5.4 Outlook and Concluding Remark

The chapter demonstrated that the Selover/Jensen model, as well as a surveyed literature on the synchronization of business cycles by means of nonlinear mode-locking mechanisms, are part of a specific, more general class of mathematical models. A generalization of this class of economic cycles' mode-lock modelling was elaborated and provided, making parts of the findings by Selover and Jensen (1999), based on simulations, obsolete.

Furthermore, an endogenous mode-locking model of national business cycle synchronization, induced by the economic behavior of internationally and interactively operating firms in the presence of information externalities was derived, calibrated, enriched with exogenous shocks and simulated on the basis of empirical data and spectral analytic findings for six of the G7 countries and the Netherlands. It was shown that the simulations' outputs accurately fit the data and reflected the empirical synchronization process. It remains for future work to bring the results even closer to the findings of the strand of empirical literature on international business cycle comovement, see e.g. Imbs (1999), concerning especially the determination and quantification of the heterogeneous forms of interactions between different countries and the global international production activity, as reflected in the presented model's parameters χ_j.

Such a model, i.e. a model with heterogeneous interaction parameters, for the synchronization of sectoral US investment cycles is motivated by empirical evidence a) for the aggregation problem arising in the course of linear models of the sectoral aggregation process and b) for sectoral cycles' synchronization in the first two chapters of the proceeding part of the monograph. Finally, in a third chapter of the following part, a model is presented that is able to capture the empirical aggregation process and synchronization phenomena across different sectors. This model is calibrated, simulated and brought into agreement with actual data and measures.

Part III

The Sectoral Constitution of Macro-Cycles

6. An Aggregation Problem for Linear Models?

Indeed, I think it is unlikely that we will ever have a clear understanding of fluctuations without a more detailed analysis of disaggregate data ... My own view is that we need much more understanding of the disaggregate data than we (or at least I) currently have ... I think it is very important that we force ourselves to think about more disaggregated models and data.
C. I. Plosser (1991)

This part of the monograph analyzes the generation of macroeconomic cycles from sectoral cycles on the basis of US investment data. The focus of the study is on the variable new real (base year 1987) capital spending, including permanent additions and major alterations to plant structures along with new machinery and equipment, taken from the NBER-CES/Census US Manufacturing Productivity Database. The dataset consists of 450 SIC[1] 4-digit industrial series, covering annual observations for the period 1958 to 1992. For further detail, see Bartelsman and Gray (1996). I test these 450 SIC 4-digit series, covering the period from 1958 to 1992, for cyclicity and estimate their central spectral features. I find that almost all of the disaggregated series, as well as the aggregate series, are strongly and significantly autoregressive. These series have complex roots that imply business cycles with traditional periods centered around five years. In this context alternative VAR specifications are tested. Their ability to explain the spectral features of constituent and aggregate series is examined in simulation experiments. I find that there is a substantial and statistically significant feedback effect from the aggregate activity on the sectoral series. In the VAR simulations the aggregate feedback acts as a common shock impinging on the sectors. The residuals, which I interpret as idiosyncratic shocks, are only weakly correlated among the sectors. In general I find that the VAR model is able to describe the cyclical characteristics of the individual time series both accurately and parsimoniously. The linear models are only partially successful in modelling the aggregation process. This points to the desirability of a nonlinear aggregation model. This is also suggested by the empirical finding that the phases and periods of the cycles are drawn together over time, cf. the preceding chapter of the present study.

---

[1] *Standard Industrial Classification* System

6.1 Description of US Business Cycles

6.1.1 Business Cycles in Central US NIPA Time Series

The central *explanandum* of this part of the monograph analysis will be the constitution of the US. manufacturing investment aggregate from its 450 four-digit sectoral disaggregated series. Nevertheless, the task of this first subsection is to assess the coherency, synchronicity and relevance of manufacturing investment itself, i.e. in total, in contributing to the dynamics of NIPA time series that are of higher statistical dimension. In line with the findings of the first chapter of part II of the monograph and the literature surveyed in the introductory sections, I find for the period 1960 to 1992 that the standard deviation of the GDP business cycle component diminishes by a rough 50 percent (47.25%), if one substracts its private total investment constituent from it. Substracting the cycle component of manufacturing investment from total private investment, leads to a reduction of its standard deviation of about 10 percentage points (9.37%). Nevertheless, the two series are quite coherent, as reflected in a *squared coherency* (*sc*) value of 0.81 and a - only slightly positive - *phase shift* (*ps*) measure of 0.47,[2] see the methodological part of the monograph for how to interpret these measures. The bivariate spectral relationship between the higher dimensioned investment aggregate total private fixed investment (TPI) and the GDP series is even more striking as reflected in a *sc*-value equalling 0.97 and a *ps*-constellation of −0.1. The GDP series also moves quite coherently in line with its manufacturing investment (MFI) constituent, as measured by a *sc*-value of 0.84 and, as does the TPI quasi-cycle, the cyclic component of GDP somewhat leads the MFI cycle: the *ps*-measure takes on a value of 0.33. It should be noted that the frequencies corresponding to these reported maxima of coherency is quite close to the periodicity of 4.48 years contained in the MFI business cycle component. These results are also graphically illustrated in the following Figures 6.1a and 6.1b.

[2] Indicating that the total private investment series, slightly leads the manufacturing investment business cycle component.

In Figure 6.1a, we graphically present the US GDP, TPI and MFI business cycle components (the applied filter is the MBK-filter, see above) for the period 1960-92 in one diagram, so as to allow one to focus directly on the degree of comovement between them. Following Christiano and Fitzgerald (1998), we divided each series by its sample standard deviation, so that the standard deviation of the displayed data is unity in each case. Figure 6.1b shows the ME-(auto)spectra of these series plotted from highest to lowest aggregate series, so as to allow a direct comparison of spectra (the dashed lines display the respective integrated spectra). Table 6.1a and 6.1b, following Figures 6.1a and 6.1b, summarize the basic spectral features (univariate and bivariate) and goodness of fit measures for this three-steps aggregation ladder: manufacturing investment (MFI) → total private fixed investment (TPI) → GDP.

Fig. 6.1a. Business cycle components of US GDP, TPI, MFI

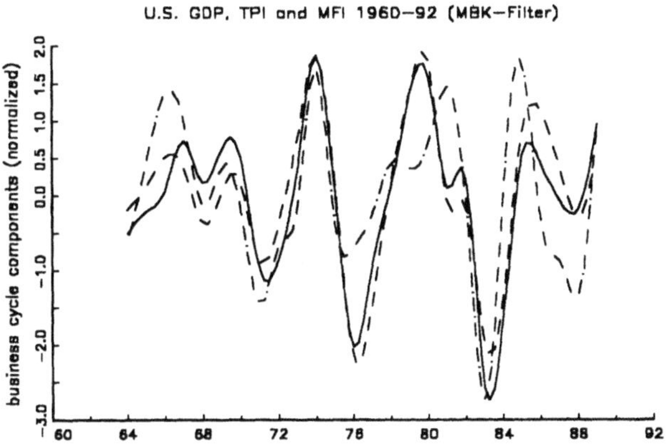

Note: solid: GDP, dashed: TPI, dotted and dashed: MFI

As can be seen from the following Figure 6.1b, it is noteworthy that the spectral properties of the US GDP and MFI series are so similar in shape and position that one is hardly able to discriminate between the two of them by a visual inspection, see Figure 6.1b below. For a quantification of how strong and in which phase position the US investment components are related to the other central US NIPA aggregates, the reader is referred to chapter 4 of part II of the monograph.

Fig. 6.1b. ME-spectra of US GDP, TPI, MFI (detrending: MBK-filter)

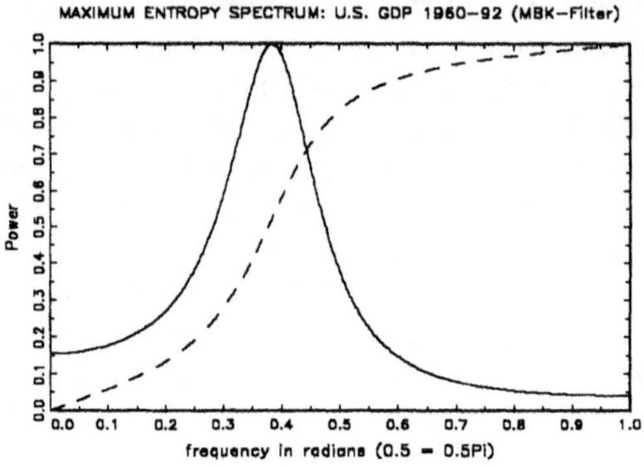

GDP → peak period: 5.13 yrs.

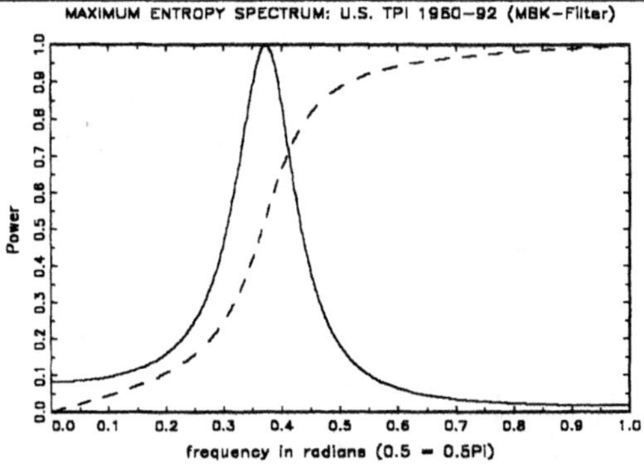

TPI → peak period: 5.39 yrs.

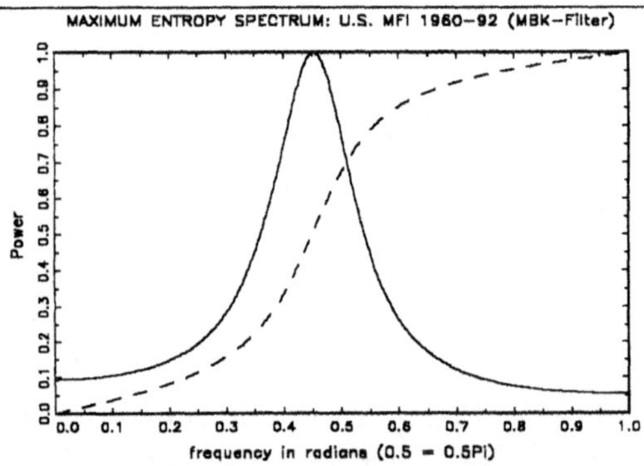

MFI → peak period: 4.48 yrs.

Table 6.1a. Univariate ME-spectral features, 1960-92[3] (MBK-filter)

series	per.	roots	mod$^{a)}$	R^2	logL	SNR	coefficients$^{b)}$	
MFI	4.48	0.12±0.73i	0.74 (0.13)	0.23	-264.3	0.48	0.25 (1.44)	-.55 (-3.08)
TPI	5.39	0.31±0.75i	0.82 (0.13)	0.47	-274.3	1.12	0.62 (3.89)	-.67 (-4.16)
GDP	5.13	0.24±0.70i	0.74 (0.15)	0.31	-126.0	0.62	0.50 (2.79)	-.55 (-3.08)

Note: Values given in parentheses are a) standard errors and b) t-values.

Table 6.1b. Bivariate ME-spectral features, 1960-92 (MBK-filter)

series	per.$^{a)}$	sc	ps	phase$^{b)}$	gain
TPI and GDP	4.48	0.97	-.10	-8.17	1.77
TPI and MFI	4.17	0.81	0.47	4.38	4.38
MFI and GDP	4.33	0.84	0.33	27.44	8.92

Note: Measures given a) at maximum of squared coherency (sc) and b)in degrees.

6.1.2 Cycles in Disaggregated US Manufacturing Investment

As already mentioned above, the study is based on the variable new real (base year 1987) capital spending, including permanent additions and major alterations to plant structures along with new machinery and equipment, taken from the NBER-CES/Census US Manufacturing Productivity Database. The dataset consists in 450 SIC 4-digit industrial series, covering annual observations for the period 1958 to 1992. For further detail, see Bartelsman and Gray (1996). To get an intuition for which industries show the highest standardized (i.e., in standard deviation terms of the manufacturing aggregate series) standard deviation, we calculate the ratios $\sigma_{y_i}/\sigma_{\sum_i y_i = y^A}$ $\forall i = 1, ..., 450$ and rank the industries, accordingly. Table 2a and 2b report the ten most variable series for the MBK- and HP(100)-filtered sectoral series, respectively.[4]

---

[3] Despite for the MFI series, where we consider the slightly longer period from 1958 to 1992.

[4] Note the SIC-codes are given in 1972 definitions. For concordance with 1987 definitions, see `http://www.nber.org/nberces/sic_72.txt`

Table 6.2a. Top 10 sectors with highest standardized variance
(applied filter: MBK: $\sigma_{y^A} = 5057.79$)

Industry	SIC4 code	σ_{y_i}	$\sigma_{y_i}/\sigma_{y^A}$
motor vehicles and car bodies	3711	777.67	0.15
petroleum refining	2911	589.76	0.12
motor vehicles parts and accesoires	3714	558.84	0.11
blast furnances and steel mills	3312	418.09	0.08
paper mills	2621	356.33	0.07
industrial organic chemicals, nec	2869	302.40	0.06
semiconductors and related devices	3674	263.44	0.05
miscellaneous plastics products	3079	239.60	0.05
paperboard mills	2631	211.13	0.04
electronic-computing equipment	3573	165.54	0.03

Table 6.2b. Top 10 sectors with highest standardized variance
(applied filter: HP(100): $\sigma_{y^A} = 5847.45$)

Industry	SIC4 code	σ_{y_i}	$\sigma_{y_i}/\sigma_{y^A}$
petroleum refining	2911	866.71	0.15
motor vehicles and car bodies	3711	743.46	0.13
blast furnances and steel mills	3312	647.75	0.11
motor vehicles parts and accesoires	3714	610.61	0.10
industrial organic chemicals, nec	2869	529.99	0.09
paper mills	2621	431.10	0.07
paperboard mills	2631	323.65	0.06
semiconductors and related devices	3674	269.88	0.05
miscellaneous plastics products	3079	244.48	0.04
electronic-computing equipment	2821	219.36	0.04

Obviously, the ranking pattern is quite robust over the two deterministic filtering methods. The first four sectors (motor vehicles and car bodies, motor vehicles parts and accessories, petroleum refining and blast furnaces and steel mills) are generally seen as key sectors and contribute more than one fifth to the standard deviation of the aggregate series (22.7%). These core sectors stem mainly from the interrelated motor vehicles and equipment (corresponding SIC2 sector is *transportation*), petroleum refining[5] (corresponding SIC2 sector is *petroleum and coal products*) and blast furnace and basic steel products (corresponding SIC2 sector is *primary metal industries*) industries, i.e. they are concentrated in sector groups producing investment in capital goods and their inputs. Furthermore, it should be noted, that substracting

[5] For the not displayed results for the higher aggregated constituent series, i.e. the 143 SIC3 and the 20 SIC2 manufacturing subsectors, the respective motor vehicles group contributes the highest part also for the HP(100)-filtered series. Furthermore, the ranking pattern is quite robust for both filtering methods for these higher aggregated sectoral definitions, too.

the first 20 series of the above ranking, i.e. less than 5% of all disaggregate series from the aggregate investment series, reduces the standard deviation of its business cycle dynamics by an overproportional approximately 45%.

Univariate spectral estimation results. According to ME-spectral estimates more than 95% of the sectoral series imply complex solutions of the adjusted AR(2)-polynomials[6] and contain a significant and prominent periodicity. Excluding the industries with non-complex AR structure in the constitution of the manufacturing investment aggregate, reduces its sample standard deviation σ_{y^A} by less than 1 percentage (0.004% - in absolute standard deviation terms by a factor of 24.47). As expected, most of these series stem from the *textile* and *food* sector that are generally agreed on to be not part of the key industrial sectors of business cyclic fluctuations.[7]

The distribution of the estimated period lengths (in years) of the remaining 430 industrial series ranges between 2.5 and 7.6 years. The distribution shows a (quite small) standard deviation of 0.63 and a mean of 4 years (remember, for comparison, the manufacturing investment aggregate showed a periodicity of 4.48 years), suggesting an existing, but fairly weak, heterogeneity in periodicity for the sectoral disaggregated series.

The distribution of the implied moduli shows a mean value of 0.6, the standard deviation of the distribution lying at 0.15. The estimated values range from 0.23 to 0.96 (remember, for comparison, the ME-spectral estimate for the manufacturing investment aggregate implied a modulus of 0.75). All estimated moduli are significant on nearly all conventional significance levels, i.e., the lowest implied t-value (the corresponding null is mod = 0) lies at 2.22. The adjusted R^2s of the underlying AR(2)-models range between 1 and 65 percent (remember, for comparison, for the manufacturing investment aggregate series the adjusted R^2 was 23 percent). The standard deviation of their distribution is 0.13. The average adjusted R^2 equals 13 percent. There are strong positive relationships between moduli, adjusted R^2s of the underlying AR models and standard errors of moduli, as well as a weak positive relationship between implied moduli and estimated period lenghts.

Bivariate spectral estimation results. Besides the univariate spectral description of the disaggregate series, I estimated their bivariate relationship to the MFI aggregate. I find that the median of estimated phase (*ps*) shifts lies at −0.07, suggesting that only few more constituent series rather lag than lead the aggregate cycle. The *ps*-values range between −5.88 and 2.36, where the lowest absolute *ps* is estimated for industry SIC 3496: 'misc. fabricated wire products' equalling 0.01 (at a frequency, corresponding to the maximum

[6] I implicitly assume that the constituent series bear a similar autoregressive structure as the resulting aggregate series and therefore fix the order for all series at $p = 2$. It is also the average order, recommended by the Bayesian (V)AR-order determination procedure suggested by Heintel (1998).

[7] Note, there is only one industry SIC 3334 'primary aluminium' that lies in the first half of the ranking *and* shows a standardized standard deviation > 1%.

of coherency of 0.84, equalling 4.03 years[8]). The standard deviation for the estimated *ps*-values is 0.94.

The distribution of estimated squared coherencies (*sc*) between aggregate and respective disaggregate business cycle components ranges between 0.05 and 0.99 with a median of 0.59 and a mean of 0.58, where the highest coherency with the MFI aggregate is estimated for industry SIC 3569: 'general industrial machinery, nec' equalling 0.99 at a period length of 4.85 years and a relative *ps* of 0.11. The standard deviation of the *sc*-estimates equals 0.21.

Do the disaggregate series share the aggregate cycle?. Before trying to answer this question, let me briefly outline the findings in Heintel (1998), where a Bayesian criterion (BAC), i.e., a Bayesian (V)AR models' order determination procedure is suggested. Heintel (1998) shows by means of 5000 Monte Carlo (MC) simulation runs that his BAC, given a simulated VAR(1)-model with cyclical structure and allowing for a highest VAR order of 6, suggests in 85.7% of all cases the correct VAR(1)-order and only in 4.6% of all cases VAR(2), i.e. more than one complex solution. For comparison, he also denotes the performances of Akaike's information criterion (AIC) and the conventional Bayesian information criterion (BIC), suggesting in 82.3% (AIC) and 42.3% (BIC) of all cases correctly VAR(1) and in 6.7% (AIC) and 0% (BIC) of all cases falsely VAR(2). Obviously, the BAC is first best in determining the adequate order of a VAR model, with regard to the decision VAR(1) or VAR(2), i.e. the question whether the two series at stake contain only one cyclicality as reflected in the (potential) one complex solution implied by a VAR(1)-model or more? Besides BAC, I also consider a comprehensive range of order selection criteria usually found in the literature, see e.g. Lütkepohl (1991), namely: the final prediction error criterion (FPE), AIC, the Hannan-Quinn criterion (HQ) and the Schwarz criterion (SC).

Allowing for a maximum VAR order of 2, we obtain the following result of suggested VAR(1)-models for the 430 disaggregate investment series with cyclic dynamics and the investment aggregate series: BAC: 1, FPE: 10, AIC: 10, HQ: 13, SC: 17. Allowing for a highest order of 6, the number of cases, where VAR(1), i.e. one single cyclicality shared by disaggregate and aggregate series, is suggested, reduces: BAC: 1, FPE: 1, AIC: 1, HQ: 2, SC: 13. In conclusion, our order determination study based on information criteria, obviously, favors a VAR(2)-modelling of the relationship between aggregate and disaggregate series.

Nevertheless, the results suggest that although the aggregate and disaggregate series might not share exactly the same cycle in the sense of one common complex root, the two share a very similar periodicity, as can be seen from Figure 6.2. Figure 6.2 displays the distribution of implied periodicities of 239 cases, where a complex solution of an adjusted VAR(1)-model

[8] In general the periodicities at maximum of coherency (aggregate to disaggregate) are distributed between 2.42 and 14.08 years with a median of 4.68 and a mean of 4.72 years. The distribution's standard deviation equals 1.18.

to respective disaggregate and aggregate series exists (white bars). For 422 of the disaggregate investment series, this is the case for the VAR(2)-model adjustment routine (black bars).[9] The median value of period lengths corresponding to the maximum of coherency in the case of the VAR(1)-model estimations (4.42 years), lies solely 0.06 years below the cycle we found in the empirical aggregate (4.48 years). This suggests that on average at least 55% of the disaggregate series share the aggregate's periodicity. But essentially, as can be seen from Figure 6.2, this seems also to be the case for the VAR(2)-models' results, for which the median value of implied period lengths (4.68 years) - at maximum of *sc* between aggregate and respective disaggregate - lies 0.2 years above the empirical aggregate's periodicity. In contrast to the VAR(1)-models' results, this finding is based on the distribution of 98% of all disaggregate series with cyclic dynamics and, as can be seen from Figure 6.2, the implied periodicities are more concentrated around the aggregate's periodicity as reflected in a standard deviation of 1.18 years for the VAR(2)-models vs. a standard deviation of 2.09 years for the VAR(1)-models.

Fig. 6.2. VAR(1) vs. VAR(2): aggregate and disaggregate series

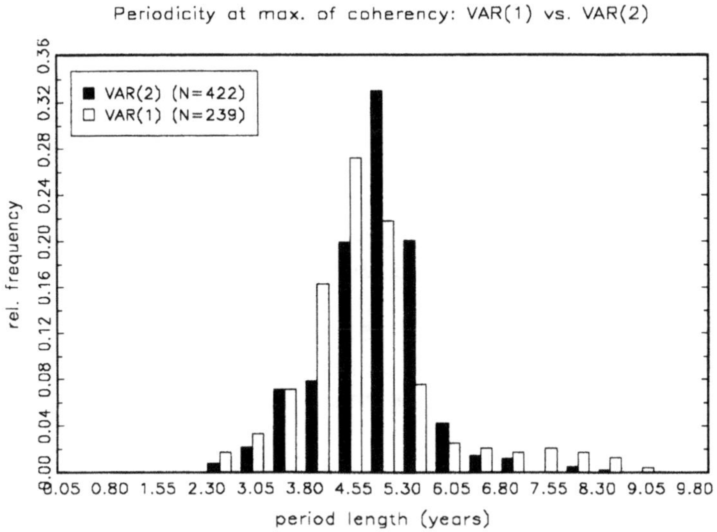

Note: for VAR(2) complex solution with highest sc-value is displayed.

[9] In 160 cases there exist two complex solutions and thereby two implied periodicities for the VAR(2)-models. For these cases Figure 6.2 displays the implied periodicity of that root that correponds to the relative higher *sc* between respective disaggregate and aggregate series. On average these second roots show a *sc*-value that is less than half that of the first root. Furthermore, the implied period lengths of the second roots are more than three times as dispersed as the ones of the first roots.

6.2 Testing Autoregressivity and Aggregate Feedback

In this section we test the detrended disaggregated 4-digit investment series for significant AR dynamics as well as for an impact from the aggregate investment activity on the respective industrial one. In detail, we are considering the following models

$$y_{i,t} = \phi_{i,1} \sum_{j \neq i} y_{j,t} + \phi_{i,2} \sum_{j \neq i} y_{j,t-1} + \Phi_i(L) y_{i,t} \tag{6.1}$$

$$y_{i,t} = \phi_{i,3} \sum_{i} y_{i,t} + \phi_{i,4} \sum_{i} y_{i,t-1} + \Phi_i(L) y_{i,t}, \tag{6.2}$$

i.e. model (6.1) is excluding the respective constituent series i in the construction of the aggregate, while model (6.2) is including it. Furthermore, we consider a lag operator $\Phi_i(L)$ of dimension 2, i.e. an AR order of $p = 2$. Since we like to test for a set of linear restrictions on the respective stochastic difference equation:

$$H_0 \ (3): \ \phi_{i,1} = \phi_{i,2} = 0 \tag{6.3}$$

$$H_0 \ (4): \ \phi_{i,3} = \phi_{i,4} = 0, \tag{6.4}$$

we test both restricted models (6.3) and (6.4) against the unrestricted models (6.1) and (6.2) via the usual F-test procedures, respectively. Table 6.3 below reports the shares of series for which the hypotheses (6.3) and (6.4) could be rejected for three significance levels and filtering methods. As one can see, on average up to about half of the sectoral series show significant (at least on the 10 percentage level) AR dynamics as well as an impact from the contemporaneous and lagged aggregate series for both definitions (6.1) and (6.2).

What we are also interested in, is the size and sign of the estimated 'aggregate impact'-coefficients $\widehat{\phi}_{i,1}$ and $\widehat{\phi}_{i,2}$. Table 6.4 below contains these informations for the different aggregate specifications (6.1) and (6.2), where

$$1/N \sum_{i} \widehat{\phi}_{i,1} \text{ and } 1/N \sum_{i} \widehat{\phi}_{i,2}$$

report the respective average relative size and

$$1/N \sum_{i} \left|\widehat{\phi}_{i,1}\right| \text{ and } 1/N \sum_{i} \left|\widehat{\phi}_{i,2}\right|$$

the corresponding average absolute size of the estimated coefficients. In the last two columns the number of coefficients estimated with negative sign is given.

Table 6.3. F-Tests on AR dynamics and aggregate feedback

significance level: 1%			
		H_0 (3)	H_0 (4)
a.	(6.1)	21.33%	17.78%
	(6.2)	21.56%	17.56%
b.	(6.1)	18.89%	15.78%
	(6.2)	19.33%	15.78%
c.	(6.1)	21.11%	15.78%
	(6.2)	21.78%	15.33%
significance level: 5%			
		H_0 (3)	H_0 (4)
a.	(6.1)	39.11%	38.44%
	(6.2)	39.78%	38.22%
b.	(6.1)	31.33%	32.89%
	(6.2)	32.00%	32.89%
c.	(6.1)	39.11%	28.67%
	(6.2)	39.56%	28,67%
significance level: 10%			
		H_0 (3)	H_0 (4)
a.	(6.1)	48.67%	51.56%
	(6.2)	50.00%	51.56%
b.	(6.1)	42.67%	45.11%
	(6.2)	43.78%	45.11%
c.	(6.1)	50.22%	40.67%
	(6.2)	50.89%	40.67%

Note: a. first log Differences, b. MBK-filter, c. HP(100)-filter

Table 6.4. Sizes and signs of estimated aggregate feedback coefficients

$\frac{1}{N}\sum_i \widehat{\phi}_{i,1}$	$\frac{1}{N}\sum_i \widehat{\phi}_{i,2}$	$\frac{1}{N}\sum_i \lvert\widehat{\phi}_{i,1}\rvert$	$\frac{1}{N}\sum_i \lvert\widehat{\phi}_{i,2}\rvert$	$\widehat{\phi}_{i,1} < 0$	$\widehat{\phi}_{i,2} < 0$
0.002 (47.5%)*	0.001 (16.6%)*	0.002	0.001	42	138
0.002 (49.3%)	0.002 (16.6%)	0.002	0.001	36	138
0.002 (40.0%)	0.000 (16.2%)	0.002	0.001	67	230
0.002 (39.7%)	-.001 (16.2%)	0.002	0.001	64	230
0.002 (41.3%)	0.000 (20.2%)	0.002	0.001	80	265
0.002 (43.7%)	0.000 (20.0%)	0.002	0.001	77	267

Note: 1st row: Log Differences, 2nd row: MBK-filter, 3rd row: HP(100)-filter. (values rounded on third digit).

*Values in brackets: shares of coefficient estimates significant on 10% level.

What is noteworthy from these results, is the fact that the majority of contemporaneous 'aggregate impact'-coefficients $\widehat{\phi_{i,1}}$ has a positive sign, suggesting a positive feedback from the aggregate investment activity. Furthermore, the impact from the aggregate series in first lag expression seems to be of negligible significance.

6.3 Linear Models of the Aggregation Process

This section of the present chapter addresses the question of how well linear models with a) a purely idiosyncratic, b) a sectorally interdependent, and c) a composed idiosyncratic and common shock structure perform in explaining integratedly the spectral features of the industrial constituent and the aggregate series. Four basic linear models with a time series and cross sectional dimension are estimated and simulated as a multiple time series system with VAR generation process, see e.g. Lütkepohl (1991), Appendix D.[10]

Reference case: idiosyncratic shocks. To assess the gain in explanatory power achieved by linear models with a sectorally correlated shock structure, one needs to consider the basic reference case of uncorrelated shocks and sectorally interdependent shocks via the variance/covariance-relationships of the estimated sectoral shock vectors.

I am considering a multiple time series model with VAR Generation Process. In the following, y_t^s denotes the disaggregated variable of industrial sector s that is analyzed. This is investment filtered by the MBK-Filter. Let me assume z_t is a vector of aggregate variables which is exogenous to the industrial sector, and which follows a first order VAR process. Such that z_t^s is a vector of sector specific exogenous variables. They are uncorrelated across industrial sectors, and also follow a first order VAR process. Furthermore, let me assume that the profit function of sector s can be approximated by a quadratic function in the lags of y_t^s, in z_t^s and z_t. Then one obtains a linear policy function (abstracting from the irrelevant constant) of the form

$$y_t^s = \sum_{i=1}^{p} \alpha_{1i} y_{t-i}^s + \alpha_2 z_t + \alpha_3 z_t^s + \text{error term} \tag{6.5}$$

In this study no effort is made to identify the exogenous variables z^s and z. However, since they are supposed to follow AR processes, one knows that they have (infinite) MA-representations in terms of their driving shocks ε^s, so that I am able to rewrite (6.5) as

$$A^s(L)\, y_t^s = B^s(L)\, \varepsilon_t^s, \tag{6.6}$$

[10] For an overview of simulation-based inference in econometrics, see Mariano, Schuermann and Weeks (2000).

where L denotes the lag operator. In a first step I estimate

$$y_t^s = \sum_{i=1}^{p} \beta_i y_{t-i}^s + \varepsilon_t^s, \tag{6.7}$$

where I suppose an AR order of 2, i.e. $p = 2$. To capture the temporal interdependencies of the industrial shocks, contained in the $\widehat{\varepsilon}_t^s$-vectors, with regard to the intended simulations, I calculate their empirical variance/covariance-matrix $\widehat{\Sigma}_\varepsilon$. To simulate the multiple time series of dimension $S = 450$ and length T, I proceed to generate a series of disturbance vectors $u_{-(p+1)}, \ldots, u_0, \ldots, u_T$. Since a series of Gaussian disturbances is desired, i.e. $u_t \sim N\left(0, \widehat{\Sigma}_\varepsilon\right)$, I choose S independent univariate standard normal variates $v_1, \ldots, v_S$ and multiply it by the $(S \times S)$ matrix $\mathbf{P}$ for which $\mathbf{PP}' = \widehat{\Sigma}_\varepsilon$, that is,

$$u_t = \mathbf{P} \begin{bmatrix} v_1 \\ \vdots \\ v_S \end{bmatrix}, \tag{6.8}$$

see Lütkepohl (1991), Appendix D. This process is repeated $T + p + 1$ times until one gets the desired series of disturbances. For a given set of estimated AR parameters $\mathbf{A}_1, \ldots, \mathbf{A}_p$, where $p = 2$ and the $\mathbf{A}_i$ are of dimension $(S \times S)$, and a given set of starting values $y_{-(p+1)}, \ldots, y_0$, the generated u_t may be used to simulate a time series $y_t, \ldots, y_T$ with VAR(p) generation process recursively as

$$y_t = \mathbf{A}_1 y_{t-1} + \ldots + \mathbf{A}_p y_{t-p} + u_t \tag{6.9}$$

starting with $t = 1$, $t = 2$, etc. until $t = T$. As argued above, the choice of initial values has some impact on the generated series, therefore I treat the first two values of the empirical (modified BK-filtered) series as presample values in the VAR model, too. This strategy ensures the starting phase constellations of the empirical micro-cycles. Since the AR coefficients estimates stem from the MBK-filtered sample of series with a length of 29 periods, also the simulations are conducted for 29 periods.

I proceed to simulate two models: namely, *model I* as described by equation (6.9) in combination with (6.8) and *model II* as given by equation (6.9) superindexed by s, where I choose $u_t^s \sim N\left(0, \sigma_{\widehat{\varepsilon}_t^s}\right)$, i.e. a model that does not consider the interdependencies of sectoral shocks contained in $\widehat{\Sigma}_\varepsilon$. The Monte-Carlo simulation strategy consists in simulating the respective model 1000 times and to calculate the standard deviation of the resulting aggregate for every simulation run to compare it with the standard deviation of the actual aggregate $\sigma_{y^a} = 5057.79$. Table 6.5 below displays the results in its first two rows. Note that there are no remarkable differences between model specification *I* and *II*. This stems from the fact that the average correlation coefficient between estimated sectoral shocks or error terms equals "only"

7% (0.073). Furthermore, one can note that on average there is roughly a 3.2 to 1 relationship between the empirical and simulated standard deviations of the aggregate investment series. This leads to the conclusion that a common shock structure, as e.g. in form of an impact by the contemporaneous aggregate activity, is in need to capture the empirical variance of the aggregate series and to explain the empirical aggregation process by means of a stochastic linear framework.

Idiosyncratic and common shocks via aggregate activity. In this subsection, I am repeating the simulation from the last paragraphs, introducing a common shock structure to the sectoral series via the impact of the contemporaneous aggregate activity. I do so by simply modifying *models I* and *II* by introducing the contemporaneous aggregate as additional explanatory variable in the estimations of coefficients and using the contemporaneous simulated aggregate in a simultaneous VAR equations framework to simulate it. In analogy to the preceding paragraph I will use the notation *model III* when $\widehat{\Sigma}_\varepsilon$ is incorporated in our simulations, else I will call it *model IV*. Once more the Monte-Carlo simulation strategy consists in simulating the respective model 1000 times and to calculate the standard deviation of the resulting aggregate for every simulation run to compare it with the empirical $\sigma_{y^a} = 5057.79$. The results are displayed in the third and fourth row of Table 6.5 below.

Once more, there are no remarkable differences between model specification *III* and *IV*. This stems from the fact that the average correlation coefficient between estimated sectoral shocks or error terms now is even smaller (since the aggregate explains variance), equalling 1% (0.014). Furthermore, one can note that now the relationship between empirical and simulated standard deviations of the aggregate investment series has switched, i.e. it is overshooted by the simulation results, equalling roughly 1 to 2.7.

Table 6.5. Standard deviations of MC-simulated aggregate series

	mean	median	max	min	std. dev.
model I	1608.97	1599.19	2575.62	963.79	252.40
model II	1580.50	1568.88	2575.50	935.05	250.34
model III	13856.89	13810.34	20447.70	8154.37	2118.24
model IV	13800.45	13729.84	21147.56	8260.93	2101.51

Assessing the spectral features of the linear models. To assess the concordance of the spectral features of the implied (for *model I*) and simulated (for all linear models) aggregate with the ME-spectrum of the empirical aggregate series, I compute the analytically implied spectrum for the aggregate series of *model I* and compute the ME-spectra for the MC-simulated aggregate series, for which the adjusted AR coefficients are the 'nearest neighbors' of the median coefficient vector of AR(2)-models adjusted to the 1000 simulated aggregate series, of *model I, II, III,* and *IV.*

Model I can be written in vectorial form as a general VAR(2)-process (for the following argumentation, see e.g. Hamilton, Section 10)

$$y_t = \Phi_1 y_{t-1} + \Phi_2 y_{t-2} + \varepsilon_t \tag{6.10}$$

with $E\left(\varepsilon_t \varepsilon_t'\right) = \Omega$. The joint spectral density at frequency ω is then

$$f_Y(\omega) = \frac{1}{2\pi}\left(I_n - \Phi_1 e^{-i\omega} - \Phi_2 e^{-2i\omega}\right) \Omega \left(I_n - \Phi_1' e^{i\omega} - \Phi_2 e^{2i\omega}\right)^{-1} \tag{6.11}$$

In general the spectrum of a linear combination $x_t = z \cdot y_t$ of the VAR(2)-process is given by

$$f_X(\omega) = z f_Y(\omega) z'. \tag{6.12}$$

One can apply these formula by expressing the sum over the sectoral y-series as linear transformation of the system, where $z = (1, 1, 1, ..., 1)$ is a unity row vector of dimension (1×450). The resulting spectrum from these analytical computations is displayed in Figure 6.3, plotted against the spectrum of the empirical aggregate series.

Fig. 6.3. VAR-spectrum (model I) vs. empirical spectrum

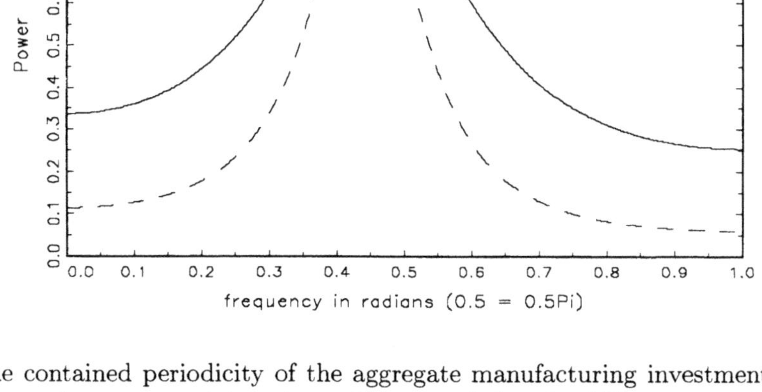

The contained periodicity of the aggregate manufacturing investment business cycle component is quite well captured, i.e. the ME-spectrum implied by the VAR(2)-model (in the formulation of *model I*, outlined above, solid line) is peaking nearly at the same frequency as the ME-spectrum for the empirical series (dashed line). The central difference is the prominence of the peak in the spectrum. The implied VAR(2)-model's aggregate shows a more flat spectrum, suggesting that the aggregate series is modeled too less volatile (cf. the results reported in Table 6.5 above) and too much noise- rather than signal-driven in contrast to the empirical aggregate.

The following Figure 6.4a, displays the ME-spectra for the MC-simulated aggregate series (solid line) , for which the adjusted AR(2)-coefficients were the 'nearest neighbors' of the median coefficient vector of AR(2)-models adjusted to the 1000 simulated aggregate series of *model I, II, III,* and *IV*. Figure 6.4b plots the corresponding simulation run's aggregate series (solid line) against the actual manufacturing investment aggregate (dashed line).

Fig. 6.4a. Spectrum of MC-simulated aggregate vs. actual spectrum

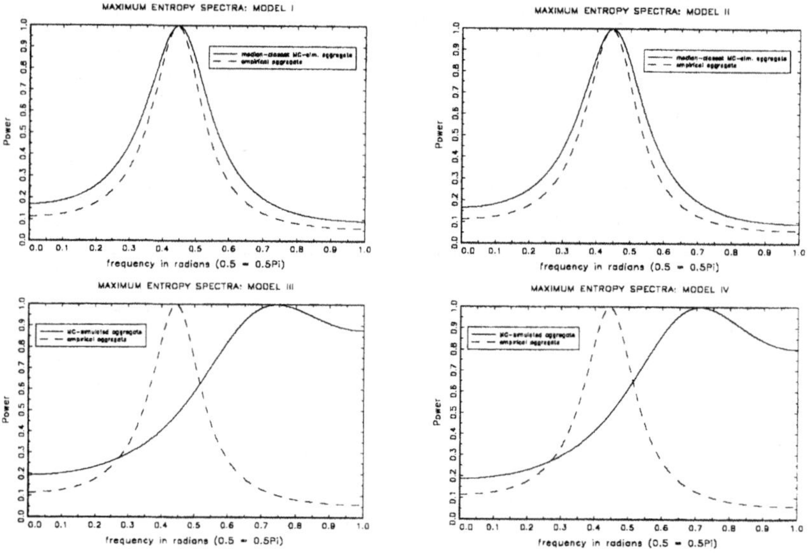

Fig. 6.4b. Corresponding MC-simulated aggregate vs. actual aggregate

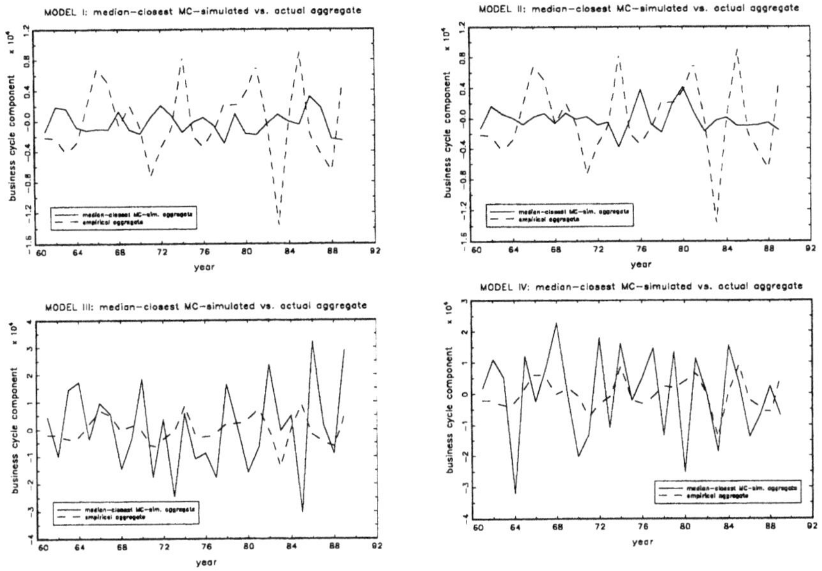

6.4 Evaluation of Linear Models

The present chapter's tests of nested models, nesting the hypothesis of autoregressive dynamics and linear feedback effects from the aggregate investment activity, as well as the VAR simulation study in the last paragraphs of the preceding section on linear models, suggest that the aggregate investment variable plays a role in determining the industrial investment behavior. Nevertheless, employing the aggregate variable in the framework of VAR simulations as a common shock variable - besides idiosyncratic and, according to my findings, only very weakly correlated sectoral shocks - leads not to a reasonable explanation of the aggregation process and thereby of the dynamics inherent in the aggregate series. It rather models its dynamics a) too volatile (see the second row of Figure 6.4b above), b) too noise-driven (see the flattening of the solidly plotted spectra in Figure 6.3 and the second row of Figure 6.4a above) and c) with a bias in periodicity (see the shifting of the spectra towards higher frequencies in the solidly plotted spectra in the second row of Figure 6.4a above). In summary these insights suggest that the aggregation process might be more adequately described and modeled by a nonlinear process, incorporating the aggregate activity as suggested for example by Hillinger and Weser (1988).[11]

[11] There is a body of (mainly) statistical and methodological literature concerned with the fundamental problem of the linear aggregation of economic dynamics. It includes the contributions by Theil (1965), who coined the term *non possumum*

Further empirical evidence in this direction can be found by applying the strategy suggested by Selover and Jensen (1999), i.e. to look at the development of phase shifts of the disaggregated series relative to the aggregate series and the periodicities of the industrial investment series *over time*[12] or other novel methods. To find evidence for sectoral cycles' synchronization and to develop and present novel methods to do so, will be the task of the proceeding chapter of the monograph.

In summary, the findings of the present chapter highlight the limits of linear models, such as first generation RBC models,[13] and give grounds for nonlinear synchronization mechanisms in the form of resonant stimulation and phase- or mode-locking of industrial investment cycles with the aggregate activity. In conclusion, the analysis of the present chapter suggests that business cycle transmission among different sectors is *not* a direct linear impulse type of phenomenon.

results for linear aggregation, van Daal and Merkies (1984), Goodwin (1984), Schlicht (1985), Barker and Pesaran (1990), Quah (1994), Uhlig (1996) and Forni and Lippi (1997).

[12] While changes of phase shifts *over time* can be accounted for in linear models (for example by means of aggregate shocks setting idiosyncratic cyclicalities in phase), varying periodicties over time can, by no means, be explained in the framework of linear models. In a similar context Haxholdt et al. (1995) note: "For linear systems the principle of superposition applies. The behavior of any variable in the system is a sum of distinct modes, or elementary excitations, where the frequencies and attenuation rates are determined by the eigenvalues of the Jacobian matrix. Different modes can exist and develop independently of one another, and the sensitivity of any mode to an external disturbance will be the same, irrespective of the phases of the others. Mode-locking cannot occur in linear systems, because the individual oscillatory modes do not affect one another," p. 179-180. The decisive point is that the modes do *not* interact in linear systems.

[13] Actually, in the RBC framework these are linearized behavioral equations of representative agents or sectors in a Ramsey model's environment.

7. The Synchronization of Sectoral Cycles

Output movements across broadly defined sectors move together.
R. E. Lucas (1977)

Macroeconomists ... have generally been less concerned with understanding the synchronized nature of this [business cycle] pattern across sectors.
L. J. Christiano and T. J. Fitzgerald (1998)

7.1 Definitions of Synchronization

Collective dynamics of (stochastic) systems, as observed in biological, chemical, economic, mechanical, statistical-physical, neurological or sociological systems, show a great variety of phenomena like pulsating patterns, frustration, synchronization or stochastic resonance, see, for example, Kuramoto and Nishikawa (1987), Selover and Jensen (1999), Sosnovtseva et al. (1999) and Néda et al. (2000a and 2000b). Recently, the natural sciences have shown a growing interest in the *measurement* and explanation of the synchronization of cyclically behaving entities, cf. the recent contribution to *Nature* by Néda et al. (2000b).

For a quantification of synchronization phenomena, a set of clear-cut definitions for different types of synchronization is needed.[1] Following Sosnovtseva et al. (1999), one can discriminate the following forms or stages of synchronization, as triggered, for example, by resonant stimulation, cf. part II, chapter 5 of the monograph:

generalized synchronization
↓
phase synchronization
↓
period and phase synchronization
↓
complete synchronization.

[1] In general it should be noted that resonance, mode-locking or entrainment are the more general phenomena. A possible manifestation of them, depending on their quantitative strength, is the more specific phenomenon of synchronization, cf. Haxholdt et al. (1995), p. 178.

The arrows mark periods of transition that may be interrupted by a frustration, i.e. the return to a more dissipative less synchronous state of the system. A frustration of the system would therefore interrupt the above sketched (temporal) process of synchronization. It may be induced for example by a large exogenous shock, cf. Néda et al. (2000a), p. 6990. Each preceding stage of synchronization is a necessary, though not sufficient, condition for the proceeding type of synchronization.

Definition 7.1.1. *Generalized* synchronization is defined as the presence of some functional relationship between time series of corresponding dynamic variables of the subsystem or between a subsystem's time series and the aggregate time series, i.e., $y_2(t) = \Im[y_1(t)]$ or $y_j(t) = \Im\left[\sum_j^N y_j(t)\right]$ for $j = 1, ..., N$. With further increase of the strength of interaction, this regime tends to phase, period and phase, and finally complete synchronization.

An 'appropriate quantity' to characterize a synchronization regime is cross-spectral density, cf. Sosnovtseva et al. (1999), p. 6561. In the methodology applied in the present work generalized co-movement implies reasonable high squared coherency (sc) values.[2]

Definition 7.1.2. *Phase* synchronization is given when phases of two cyclic components, e.g. contained in constituent and aggregate time series, lock on to each other while their amplitudes remain uncorrelated and sustain an irregular motion of their own.

In the methodology of the monograph phase synchronization implies reasonable small values of the absolute value of the phase shift (ps) measures.

Definition 7.1.3. *Period and phase* synchronization is defined as the case when phases and period lengths of two cyclic components, e.g. contained in constituent and aggregate time series, parallelly lock on to each other.

In the methodology of the present work, period and phase synchronization implies reasonable small values of the absolute value of the ps measures, paralleled by a reasonable degree of homogeneity in period lengths.

Definition 7.1.4. *Complete* synchronization is present in the case of two cyclic components, e.g. contained in constituent and aggregate time series, coinciding completely, such that their cyclic dynamics exactly equal each other, i.e., $y_1(t) = y_2(t)$ or $y_j(t) = y_{j+1}(t) = ... = y_N(t)$.

---

[2] For formal defintions of spectral measures the reader is referred to the methodolgical part of the thesis. For bivariate, i.e. cross-, spectral estimations in the context of US sectoral investment cycles, see the results reported in the preceding chapter.

7.2 A Recent Approach: Method and Findings

To the best of my knowledge, Selover and Jensen (1999) made the first and so far unique attempt to investigate empirically the synchronization of business cycles, in the light of the mode-locking hypothesis. They analyze the implication of the mode-lock concept that nonlinear entrainment of the cyclic components of the observed fluctuations would lead to a setting into phase (*phase* synchronization), paralleled by a high degree of homogeneity in the period lengths of the constituting cycles (*phase and period* synchronization).[3] The crucial point is that the drawing together of different phases and period lengths does not happen instantaneously according to a potentially underlying phase-/mode-locking regime, as would be the case in a common shock scenario, but rather develop over time until synchronization reaches the full impact or a temporary state of frustration. An adequate technique to investigate this phenomenon is multivariate spectral analysis. Table 5.1 of part II, chapter 5 of the monograph, displays the findings of Selover and Jensen (1999), based on classical uni- and bivariate spectral analysis, for monthly industrial production series of seven major industrial economies. Their strategy (in the following: SJ-method) consisted in dividing the sample into three sub-intervals, namely an early period (from 1958:01 to 1973:09), followed by the turbulent oil price shocks period (from 1973:10 to 1979:12),[4] and finally a late period (from 1980:01 to 1995:12). Their investigations focus on the early and late period, while the period including the two major oil shocks and the change in exchange rate regime in 1973 is left out of the analysis. The spectral analytic findings, displayed in Table 5.1 of part II, chapter 5 of the monograph, essentially document two main results: There seems to be a strong tendency towards a similar phase position and parallely towards a similar, or even equal, periodicity of the national cycles. Furthermore, this phase and period synchronization has developed over time, i.e. from an early to a late period. Selover and Jensen (1999) note: "This synchronization, with its convergence in frequency and in phase angles is evidence in support of the mode-locking hypothesis," p. 607.

Several problems existed in applying the SJ-method to the sectoral NBER dataset, described in the preceding chapter, by means of the spectral instruments, outlined in the methodological part of the monograph: The annual frequency of the data virtually does not allow the division of the observation period into three sub-intervals and the parametric estimation of

[3] Somehow similar, there is a recent research effort, based on dynamic factor analysis, to extract the common supranational (as opposed to a remaining idiosynchratic national) component from a variety of different national time series in the frequency domain, see Reichlin (2000). According to the definitions, outlined above, this strategy investigates the stronger phenomenon of (close to) *complete* synchronization.

[4] The Arab oil embargo in 1973 led to a jump in the global market's price per barrel from roughly US \$1.50 to US \$10. The Iran-Iraq tensions in the late 1970s caused world oil production to drop approximately 7.2%.

the uni- and bivariate ME- (or AR-)spectral densities and measures. To adjust the underlying (V)AR models to series with an observation horizon of $t = 1, ..., T$, where $T \leq 10$, would induce small sample biases and lead to unreliable results. Nevertheless, both the latest MBK-detrending technology, though shortening the observation period by three data points at the beginning and end of the time series, and the ME-spectral estimation procedure are strictly preferable to conventional methods, like HP-filtering or classical non-parametric estimates of the spectra, cf. the methodological part of the monograph. A straightforward solution to overcome this dilemma is to employ a non-parametric spline smoothing procedure. In addition, this strategy is in the same spirit as the continuous time formulations of the models presented in the course of the present work[5] since it presumes that the data-generating process is a (quasi-)continuous process of the form $y(t) = f(t) + \varepsilon(t)$. The time index variable t is observed only in finite values. In the terms of the statistical literature on non-parametric splining these are so called 'knots' at which the actual values for y are recorded. In the present case the knots $t_1, ..., t_n$ correspond to the actual observations $y_1, ..., y_n$. Between two neighboring points in time t_j and t_{j+1}, where $j = 1, ..., n$, of the observed time series y_t, the following cubic functional form is supposed, i.e., in formal terms, if $t_j \leq t \leq t_{j+1}$:

$$s_j(t) = a_j + b_j t + c_j t^2 + d_j t^3, \quad \text{s.t.} \tag{7.1}$$

$$a_{j-1} + b_{j-1}t_j + c_{j-1}t_j^2 + d_{j-1}t_j^3 = a_j + b_j t_j + c_j t_j^2 + d_j t_j^3, \tag{i}$$

$$b_{j-1} + 2c_{j-1}t_j + 3d_{j-1}t_j^2 = b_j + 2c_j t_j + 3d_j t_j^2, \tag{ii}$$

$$2c_{j-1} + 6d_{j-1}t_j = 2c_j + 6d_j t_j, \tag{iii}$$

$$c_0 = d_0 = c_n = d_n = 0. \tag{iv}$$

The first three restrictions (i) to (iii) ensure the continuity of the cubic spline at the knots, while (iv) ensures that the spline is a linear function outside the range of the knots. For the above cubic spline (7.1), the functions $s(t)$, $s'(t)$ and $s''(t)$ are in every knot t_j of the time series continuous functions. However, (7.1) has a discontinuous third derivative, i.e. $s'''(t) = dj$ if $t_j \leq t < t_{j+1}$. The cubic spline property is achieved by choosing the parameters in (7.1) such that the actual interpolating function minimizes the integrated squared second derivative of $s(t)$, i.e. $\int_{y_1}^{y_n} [s''(t)]^2 dt$. The term $\int_{y_1}^{y_n} [s''(t)]^2 dt$ therefore acts as a roughness penalty. It takes on relatively small values for smooth or slowly varying curves. In other words, it measures the smoothness of the approximating global function. Fitting a cubic spline which minimizes the residual sum of squares with a restriction on the smoothness of the resulting cubic spline is therefore achieved by using a modified sum of squares of the following form

[5] As presented in part II of chapter 5 and the proceeding chapter of the present part of the monograph.

$$S(p) = p \sum_{j} [y_j - s(y_j)]^2 + (1-p) \int_{y_1}^{y_n} [s''(t)]^2 \, dt. \tag{7.2}$$

The cubic spline given by (7.1) and (7.2) is called an interpolating cubic spline. The minimization of the roughness penalty allows a reasonable and continuous supplement of the existing discrete time series via the generation of in-between values. It is applied throughout this chapter.

Fig. 7.1. Exemplary business cycle component: raw vs. splined

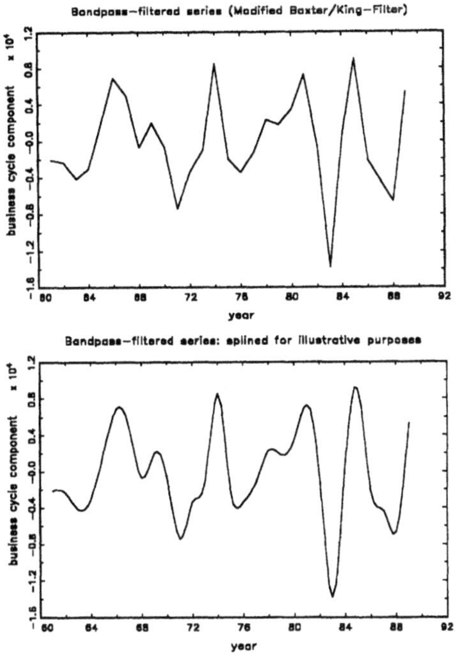

For illustrative purposes the above Figure 7.1 displays the business cycle component of the US MFI aggregate series in annual observations and its cubic splined analogue (see also Figure 6.1a of the preceding chapter).

To apply the SJ-method to the NBER dataset under investigation, all 450 industrial business cycle components, extracted by means of the MBK-filter, are splined according to (7.1) and (7.2) so that for a pair of actual datapoints three in-between points are generated, making a total of $n = 113$ datapoints (remember the MBK-filtered series contain $T = 29$ annual observations, respectively). In a next step the sample is divided on its temporal dimension into an early and late period. Furthermore a second narrowed definition of the late period is considered to a) check the robustness of results and b) account for the fact that the second oil crisis is, in contrast to the practice of Selover and Jensen (1999), usually dated the early 1980s (keep in mind that Iraq and Iran were not officially at war until 1980), cf. also, Figure 7.1 above.

The resulting sub-intervals range from 1962:1 to 1973:4, making a total of $n = 48$ datapoints (early period), from 1980:1 to 1990:1, making a total of $n = 41$ datapoints (late period in definition I), and finally from 1983:1 to 1990:1, making a total of $n = 29$ datapoints (late period in definition II). The number of datapoints of the subsamples now ensures the application of ME-spectral instruments as well as the completion of, at least on average, two full cyclical fluctuations in the range of the respective subsample.[6] To find empirical indications for *phase* synchronization, I estimate the bivariate phase shift (ps) measures, i.e. phase leads and lags at maximum of squared coherency (sc), for every constituent series relative to the MFI aggregate investment cycle component for the respective sub-interval and analyze their distributions by standard descriptive techniques in the form of histograms and boxplots. The results of the histogram analysis, reported in Table 7.1 below, show that the modal value of estimated phase shifts, covered by around one fifth of all sectors, more than halves from the early to the late period and tends to take on a zero-value, made up by 40% (in definition I of the late period) up to more than 50% (in definition II of the late period) of all sectoral series. The means of the absolute values[7] of estimated phase shifts point clearly in the same direction. The boxplots, displayed in Figure 7.2 below, are of statistical standard with the minimum and maximum of the whiskers calculated according to the interquartile range: The bottom of the box corresponds to the 25th percentile, the line drawn through the box marks the 50th percentile (median) and the top of the box the 75th percentile of the distribution. The minimum whisker limit is given by the 25th percentile $-1.5\,(iqr)$ and the maximum whisker limit by the 75th percentile $+1.5\,(iqr)$, where $iqr \equiv$ interquartile range, defined as the length of the box, i.e. 75th percentile minus 25th percentile of the distribution. As can be seen from the first window of Figure 7.2 below, the whiskers of the distribution of relative ps estimates $\Delta\,(ps)$ shrink from the early to the late period, while the median throughout takes on a value of approximately zero. For the distribution of absolute ps measures $\Delta\,(|ps|)$, displayed in the second window of Figure 7.2 below, the median reduces from the early to the late period, while the whiskers shrink, too. In summary, these results are clear evidence in support of *phase* synchronization as defined in the preceding section.

To investigate the stronger hypothesis of *phase and period* synchronization, especially with regard to the limited explanatory power of linear models (cf. the argumentation in the preceding sections), I also estimate the period lengths for the early and the late period by means of univariate ME-spectral analysis. The results are presented in the polardiagrams of Figure 7.3 below. Every circle of the polardiagram marks a period length in years, every ray one

[6] According to the prior of a mean period length of the industrial investment series of about 4.5 years, as reported in the estimation results from the preceding chapter.

[7] Taking absolute values ensures that phase leads and lags do not cancel out in the course of the computation of mean values.

sector, so that the estimated period lengths are positioned on different rings of the two diagrams, representing period lengths in years. The thick lines pointing in the centre of the polardiagram mark sectoral series that contain no cyclicality, i.e. imply no complex solution for the estimated underlying AR model. A thorough visual inspection of the two polardiagrams reveals the fact that for the late period (in definition I) the estimated period lengths are more concentrated on a band of rings, consisting of circles or *annuli*, covering estimated period lengths from 3 to about 7 years, while for the early period this concentration is to a lower degree with quite a few more estimations overshooting this band. Furthermore, the standard deviation of the distribution of estimated sectoral periodicities (in years) about halves from the early to the late period (in definition I), namely from 2.81 to 1.47 years. In conclusion, the findings of the present section, based on the SJ-method, give unambiguous grounds for *phase and period* synchronization of sectoral investment cycles. Nevertheless, in some respects there is space for improvement of the method, as well as for bringing it closer to related methods like Bayesian models with changing coefficients based on the Kalman-filter algorithm. The following section seeks to improve the method and to gain a more detailed insight and evidence with regard to sectoral cycles' synchronization.

Table 7.1. Distributions of phase shifts $\Delta(ps)$ at maximum of sc

	modal value of $\Delta(ps)$	mean of $\Delta(\lvert ps \rvert)$
Early period 1962:1 - 1973:4, n = 48	− 1.5 (22%)*	4.45
Late period, def. I 1980:1 - 1990:1, n = 41	− 0.4 (40%)*	3.97
Late period, def. II 1983:1 - 1990:1, n = 29	+ 0.3 (53%)*	2.89

* Relative frequencies; categories of underlying histograms rounded on 1st decimal

Fig. 7.2. Distributions of ps (rel. / abs.): $\Delta(ps)$ / $\Delta(\lvert ps \rvert)$

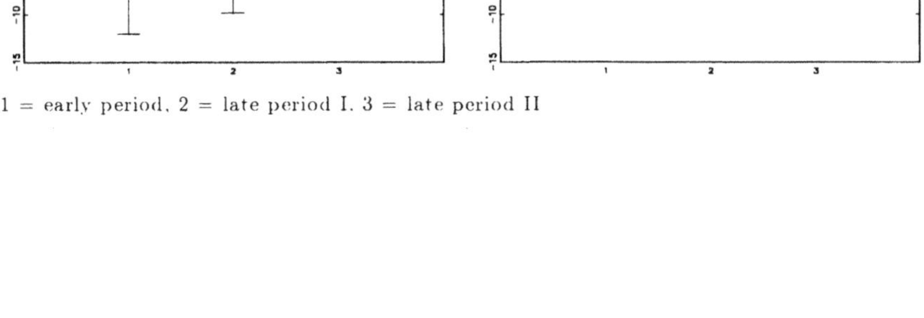

1 = early period, 2 = late period I, 3 = late period II

Fig. 7.3. Development of estimated sectoral periodicities (years) over time

Polar diagram: Estimated period lengths: Early period; std. dev.: 2.81

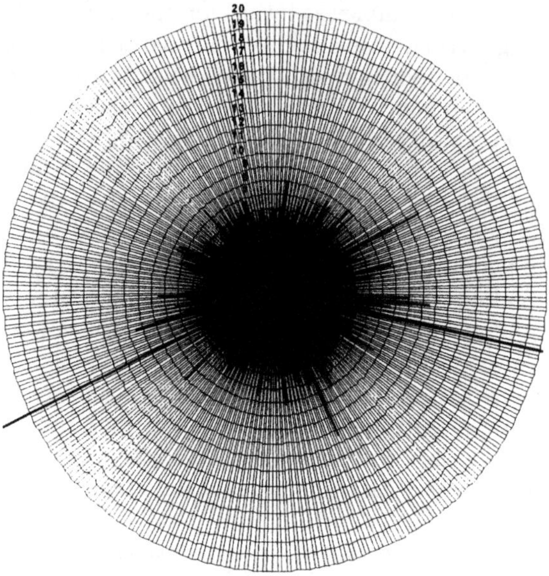

Polar diagram: Estimated period lengths: Late period (def. I); std. dev.: 1.74

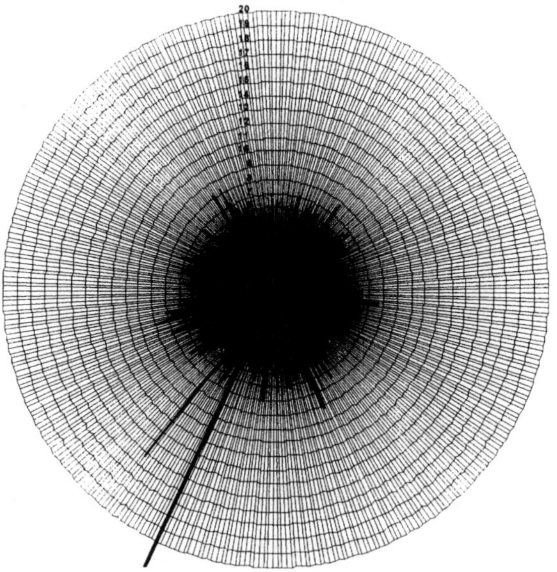

7.3 The "Shift-Win"-Approach: Method and Findings

In the course of this section the SJ-method is refined so as to get further evidence and more detailed information regarding the synchronization of sectoral business cycles.[8] One may ask why Bayesian VAR (BVAR) models are not considered that allow for the updating of time-varying parameters and coefficients by applying the Kalman-filter algorithm[9] to estimate time-dependent spectral measures - a strategy, for example, followed by Ritschl and Woitek (2000), based on the BVAR approach of Doan, Litterman and Sims (1984).[10] The central reason is that there exists no real prior for the updates of the coefficients. In contrast to a BVAR approach, the shifting window approach, suggested in the following, refrains from any prior information or prior beliefs as for example the standard Litterman prior, according to which each time series is characterized by an AR(1) process, cf. Ritschl and Woitek (2000) or in general Uhlig (1994).

Under the same argumentation as in the preceding section, I adopt the cubic spline smoothing philosophy and rely on the same smoothed dataset, covering the years from 1962 to 1990 and consisting of $n = 113$ datapoints from 1962:1 to 1990:1. The central idea is to shift a window with fixed length in incremental steps over the datapoints, adjust AR and VAR models to the industrial series covered by the range of the respective window position and to estimate the uni- and bivariate spectral measures, i.e. period length and *ps* relative to the MFI aggregate. I do so for all 450 sectors, respectively, and analyze their distributions. To place emphasis on the time-dependent nature of the system, the window positions, as defined in the following, overlap each other. The length of the window is chosen to allow the completion of, at least on average, three full cyclical fluctuations in the range of the respective window position: $n_w = 60$ (15 years). In the following this shifting window approach is denoted the SW-Method.

Displayed in Table 7.2 below, the following 27 window positions are considered:

[8] I am indebted to Stephan Klasen for his encouragement to consider this approach once more and to develop the described method. I wouldn't have pursued it further without his suggestion to do so during an oral presentation of my preliminary results at the Forschungsseminar (research seminar) of the Department of Economics, University of Munich.

[9] The relationship of signal extraction via spline smoothing to the Kalman-filtering procedure is established and discussed by Wecker and Ansley (1983).

[10] Another approach to take account of temporally varying coefficients in the context of sectoral business cycles is followed by Fioretti and Süssmuth (2001), who apply a neural network of the Kohonen type.

Table 7.2. Window positions of SW-Method to detect synchronization

window	*range*	*window*	*range*	*window*	*range*
position 1	62:1 - 77:1	position 11	67:1 - 82:1	position 21	72:1 - 87:1
position 2	62:3 - 77:3	position 12	67:3 - 82:3	position 22	72:3 - 87:3
position 3	63:1 - 78:1	position 13	68:1 - 83:1	position 23	73:1 - 88:1
position 4	63:3 - 78:3	position 14	68:3 - 83:3	position 24	73:3 - 88:3
position 5	64:1 - 79:1	position 15	69:1 - 84:1	position 25	74:1 - 89:1
position 6	64:3 - 79:3	position 16	69:3 - 84:3	position 26	74:3 - 89:3
position 7	65:1 - 80:1	position 17	70:1 - 85:1	position 27	75:1 - 90:1
position 8	65:3 - 80:3	position 18	70:3 - 85:3		
position 9	66:1 - 81:1	position 19	71:1 - 86:1		
position 10	66:3 - 81:3	position 20	71:3 - 86:3		

Figure 7.4 below displays the findings with regard to the less strong hypothesis of *phase* synchronization as a pre-condition of the more stronger hypothesis of *phase and period* synchronization. The first thing to note, regarding the distributions of *ps* estimates reported in Figure 7.4, is that the median values behave quite stationary for the different window positions, taking on close to zero-values or, at least, values $<< |1|$ year. The whiskers and the *iqr*(-boxes) reduce for the data range covered by the first window position to the respective one covered by the last position by roughly 5.5%. The whiskers and the *iqr* reach their maximum, implying the highest dissipation in sectoral cycles' phase positions, for window position 12 (67:3 - 82:3), i.e. as soon as the mid point of the years 1982/83 is included. They take on values approximately 27% higher than for window position 1 (64:1 - 79:1) and about 35% higher than for window position 27 (75:1 - 90:1). Fitting an OLS-regression line to the upper as well as lower whisker (or *iqr*-boxes') limits, would lead to a close to horizontal line, if one considers all window positions. But performing the same beginning with window position 8 (65:3 - 80:3) or 9 (66:1 - 81:3), the OLS-regression line would be negatively sloped for the upper, positively sloped for the lower limits. This suggests the following interpretation:

There are indications for the end of a phase synchronization regime after the first four window positions (ranges, see Table 7.2 above),[11] followed by an asynchronous phase regime, i.e. from position 5 (64:1 - 79:1) to position 12 (67:3 - 82:3), proceeded by another obvious phase synchronization regime from position 13 (68:1 - 83:1) to position 27 (75:1 - 90:1). With regard to the asynchronizing (second profoundly synchronizing) phase regime, the inclusion of the datapoints 79:1 - 82:3 (83:1 - 90:1) at the end of the window range seems to be crucial. These findings are congruent with the results obtained by means of the SJ-method, documented in the preceding section, where this intermediate period covering the two oil price crises was left out of the

[11] A historiographical outline of the US economy from the 1961 expansion over the Korean War boom, followed by the decline during the Vietnam War years and the proceeding boom is given for example by Perlo (1974).

analysis. An interplay between synchronized and unsynchronized regimes is a feature that is observed also in other sociological contexts and systems, like the rhythmic applause in concert halls, see Néda et al. (2000a and 2000b).[12]

Fig. 7.4. Distributions of phase shifts $\Delta(ps)$ at max. of sc, SW-method

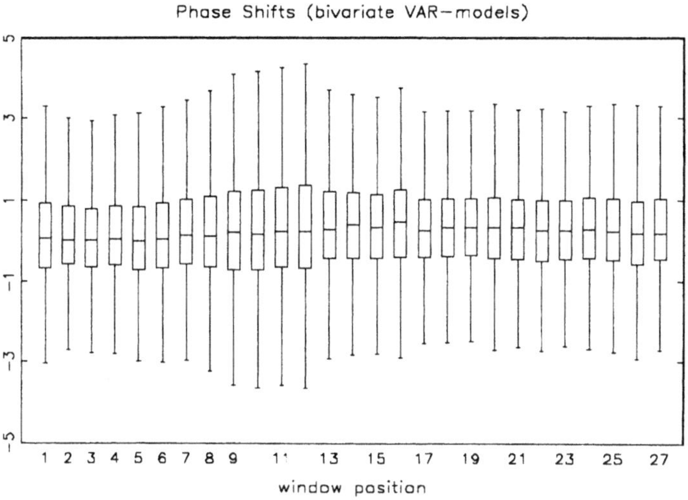

Obviously, the most dissipative state of the sectoral cyclicalities' phase positions is measured when data corresponding to the turbulent oil crisis' years (79:1 - 82:3) are included at the end of the analyzed sub-intervals. This stands in stark contrast to an aggregate shock scenario that would lead to a setting into phase of sectoral cyclicalities - though one may argue this happens with a certain time lag. But even if one considers such a lag structure or models incorporating sectoral shocks, propagated via intermediate input relationships,[13] as recently suggested in a series of articles on multisector RBC models, following the track of Long and Plosser (1983), see *inter alia* Hornstein and Praschnik (1997) and Horvath (1998a and 1998b), potential *period* synchronization cannot be explained.

---

[12] It is noteworthy that these recent contributions on the self-organization, physics and dynamics of the rythmic applause share with the present study the problem of "short sampling time," i.e. relatively short time series, cf. Néda et al. (2000a), p. 6989.

[13] Preventing independent sectoral shocks, as reported in Long and Plosser (1987) and Burnside, Eichenbaum and Rebelo (1996), from cancelling out according to the law of large numbers or similar laws, see Horvath (1998a and 1998b).

Fig. 7.5a. Distributions of per. at max. of *sc* (SW-method): bivariate VAR

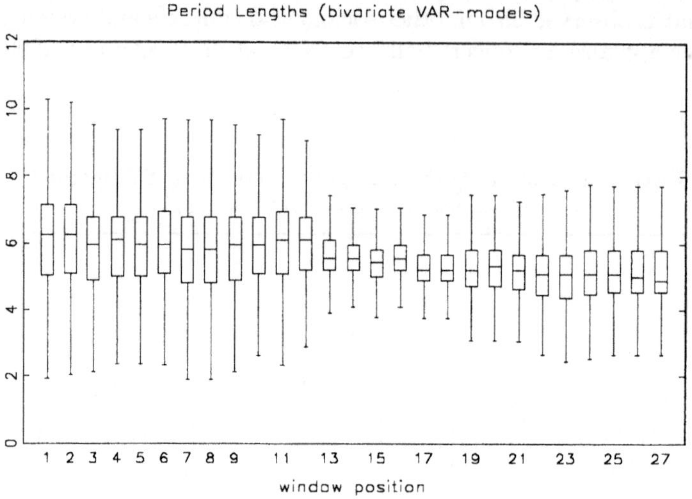

Fig. 7.5b. Distributions of per. (SW-method): univariate AR

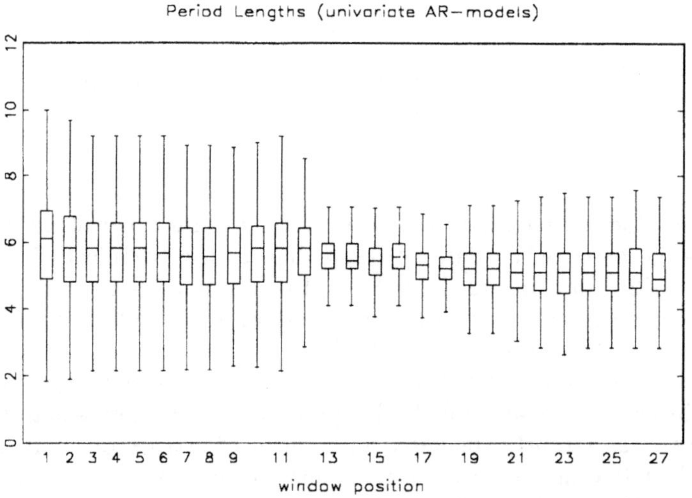

Figure 7.5a and 7.5b display the distributions of estimated period lengths on the base of a) bivariate spectral estimates at maximum of *sc* with the cycle component contained in the MFI aggregate series (VAR model adjustments) and b) univariate spectral analysis (AR model adjustments). They show a quite homogenous pattern. The first result to note is that for both estimation strategies the median period length drops over time from > 6 years for window position 1 to a period length < 5 years, corresponding to the MFI aggregate series' frequency of about 4.5 years for the last window position. For both strategies, the whiskers and the *iqr*(-boxes) reduce for the data

range covered by the first window position to the respective one covered by the last position by about 40 to 45%. Nevertheless, they do not reflect the respective global minima of whiskers and inter quartile ranges for all window positions. In both cases the reduction is especially outnumbered by a reduction in whisker lengths and the *iqr* of approximately 64% for position 14 (68:3 - 83:3) and position 16 (69:3 - 84:3), respectively. The frequencies of the contained cyclic components seem to be the most homogenous roughly for positions 13 to 18 (in total, covering the period 68:1 - 85:3), but the median of periodicities is not stable and sizeably jumps in the range of 5 to about 5.8 years during this period. Though there is an observable but relatively slight incline of the dispersion of estimated sectoral periodicities with the inclusion of the year 1986, the distributions become stable with regard to their median values and roughly match the aggregate cycle's periodicity. Fitting an OLS-regression line to the upper as well as lower whisker (or *iqr*-boxes') limits, would lead to a negative slope for the upper, a positive slope for the lower limits.

In summary, the analysis of the present chapter suggests that there is evidence for *phase and period* synchronization of sectoral business cycles that is clearly in favor of a nonlinear synchronization mechanism, as opposed to a linear shock-driven class of models.

8. A Non-Linear Synchronization Model

I can calculate the motions of heavenly bodies, but not the madness of people.
I. Newton (1720)

This example [of a simple herding model] and others like it hold out some hope that a fully developed business cycle model incorporating information externalities might exhibit the synchronization of behavior across economic sectors that we observe over the business cycle.
L. J. Christiano and T. J. Fitzgerald (1998)

The bottom fell out on the demand side, in tandem with a global economic slowdown. Exacerbating the situation was the DRAM industry's relentless drive to expand production even as prices plummeted further. And despite their woes, none of the biggest manufacturers appear ready to cut back on production ... "Nobody likes to do it alone ...," said Mr. Ross of Goldman Sachs.
T. Uimonen (staff reporter) in *Wall Street Journal Europe* (July 5, 2001)

The model outlined in the following essentially takes up the track of the model by Weser (1992) to portray and explain the interacting US manufacturing sectors' investing behaviors, empirically described in the preceding chapters of the present part of the monograph. The original structure is in several parts maintained. Nevertheless, central innovations necessary:

1. to take a natural rate of damping of the observed sectoral investment cycles into account,
2. to allow for heterogeneous degrees of interaction between the interacting sectors,
3. to take exogenous (stochastic) shocks into accout, and
4. to simulate it, for the first time, on the base of real world data and estimations,

are undertaken to ensure that the model exhibits the synchronization of behavior across economic sectors that is observed and documented in the preceding two chapters of the present part of the monograph. In a first step the model is related to an argumentation based on the recent literature on herding. Proceedingly, it is stringently and reasonably calibrated on the base of the empirical findings reported in chapter 6 and 7. Finally, the model in its stochastic version is Monte Carlo (MC-) simulated to assess an agreement between model and data.

It is noteworthy that there exists some relationship of the model to the strand of literature on (nonlinear) system dynamics and complex economic dynamics, see Mass (1975), Forrester (1977), Weidlich and Haag (1983, chapter 5), Sterman (1989), Radzicki and Sterman (1994), Bak et al. (1993), i.e. the 'Scheinkman-Woodford Sandpile Model', Tvede (1997, part III) and Rosser (1999). This relationship is not further deepened and is present, inasmuch similar models with an origin in the system dynamics approach developed parallely to the one of Hillinger and Weser (1988a) and Weser (1992) but remained somehow scattered, complex, stylized in nature and, in comparison, less meaningful in their economic interpretation. The central task of this chapter is to refine the model of Weser (1992), to make it even more economically meaningful, and to bring it, as much as possible, in concordance to the empirical findings.

8.1 Theoretical Underpinning of the Model

Let us consider $i = 1, ..., N$ investing sectors or firms, each sufficiently homogeneous to be represented by a single decision maker i. The model has two dimensions: a medium run investment objective and a myopic one. I will start the outline with the medium run objective of the decision makers, before going over to describe the "moving in the margin", i.e., the myopic behavior of timing the triggering of a certain investment project. The results of the myopic model will have direct implications for the previously outlined medium run model and will be implemented in an integrated model in which the rate of capital adjustment is endogenized, i.e., the individual adjustment coefficients will depend on the overall aggregate behavior. This integration underlies a modular approach, in that the integrated model is not developed from a unique calculus. Nevertheless, it should be noted that the idea to discriminate a myopic and a medium-term firm behavior is not novel, see for example Matsumoto (1997), who suggests in his nonlinear macro model of endogenous inventory oscillations, that there "exists a case in which the firm takes account of two time horizons when making the optimal plan," p. 107. Actually, he also discriminates a myopic time horizon ($t - T$, where T is infinitesimally short, i.e. $T \to 0$, cf. section 8.1.2 of the present paper) and a "longer time horizon," where the firm has to adopt an auxiliary hypothesis about profits beyond $t - T$, cf. the following section 8.1.1. The linking of these two time horizons of the present paper's model is outlined in section 8.1.3.

8.1.1 The Medium-Term Investment Objective: Smoothing

The long run components of the model are assumed to be exogenously given and left out of the explanation. This holds true for the desired fixed capital stock K_i^* of a firm as well as for its time derivative. They are regarded as products of long-term planning and assumed to be exogenously given. Therefore the analysis is limited to the minimization of costs due to capital deficit and adjustment processes arising in the medium-run investment behavior. All costs are formulated in terms of deviations k_i of the actual capital K_i from its desired value K_i^*; i.e., $k_i = K_i^* - K_i$, $k_i^{'} = \frac{d}{dt}(K_i^* - K_i)$, etc. These costs may be expressed as a sum of contributions each quadratic in k_i, $k_i^{'} = i_i$ and $k_i^{''} = i_i^{'}$, where $i_i = k_i^{'}$ denotes the individual investment deficit. The microeconomic underpinning of the medium run model of this section is an intertemporal optimization calculus in the presence of these three quadratic adjustment cost components outlined in more detail in the following three assumptions:

Assumption 8.1.1. Costs arise due to the individual capital deficit or excess of capital: $k_i > 0$ expresses excess capital of an industry leading to inflexibility and enhanced depreciation causing costs. $k_i < 0$ stands for an underequipment with capital, i.e., a capital deficit of a firm. This leads to missing production possibilities and excessive capacity utilization.

Assumption 8.1.2. Costs arise due to changes of the individual capital stock: $k_i^{'} > 0$ and $k_i^{'} < 0$ mark situations where imperfect substitutability with other production factors leads to costs or, in the case of close to perfect substitutability, leads to a subefficient use of the other input factors and thereby cause costs.

Assumption 8.1.3. Costs arise due to changes of the individual investment strategy: $k_i^{''} = i_i^{'} > 0$ and $k_i^{''} = i_i^{'} < 0$ reflect changes in the medium run investment strategy of a firm. Changes of contractual commitments and supplier's arrangements are costbearing consequences of this behavior.

Taking all the components expressed in these assumptions into account we can formulate the following cost function for investor i:

$$C_i\left(k_i, k_i^{'}, k_i^{''}\right) = \alpha_i k_i^2 + \beta_i \left(k_i^{'}\right)^2 + \gamma_i \left(k_i^{''}\right)^2 . \tag{8.1}$$

Every firm determines the time paths of her production capital in such a way that the present value of all potential medium-term cost components, i.e. (8.1) discounted with an appropriate discount rate, is minimized. Since we are concerned with a medium-term objective focusing, e.g., on labor force's training costs (assumption 2) or institutional costs due to changing suppliers (assumption 3), etc., we are confronted with a situation of imperfect foresight. Hence, the relevant discount factor for an intertemporal optimization calculus is the medium-term discount rate ρ^m, where naturally $\rho^m > \rho^l$, i.e., the long-term discount rate ρ^l (as reflected in the market discount rate) usually takes on lower values than ρ^m:

$$\min_{k_i(t)} \int_{t_0}^{\infty} \left[\alpha_i k_i^2 + \beta_i \left(k_i^{'} \right)^2 + \gamma_i \left(k_i^{''} \right)^2 \right] e^{\rho^m (t_0 - t)} dt. \tag{8.2}$$

As demonstrated in Hillinger, Reiter and Weser (1992) this optimization leads to the following second order differential equation:

$$I_i^{'} = K_i^{''} = \frac{\alpha_i}{\gamma_i (\rho^m)^2} (K_i^* - K_i) - \frac{\beta_i}{\gamma_i \rho^m} K_i^{'} = a_i (K_i^* - K_i) - b_i K_i^{'}, \tag{8.3}$$

$$\text{where } a_i = \frac{\alpha_i}{\gamma_i (\rho^m)^2} \text{ and } b_i = \frac{\beta_i}{\gamma_i \rho^m}.$$

The second order accelerator (SOA) equation (8.3) reflects the inertia of the investment process due to institutional medium-term frictions. It expresses the acceleration $K_i^{''}$ of the individual capital stock K_i or, in other words, the rate of change of individual investment behavior $I_i^{'}$ in the medium run. Accordingly, parameter a_i is mainly responsible for the rate at which individual investment is adjusted. While parameter a_i is mainly responsible for the period length of the cyclic series described by equation (8.3), parameter b_i determines the rate of damping.

8.1.2 The Short-Term Investment Objective: Herding

The following paragraphs outline the myopic investment behavior on the basis of a basic herding scenario. The outline is in its main parts adopted from Gale (1996a) and Sgroi (1999). In the course of this section, the basic setting will be extended to the more general one, in which one agent interacts with the observable or reported aggregate behavior. At the end of this section, the qualitative main results and implications for the medium-term investing activity are summarized in the form of propositions to be later on embodied in an integrated model. According to the classification by Hors and Lordon (1997), it is a model of global interactions between non-localized agents, in which agents "react to the situation prevailing at the macroscopic level, just if an agent was interacting with all the other agents," p. 359.

Initially, let us consider $N = 2$ agents. These agents face a myopic two-sided investment decision problem: whether and if so when to run a certain investment project. This project has a specific value equaling the state of the world, w, which in the simple base case is assumed fixed at the beginning of time. We define a myopic point in time as $\tau = t - T$, where T is infinitesimally small, i.e. $T \to 0$, and is equi-spaced. Accordingly, we can index the myopic time horizon by $\tau \in \mathbf{T}_{++}$, e.g. days, weeks or months, i.e. for reasons of simplification, we assume to "move discretely in the margin" of a continuous time world. Gul and Lundholm (1995) have shown that in the more complex framework of continuous time, the results of the herding model of investment remain qualitatively the same. Put it differently the reason for gradual investment, i.e. strategically delayed investment and disinvestment, in this kind of models is due to the informational externality and is not an artifact of a (quasi-)discrete-time framework. This was already noted and shown in Caplin and Leahy (1993). Agents do not directly observe w, instead they receive a signal, μ, at $\tau = 1$. In the following, we use superscript to index agents and subscript to index time, so μ_i^τ is the signal of agent $i \in \{1,2\}$ at time τ. We will use i and j to denote our two agents. Assume for the sake of simplicity that the signals μ^i and μ^j are independent and identically drawn from a uniform distribution with range $[-1,1]$, so $\mu^i \sim U[-1,1]$ for $i \in \{1,2\}$. These signals do not change over time, and the state of the world w is set equal to the sum of all signals, $w = \mu^i + \mu^j$. Actions are defined as: $x^i = 1 \iff$ "invest"; and $x^i = 0 \iff$ "do not invest". An agent can observe his own signal, but not the signal of the other agent. In each period actions are made simultaneously, so the two agents cannot observe each others' actions. However, in period 2, the agent will know the action that the other agent performed in period 1, and through the observed choice of activity some information about the nature of the other agent's signal may be revealed. I abstract from pre-play communication that would give the agents a possibility to meet and reveal their signals. The final ingredient of the basic setting are payoffs, π_τ^i, where $\tau \in \mathbf{T}_{++}$ and $i \in \{1,2\}$, discounted strictly by a short-term rate ρ^s[1]

$$\pi_\tau^i = \begin{cases} (\rho^s)^{\tau-1} w & \text{if } x^i = 1 \\ 0 & \text{if } x^i = 0 \end{cases} . \tag{8.4}$$

To solve the short-term decision problem, we consider the problem faced by agent i: whether, and if so, when to invest. Myopically, we can consider the following simple rules: (i) invest (i.e., $x^i = 1$) if and only if $E[\pi_\tau^i] > 0$; (iia) if an investment is to be made, then make it at $\tau = 1$ if and only if $E[\pi_1^i] > E[\pi_2^i]$, otherwise wait. In these rules the profit function explicitly includes discounting the short run time horizon. This might seem a sensible rule to adopt, but while this captures a notion of the cost of delay since there is an implicit $\rho^s < 1$ in the second period payoff, the benefit of delay, namely the *option value* of waiting, is not captured. This option value comes about because of the possibility that for some reason agent i may have invested at time 1 even though doing so was foolish given the information available to him at time 2. I will consider the cost and benefit of delay in turn, but first let me define a symmetric signal value $\bar{\mu}$ such that $\mu^i > \bar{\mu} > 0 \iff x^i = 1$. I have not yet said anything about what to do at $\tau = 2$, but an alternative decision rule for $\tau = 1$ is already defined: (iib) invest at $\tau = 1$ (i.e. set $x_1^i = 1$) if and only if $\mu^i > \bar{\mu} > 0$.

Proposition 8.1.1. *There is some symmetric $\bar{\mu}$ such that it is optimal for agent i to invest at time $\tau = 1$ if and only if $\mu^i > \bar{\mu} > 0$.*

Proof. See Gale (1996a).

[1] Since uncertainty grows and the relatively more distant future has relatively less impact on actual decisions, the inequality $\rho^s > \rho^m$ holds.

Proposition 8.1.2. *(a) The game will end at $\tau = 2$, i.e. if agent i did not invest at time $\tau = 1$ he will either invest when $\tau = 2$ or never invest. (b) Agent i will only invest at $\tau = 2$ if agent j invested at $\tau = 1$.*

Proof. See Gale (1996a).

So far the basic ingredients of the investment herding model are specified. However, there is already a number of interesting results noteworthy. From now on I will refer to the value $\bar{\mu}$ established above as $\bar{\mu}(\rho^s)$ since it can be shown to be a function of ρ^s only, see Sgroi (1999). The features that characterize the above model as a herding model are: information is not fully revealed, there is no direct mapping from signal to action which can be inverted to reveal agents' signals; errors are made and private information may be ignored, in particular even if $\mu^i > 0$ for $i = 1, 2$ neither of the players will invest unless $\mu^i > \bar{\mu}(\rho^s)$ for at least some player i. There will be short-term delay in this model. This scenario clearly describes what Bikhchandi, Hirshleifer and Welch (1992) entitled an *informational cascade*: An individual, having observed the actions of those ahead of him in a sequence, who follows the behavior of the preceding individual, without regard of his own information, is said to be in a cascade. It embodies also a *herd externality* in the definition of Banerjee (1992); accordingly, a herd externality is the loss of information contained in later agents' private signals that comes about when individuals in a sequence ignore their own private information and join a herd. This is also captured since in this basic setting the game will effectively end at $\tau = 2$, beyond this point agents have either invested in the project or will never do so. In a dynamic interpretation the flow of starting projects is interrupted, i.e. investment acceleration will slow down. The addition of further agents would allow the game to continue beyond two periods of interest, but at least one agent is needed to invest in a myopic time interval or investment will stop, the flow of starting projects *retards* and acceleration *reduces* as in the two agents case.

Proposition 8.1.3. *Investment at $\tau = 2$ takes place if at least one agent invested at $\tau = 1$. A single period of no investment will end the prospect of any further investment in a model with $N \in \mathbf{N}_{++}$ agents: A Lemmings-Effect is triggered.*

Proof. See Gale (1996a).

8.1.3 The Integrated Model: Smoothing and Herding

It should be noted that propositions 1, 2 and 3 of the preceding section could be extended to the case of disinvestment, i.e. one can simply reformulate them including the case of agent i facing a disinvestment decision. By disinvestment, not disinvestment in the narrow sense of a firm's accounting but rather decisions like closing a specific production plant, shutting down machinery equipment or firing staff, i.e. observable disinvesting activities, are meant. This inclusion is just the other side of the same coin and it should be evident that the informational herding results derived and outlined in 8.1.2 hold analogously in an investment or disinvestment scenario. This extension although quite obvious is crucial in making the model symmetric in contrast to the ones of Gale (1996b) and Chalkley and Lee (1998) who challenge the explanation of potential asymmetry in investment cycles. There is no argument in the derivation of section 8.1.2 that should prevent the herding results of propositions 1, 2 and 3 from occurring also in the disinvestment case. Propositions 1, 2 and especially proposition 3 then have a direct implication on the individual acceleration rate of capital a_i in equation (8.3) above, in making it a function of the other agents' investment activity:

$$a_i = a_i \left(\sum_j I_j \right) \Rightarrow I_i^{'} = f \left(\sum_j I_j \right), \text{ where } i \neq j. \tag{8.5}$$

This influence could be quite heterogeneous between different firms, industries or sectors i and j and, even needs not to hold true at all for some i (in the following: *Type II Agents*, as opposed to influenced *Type I Agents*), depending on short-term characteristics (especially the short-term discount factor ρ^s). According to proposition 1 to 3 the functional relationship (8.5) applies for all agents i whose short-term characteristics are such that:

$$\mu^i < \bar{\mu} \left(\rho^s \right) < 0 \Longrightarrow E \left[\pi_1^i \right] < E \left[\pi_2^i \right], \tag{8.6}$$

where π_τ^i is the respective payoff in the investment or disinvestment (in terms of avoided costs of production factors) case for the short-run instance τ. Therefore one can discriminate two types of agents: Industries who, due to their short-term characteristics as reflected in the inequality relations (8.6), tend to be influenced by the aggregate investment behavior, i.e. more precisely their probability to strategically delay and to get locked into a herding cascade is *a priori* positive

$$\Pr \left[I_i^{'} = f \left(\sum_j I_j \right) \right] > 0, \tag{8.7}$$

and those who do not. The logic of the integrated model can best be illustrated by a game tree-like scheme as given in Figure 8.1. It consists in five stages of possible alternatives and gives a chronological order of the events: Type of agent: influenced by aggregate behavior vs. not influenced by aggregate behavior, type of game: investment vs. disinvestment, observation: aggregate activity vs. aggregate inactivity or destructivity, timing: follow vs. delay and finally action: speed up smoothing vs. delay (smoothing) induced by herding.

Consider first the leftmost branch of the game tree, displayed in Figure 8.1 below. Here, we face a type I agent's decision fulfilling (8.6) and (8.7) who is confronted with an individual capital deficit $(K_i^* - K_i) > 0$, i.e. who is about to "play the investment game". On the next stage, he observes at an arbitrary point in time $\tau = 1$ that the other industries $j = 1, ..., J$ of his sector constituting "the aggregate" invest, i.e. take the opportunity in $\tau = 1$ and make an investment in the project at stake. So does agent (subsector, industry or firm) i and he does it immediately at the myopic point in time $\tau = 1$. Since the starting of the additional projects is time consuming, the agents have an incentive to *speed up* the smoothing of their capital stocks. They do so with regard to the prospect to be ready in the (rat) race for additional upcoming investment opportunities in the myopic time horizon

Fig. 8.1. Order of events

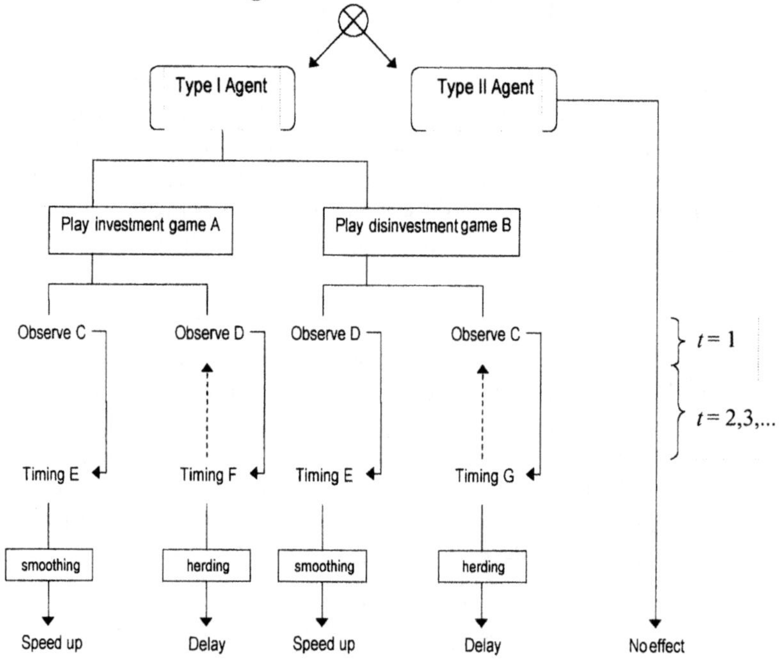

Fig. 8.1. (continued): Order of events

type of game		observation		timing
A: $K_i^* - K_i > 0$	$\rightarrow$	C: $\sum_j K_j^{'} = \sum_j I_j > 0$	$\rightarrow$	E: $\frac{\partial I_i^{'}}{\partial(\sum_j I_j)} > 0$
B: $K_i^* - K_i < 0$	$\rightarrow$	D: $\sum_j K_j^{'} = \sum_j I_j < 0$	$\rightarrow$	E: $\frac{\partial I_i^{'}}{\partial(\sum_j I_j)} > 0$
A: $K_i^* - K_i > 0$	$\rightarrow$	D: $\sum_j K_j^{'} = \sum_j I_j < 0$	$\rightarrow$	F: $\frac{\partial I_i^{'}}{\partial(\sum_j I_j)} < 0$
B: $K_i^* - K_i < 0$	$\rightarrow$	C: $\sum_j K_j^{'} = \sum_j I_j > 0$	$\rightarrow$	G: $\frac{\partial I_i^{'}}{\partial(\sum_j I_j)} > 0$

Next consider a type I agent playing the investment game and observing the aggregate not investing or disinvesting in $\tau = 1$: Agent i does not start an investment project and waits like the other agents j do. A vicious circle or informational cascade is triggered for $\tau = 2, 3, \ldots$ as suggested in proposition 3 above and indicated by the backward loop in Figure 8.1. This strategic delay induced by herding behavior has now a longer lasting effect that even impacts medium-term behavior by slowing down the pace of the medium-term investment flow. The argumentation for a firm i playing the disinvestment game would proceed analogously to the investment decision case.

In the definition of Cooper and John (1988) this scenario describes a *strategic complementarity*, inasmuch, "[s]trategic complementarities arise when the optimal strategy of an agent depends positively upon the strategies of the other agents," p. 441.[2]

Now let me turn to combine the arguments brought forward in the herding model with the medium-term objective meeting the argumentation of the last paragraphs and in Figure 8.1. As Weser (1992) suggests and Cont and Bouchaud (2000) note,[3] a most straightforward and "simple way to introduce interactions among agents is through an aggregate variable," p. 17. Concretely, the synthesis is achieved by modifying the model of equation (8.3) in the following way, cf. Weser (1992):

$$I_i^{'} = K_i^{''} = a_i \left\{ 1 + \chi_i \cdot \Psi \left[(K_i^* - K_i) \sum_j I_j \right] \right\} (K_i^* - K_i) - b_i K_i^{'}, \text{ where} \tag{8.8}$$

Ψ is defined as a transform function of the simple form:

$$\Psi[x] = \begin{cases} +1 & \text{for } x > 0 \\ 0 & \text{for } x = 0 \\ -1 & \text{for } x < 0 \end{cases} \quad \text{and} \tag{8.9}$$

[2] In modern game theory, similar scenarios are well-known as 'chicken games' in combination with 'vicious circle games', cf. Iwanaga and Namatame (2000).

[3] In the context of modeling aggregate fluctuations in financial markets by means of herding.

parameter χ_i can be interpreted as the strength of individual interaction with the aggregate behavior.[4]

In contrast to the models of Caplin and Leahy (1993) and Zeira (1994), the cyclicality in the model presented here is not *generated* by changes in investors' information on demand and certain transmission mechanisms of demand shocks. The informational interplay just *influences* the pace of an endogenously modeled capital adjustment process.

8.1.4 The Synchronization Mechanism

This section briefly outlines the potential of the model basically described by equations (8.8) and (8.9) to synchronize heterogeneous microeconomic fluctuations resulting in a robust macroeconomic cyclic pattern of the aggregate investment series. A strong criticism that multi-sector models or, generally speaking, business cycle models with disaggregative structure have been confronted with is the reasoning that "as definition of sectors became more disaggregate, aggregate volatility converged to zero at the rate implied by the law of large numbers," see Horvath (1998a and 1998b). The reason of why it does not apply in our model is the synchronization of heterogeneous individual cyclic investment behavior, which is produced by the model, given by the equation system (8.8) and (8.9). Several authors like Mosekilde et al. (1992), Larsen et al. (1993) and Sterman and Mosekilde (1994) applied a similar mechanism in a simple model of the interplay between medium-term and long-term economic cycles.

But how does this synchronization actually come about in the model? Where do we find the interaction of oscillators leading to *resonant stimulation*, as described in Weser (1992)? To illustrate this, let me reconsider equation (8.8) above. It is an equation of the so called *Hill's class* of equations, since it assigns the second temporal derivative of a variable $K_i^{''}$ to a function including a temporally variable coefficient $a_i\left[K_i\left(t\right), I_j\left(t\right)\right] \Rightarrow a_i\left(t\right)$, see Arnol'd (1983). Consider next the case of quasi-cyclic investing behavior on the sectoral or individual level, such that I_i idealistically fluctuates according to a sinusoidal function depending on microeconomic characteristics as outlined in section 8.1.1 and contained in a_i, e.g. $\cos\left(a_i t\right)$. For a sufficiently strong prominence of this cyclic component in the individual investment activity, i.e. for a relatively small damping corresponding to relatively small values of b_i, we can write

$$K_i^{''} = I_i^{'} = f\left[\left(K_i^{*} - K_i\right)\right] \rightarrow \cos\left(a_i t\right).$$

[4] Note, depending on the atomistic structure of the investing units (for the proceeding simulation study $i = 1, ..., I$ sectors, where $I >> 10$) $\sum_j I_j$ can accurately be approximated by $\sum_i I_i$. This is also justified, inasmuch an investor is usually informed by the diverse media about the total investment activity $\sum_i^I I_i$, i.e. including his own investment activity.

Suppose now that the aggregate investment series is constituted by many such quasi-cycles with roughly equal periodicities, cf. the univariate findings of section 6.1.2 in part III above, so that the sum of its first-order term follows approximately the same cyclical dynamics than $I_i^{'}$, i.e. $\cos(a_i t)$. This implies that

$$\sum_j I_j \approx \int_t^T I_i^{'} dt = \int_t^T f\left[(K_i^* - K_i)\right] dt \rightarrow \sin(a_i t).$$

To summarize this idealistic reference case, let us assign an inner (*in*) and outer (*out*) frequency to the system described by equation (8.8):

$$\underbrace{I_i^{'} = K_i^{''} = a_i \left\{ 1 + \chi_i \cdot \Psi \left[\underbrace{\underbrace{(K_i^* - K_i)}_{\cos(a_i t)} \cdot \underbrace{\sum_j I_j}_{\sin(a_i t)}}_{\frac{1}{2}\sin(2a_i t) \Rightarrow in=2a_i} \right] \right\} (K_i^* - K_i) - b_i K_i^{'}}_{\cos(a_i t) \Rightarrow out=a_i}.$$

Arnol'd (1983) notes: "Equations or systems with constant coefficients in the leading term and with coefficients in the form of trigonometric polynomials in the lower-order terms have special properties, and can be called equations of *Mathieu type*," p. 216. Obviously, equation (8.8), in its above idealistic interpretation, represents an equation of the *Mathieu type*. The special property of such an equation or system lies in its potential to resonantly stimulate different phases (*parametric resonance phenomenon*) and periodically entrain them, see Arnol'd (1983), Hillinger and Weser (1988) and Norris (1993). This effect depends on what is usually called forcing amplitude or depth of modulation, corresponding to the strength of interaction with the aggregate, in our notation χ_i. The general restriction is $\chi_i \in [0, 1)$. The other *conditio sine qua non* is a certain constellation of outer to inner frequency (*in* is sometimes also called perturbation or frequency of driving signal): If many such constellations for different values of χ_i exist, these zones of parametric resonance or periodic entrainment are usually visualized in so called *Arnol'd tongues*, see Arnol'd (1983) and Norris (1993) in general and Mosekilde et al. (1992) or Sterman and Mosekilde (1994) for applied examples of the *Arnol'd tongue* concept. For systems of Mathieu type the by far largest zone of periodic entrainment lies for a depth of modulation $\chi_i \in [0, 1)$ at the constellation of

$$\frac{out}{in} \approx \frac{1}{2},$$

see Arnol'd (1983) or Hillinger and Weser (1988). The approximate equality comes about, since this large area of parametric resonance also captures many constellations of *out* to *in* that only roughly equal 0.5. As outlined above the system characterized by equation (8.8), idealistically interpreted, exactly matches this condition, since

$$\frac{out}{in} = \frac{a_i}{2a_i} = \frac{1}{2}.$$

The expression "idealistic" now gets a more meaningful interpretation, since for all defined values of χ_i periodic entrainment is guaranteed. It should be noted that even deviations (as long as they are not major ones) from this ideal case are capable of producing resonant stimulation and mode-locking, potentially inducing period and phase synchronization; see the definitions in section 7.1 above.

8.2 A Thorough Simulation Study

8.2.1 Calibration as an Alternative to Estimation

To estimate a nonlinear model of the form (8.8) in combination with (8.9) in continuous time is rather difficult, though not impossible, given for example the possibility of employing the cubic spline smoothing strategy outlined in chapter 7. Nevertheless, the present study follows a different approach, namely to calibrate the model on the base of spectral estimations of the discrete analogues of the underlying SOA equations and empirical initial values, cf. the argumentation and strategy outlined in section 5.3.3, part II of the monograph. As shown in 5.3.3 this strategy meets all the requirements of a stringent calibration study stated, for example, by Cooley (1997). Calibration practices and Monte Carlo (MC-) simulations, sometimes also labeled 'quantitative theory', see Quah (1995) or Gregory and Smith (1995), as opposed to estimation have recently become a most popular, if not the predominating, approach to evaluate business cycle models. Empirical practice involving calibration and the use of simulations to derive operating characteristics of the models is done mostly in the context of RBC research, but there are as well applications for models of a Keynesian origin, see Quah (1995), p. 1595. Gregory and Smith (1991) elaborate and establish the nexus of calibration and simulation strategies of stochastic macro-models to their testing and estimation from a methodological perspective. Criticism like the one brought forward in Hartley, Hoover and Salyer (1997), who claim that "it is [...] standard practice to HP filter the predicted series generated by the [RBC] model before checking their intercorrelations and comparing them to the HP-filtered actual data," p. 48, does hold for standard RBC research, but *not* for the present study. Since model (8.8), (8.9) obviously stems from the dynamic disequilibrium class of models, there is no reason to detrend the simulated series. They are stationary by nature. Furthermore, the simulations of the model and their fitting of data are thoroughly examined in the course of the

present chapter. This implies evaluating them with respect to matching several features and measures of the actual data, including not only (second) moments, as is common practice in the RBC research agenda, but also spectral measures of the real world series. The examination of frequency domain features of the simulated series is a test that is either not conducted for standard RBC models or they fail to pass it, see Watson (1993) or Söderlind (1994).
To calibrate the equation system, consisting of (8.8) and (8.9), the following set of information is needed:

(a) initial values of the sectoral capital stocks in detrended form, i.e. $K_i(0)$,
(b) initial values of the sectoral investment series in detrended form, i.e. $K_i'(0) = I_i(0)$,
(c) estimates of the sectoral moduli (of implied complex roots of the correspondingly underlying AR models) to determine respective values for the structural parameter b_i in (8.8) and (8.9), according to equation (5.27) above,
(d) univariate spectral estimates of the sectoral period lengths to determine respective values for the structural parameters a_i in (8.8) and (8.9), according to equation (5.28) above.

Concerning (a) the data are provided in the supplementary part of the NBER-CES/Census US Manufacturing Productivity Database. The variable is real capital stock (in millions of 1987 US$), consisting in the sum of real equipment and real structures capital stock, provided for the 450 SIC 4-digit industries in annual observations for the period 1958 to 1992. For further detail, see Bartelsman and Gray (1996). After detrending by means of the MBK-filter procedure, the initial period 0 corresponds to the year 1961. The end point of the simulation horizon, i.e. after the simulation of 28 periods, corresponds to the year 1989. The required data, stated in (b), are given analogously by the new capital spending series of the same dataset which was analyzed in the course of the preceding chapters; see section 6.1 for a more thorough definition of this variable. Finally, the requirements (c) and (d) are met by the estimates undertaken and outlined in section 6.1.2 above. Concerning the values for the desired levels of capital $K_i^*(t)$, I follow the argumentation in Reiter (1995, section 5.1). Accordingly, for an empirical application or calibration of the model these quantities must be expressed in terms of observable quantities, typically current sales and some measures of the cost of capital. While for current sales data on the 4-digit level are available from the NBER Manufacturing Database, cost of capital are not available on this level of disaggregation and in general difficult to measure. Reiter (1995) notes: "Relating desired capital to current sales is unsatisfactory, because equipment is intended to serve as a means of production for many years; therefore, the desired level should not be dominated by short-run fluctuations, but rather by long-run expectations. Desired capital therefore reacts only to permanent changes in sales, as was first pointed out by Eisner (1960)," p. 54. Furthermore, he finds that the permanent component of sales is adequately captured by the trend, and therefore the desired capital stock follows the trend path only. Since model (8.8) in combination with (8.9) is a model from the disequilibrium class of models, expressing the variables as deviations from trend, desired capital stocks are zero. They are therefore throughout set to zero in the course of this section's simulations: $K_i^*(t) = 0$ for all t simulation periods.

8.2.2 Setting Up the Simulation Strategy and Determining Priors

For pragmatic reasons of tractability of the simulations, I decided to focus on the top 135 sectors in standardized variance terms, cf. Table 6.2a and 6.2b above. According to the CTS measure, defined in equation (3.6) above, these sectoral investment series contribute 82% in standard deviation terms to the standard deviation in the total manufacturing investment aggregate. Furthermore, following the argumentation of section 7.1 and the preceding section 8.1, the sectors are divided into a part of sectors that interacts with the aggregate investment behavior (type I industries) and a non-interacting part (type II industries).[5] The classification will be conducted in accordance with the argumentation in the first paragraphs of section 7.1. Accordingly, generalized synchronization, as adequately measured by the bivariate *sc* estimates of aggregate and disaggregate cyclicalities, is a prerequisite for the stronger forms of synchronization, namely phase synchronization and phase and period synchronization. If a sectoral series shows weak or no indications of generalized synchronization over the whole observation period, it should be modeled by a non-interacting SOA equation of the form (8.3).

To get an impression of which sectors show a reasonable degree of generalized synchronization and which do not, I ranked the selected 135 sectors according to their estimated *sc* values (for each series with the aggregate series) and plotted it in line as well as in bar type graphs, see Figures 8.2a and 8.2b below. *Prima facie*, there is a structural break in the slope of the function at approximately rank 110, corresponding to an estimated *sc* value of 0.45. From this point on, i.e. for $sc < 0.45$, the coherence of the sectoral cyclicalities with the aggregate cycle conspicuously falls with a steeper gradient. From a heuristic and pragmatic point of view, I treat these first 110 industries as type I, the remaining 25 sectors as type II industries.

---

[5] This kind of classification, as originally suggested for the present model by Weser (1992), is also common practice in dynamic systems of statistical physics. See for example Kuramoto and Nishikawa (1987), who note: "A notable feature of our system is that it clearly splits into two subsystems in the presence of collective oscillation, namely a synchronized part of the population and a desynchronized one," p. 571.

Fig. 8.2. Top 135 CTS sectors

a. Line chart: *sc* value ranked

b. Bar chart: *sc* value ranked

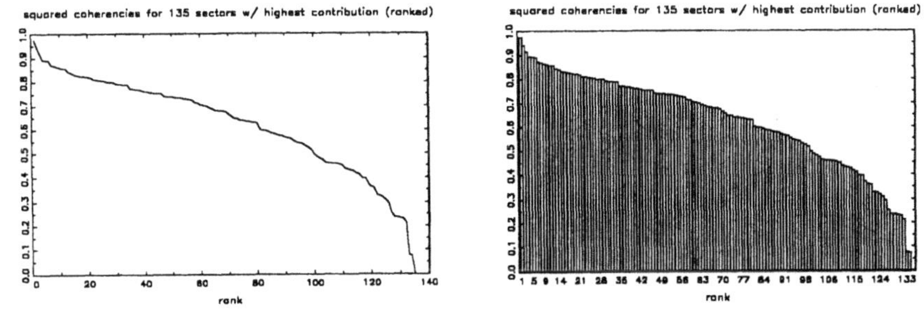

The remaining parameters that need to be determined for the simulation of the model in its deterministic form are the heterogeneous interaction parameters χ_i of equations (8.8). Again it is a straightforward strategy to suppose a relationship of these strengths of interaction with the bivariate *sc* spectral estimates. Before establishing this relationship with regard to the reduction of the 'free' parameters of the model to a single one,[6] it is of importance to gain a reference or prior value for $\overline{\chi}$ for the heterogeneous χ_i, where $i = 1, ..., 110$. The idea is to proceed analogously to the simulation of section 5.3.3: In a first step I suppose a unique value for the interaction parameters, i.e. $\chi_i = \overline{\chi}$, for all $i = 1, ..., 110$, and minimize the discrepancy between resulting simulated aggregate cycle and empirical aggregate cycle. This is done by means of a simple grid search, where the aforementioned discrepancy is measured by the standard prognostic measures mean squared error (MSE), mean absolute error (MAE) and root mean squared error (RMSE). Considered $\overline{\chi}$-values stem from the range 0.001 to 1.500[7] and were changed gradually by 1/1000 for each numerical simulation. A local (or global in the range $\overline{\chi} \in (0.001, 1.500)$) minimum for MSE, MAE and RMSE is found for $\overline{\chi} = 0.626$.[8] In the following this value is employed as a prior for the average strength of interaction of the interacting sectoral investors with the aggregate investing behavior.

Let me now turn to establish the relationship of the strengths of interaction with the bivariate *sc* estimates. The following linear-proportional relationship is supposed

$$\chi_i - \overline{\chi} = \gamma \left(sc_i - \overline{sc} \right), \tag{8.10}$$

where $\overline{sc}$ denotes the mean of estimated *sc* values, i.e. $\frac{1}{110} \sum_{i=1}^{110} sc_i$, and γ represents the factor of proportionality. In other words, it is assumed that the sectorally heterogeneous sc_i values are dispersed around their mean value linearly proportional to the sectorally heterogenous χ_i, dispersed around the

[6] In order to operationalize the simulation and optimize the simulation outputs according to this parameter.

[7] Which showed in previously conducted preliminary simulation runs good fits both on the sectoral and aggregate level.

[8] Corresponding prognostic measures are MSE = 0.124, MAE = 0.121, RMSE = 0.353.

reference strength of interaction $\overline{\chi}$. Consider now a single trial value $\widetilde{\gamma}$ for the relationship in (8.10). The unknown χ_i are then determined solely by known parameters, according to

$$\chi_i = \widetilde{\gamma}\left(sc_i - \overline{sc}\right) + \overline{\chi}, \tag{8.11}$$

allowing the model equations (8.8), (8.9), as well as (8.3) for type II industries, (in their deterministic versions) to be simulated and optimized with respect to $\widetilde{\gamma}$, so as to bring the simulation outputs in line with the sectoral and aggregate spectral and volatility features of the actual data. It is noteworthy, that besides its proportionality interpretation reflected in (8.10), there is another interesting interpretation of the parameter γ: Since we know *a priori* from the results reported in section 6.1.2 that $|(sc_i - \overline{sc})| \neq 0$ for all $i = 1, ..., 110$, γ can, at least in the lower extreme, be interpreted as the degree of heterogeneity in sectoral interaction. To make this point more clear, consider the following transformation of the relationship (8.10):

$$\gamma = \frac{\chi_i - \overline{\chi}}{sc_i - \overline{sc}}. \tag{8.12}$$

Obviously, given $|(sc_i - \overline{sc})| \neq 0$ for all i, this expression for γ equals 0 only in the case, where $\chi_i = \overline{\chi}$, for all $i = 1, ..., 110$, i.e. in the case when every sector interacts with a unique average intensity with the aggregate behavior. Therefore the reference case $\gamma = 0$ corresponds to the case of complete sectoral homogeneity in interaction.

8.2.3 Monte Carlo Simulations of the Model Incorporating Shocks

As outlined above, a further central innovation in comparison to the earlier versions of the present model by Weser (1992) is the inclusion of exogenous shocks. To incorporate stochastics in the sectoral SOA equations and to take the assumption $K_i^*(t) = 0$ into account (cf. the above argumentation), the following modification of equation system (8.8) is considered

$$\begin{aligned} I_i'(t) = K_i''(t) = \; & -a_i\left[1 + \chi_i \cdot \Psi\left(-K_i(t)\textstyle\sum_{i,j} I_{i,j}(t)\right)\right] K_i(t) \\ & -b_i K_i'(t) + \xi_i(t), \end{aligned} \tag{8.13}$$

where Ψ is further on defined as the transform function given in (8.9) above. Subscript i denotes type I industries, subscript j type II industries, respectively. In addition the idiosyncratic shock terms are assumed to be Gaussian distributed according to $\xi_i(t) \sim N\left(\mu_i^{AR}, \sigma_i^{AR}\right)$, where μ_i^{AR} denotes the mean of the error vector of the respective AR model underlying the ith sectoral ME spectral estimation model and σ_i^{AR} the corresponding standard deviation of the ith error vector.

To investigate and control for the relative importance of the idiosyncratic sectoral shocks, I introduce another parameter ϑ and implement in the simulations of equations (8.13) in combination with (8.9) in the following way:

$$\xi_i(t) = \vartheta \epsilon_i(t), \tag{8.14}$$

where now $\epsilon_i(t) \sim N\left(\mu_i^{AR}, \sigma_i^{AR}\right)$ for all $i = 1, ..., 110$ interacting sectors (type I industries).

The model, consisting of a) 110 equations of the form (8.13) in combination with (8.9), (8.11) and (8.14), and b) 25 equations of the form

$$I_j'(t) = K_j''(t) = -a_j K_j(t) - b_j K_j'(t) + \xi_j(t), \text{ where} \tag{8.15}$$

$\xi_j(t) = \vartheta \epsilon_j(t)$ and $\epsilon_j(t) \sim N\left(\mu_j^{AR}, \sigma_j^{AR}\right)$ for all $j = 1, ..., 25$ non-interacting sectors (type II industries), is now ready for a numerical simulation exercise.

For every combination of control parameters concerning strength of interaction and importance of stochastics, i.e. for every tuple of parameter values $[\gamma, \vartheta]$, 50 simulation runs were conducted and the respective absolute differences are calculated for the following:

(i) period lengths of the respective simulated aggregate series and empirical aggregate investment series, i.e. of the respective $\sum_{i,j} I_{i,j}$ at the discrete points of observation,[9]
(ii) moduli of the respective simulated aggregate series and empirical aggregate series,
(iii) standard deviations of the respective simulated aggregate series and empirical aggregate series, as well as additional prognostic measures, namely
(iv) the RMSEs between the respective simulated aggregate series and the empirical aggregate series.

It should be noted that the considered tuples $[\gamma, \vartheta]$ include cases, where either $\gamma = 0$, i.e. the case of no interacting SOAs, or $\vartheta = 0$, i.e. the deterministic case of the model. During the MC-simulations the γ- and ϑ-values are changed gradually in steps of first decimal digits. For every $[\gamma, \vartheta]$-combination, from the considered value ranges $\gamma, \vartheta \in [0, 1.5]$, 50 simulations are conducted and the respective median value of the distributions of (i) to (iv) calculated. The results are presented in the 3D-plots displayed in Figures 8.3a to 8.3d, where the x-axis maps γ-, the y-axis maps the ϑ-values and finally the z-axis measures the respective median value for the distributions of (i) to (iv).

[9] Confirmed in a series of previous experiments in the early experimental phase of the simulation study, the simulated and empirical sectoral series move closely in line for a wide range of $[\gamma, \vartheta]$-combinations. So I decided to concentrate the simulation's objective primarily on discrepancies of the two aggregate series. A sample demonstration of how well the sectoral series are captured by the model is given in the proceeding section of the present chapter.

Fig. 8.3a. Absolute per. (yrs.) discrepancy

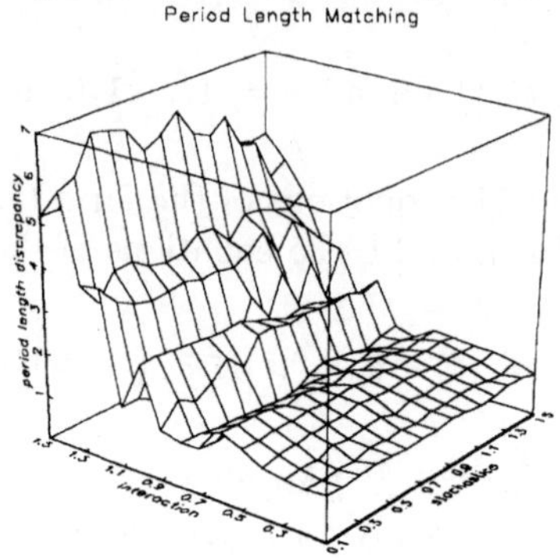

Fig. 8.3b. Absolute mod discrepancy

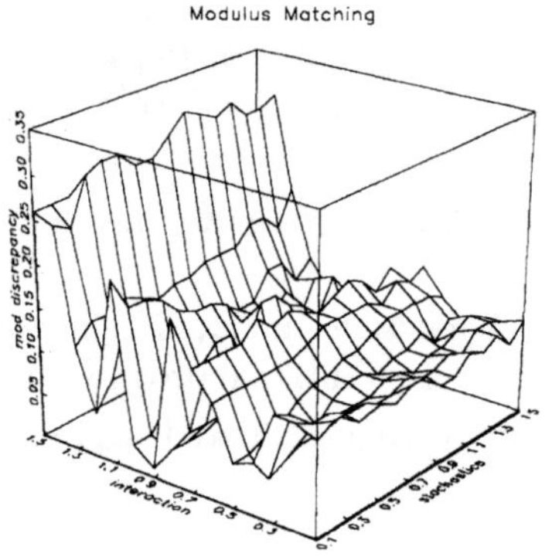

Fig. 8.3c. Absolute std. dev. discrepancy

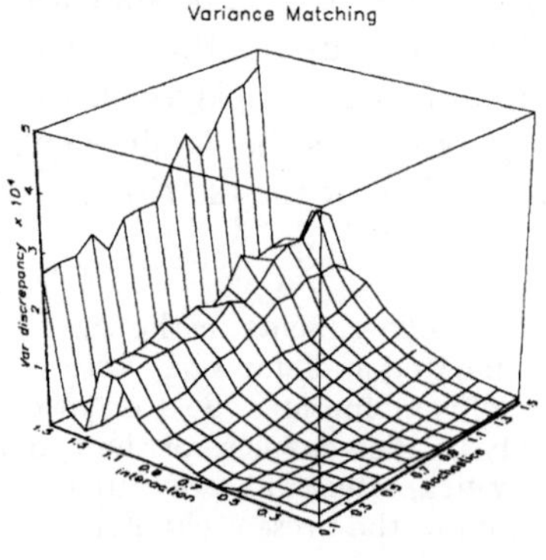

Fig. 8.3d. RMSE performance

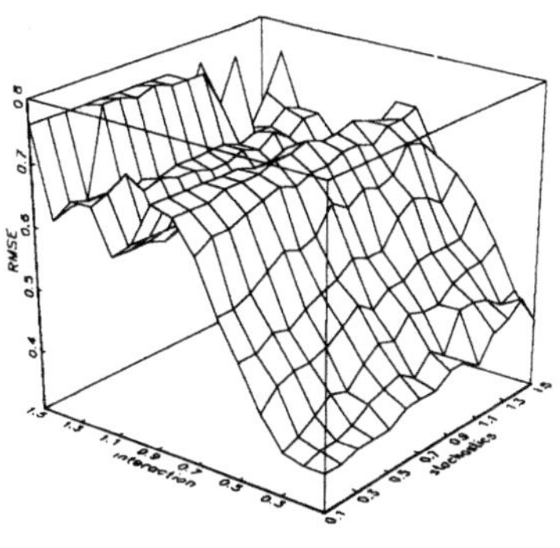

8.2.4 Evaluation of the Model and Outlook

The results presented in Figures 8.3a to 8.3d convey a clear message: First, the simulated model's aggregate captures the central spectral and volatility features of the empirical aggregate very well in a certain region of $[\gamma, \vartheta]$-combinations. This region is unique and can reasonably be approximated and defined. Second, changing the stochastics-parameter, i.e. ϑ-values, has in general considerably less impact on the results, in comparison to changing the interaction-parameter γ. Third, the best performance in terms of all four measures is achieved for $[\gamma, \vartheta]$-constellations, where γ is taking on values between 0.2 and 0.4 and ϑ equalling about 1. This region of parameter values generates (top) minimal absolute values of discrepancy (i) in period lengths of about 0.5 years, (ii) in moduli terms of about 0.01, (iii) in standard deviation terms of about 10, and finally implies (iv) RMSE-values of approximately 0.3. It should be noted that the most sensitive of all four considered performance measures is the absolute discrepancy of standard deviation terms between simulated and empirical series. This becomes evident by looking at the dimension of values denoted on the z-axis of Figure 8.3c.[10] Obviously, the absolute discrepancy in standard deviation terms is the central "limiting factor" or narrowing measure concerning the optimal region of $[\gamma, \vartheta]$-values: A careful inspection of Figure 8.3c reveals that there is a clear valley in the $[\gamma, \vartheta]$-space, corresponding to standard deviation discrepancies $< |100|$. It is defined for values γ (interaction parameter) between 0.2 and 0.4 and ϑ-values (stochastics parameter) between about 0.8 and 1.1. This region defined in the $[\gamma, \vartheta]$-space corresponds to (at least local) minima for the other three performance criteria, cf. Figure 8.3a, 8.3b and 8.3d, which are not especially

[10] A further argument for the importance of this measure is the following: Since the linear models investigated in section 6 of the present work clearly failed to replicate the variance of the empirical aggregate manufacturing investment series, one should be especially concerned with the replication of the volatility of the actual series.

sensitive (concerning the magnitude of effects) to changes in the interaction- and stochastics-parameters.

The following Figures 8.4a to 8.6b display the outcome of three sample simulation runs for the parameter constellations $\gamma = 0.3$, $\vartheta = 1$; $\gamma = 0.2$, $\vartheta = 1.1$ and $\gamma = 0.4$, $\vartheta = 0.8$, respectively. This is done in a first set of diagrams on the sectoral as well as in a second set for the aggregate MFI level. It is virtually impossible and cumbersome to show all 135 simulated sectoral series and confront them with their empirical counterparts, so I decided to exemplarily display the first and last five of the top 135 (according to contributed standard deviation terms) industries only. For all three Figures 8.4a, 8.5a and 8.6a the simulated industrial series move reasonably in line with their actual counterparts. The dotted parallels to the ordinate of the respective window are intended to help to reveal the synchronization process by means of a visual inspection. Concerning the replication of the actual MFI aggregate series' volatility and spectral features, the results presented in Figures 8.4b, 8.5b and 8.6b are striking. While for these sample simulation runs the simulated period lengths and moduli, compared to the ones of the empirical aggregate cycle, are slightly biased upward, the standard deviations of the simulated aggregate series are virtually identical to their empirical counterpart. These findings clearly indicate the potential of the model consisting of equations (8.13), (8.9), (8.11), (8.14), and (8.15) to model and replicate the empirical aggregation and synchronization (cf. the preceding chapter 7) process, in contrast to the linear models investigated in chapter 6 of the monograph that particularly under- or overshot the empirical variance of the aggregate by multiples; see the results reported in section 6.3 above.

It remains for future work to check the robustness of the results by means of an estimation of the model either in the course of a continuous time estimation exercise or in the course of a conventional estimation exercise employing the spline smoothing strategy outlined in chapter 7. Furthermore, the optimization in the course of the calibration study could be refined with regard to several aspects. After the definition of a clear cut objective function, consisting of the four performance measures and maybe also a weighted set of them, one could consider gradient based methods or Newton-Raphson algorithms to exactly determine an optimal $[\gamma, \vartheta]$-combination.

Fig. 8.4a. Disaggregate dynamics - sample simulation run: $\gamma = 0.3$, $\vartheta = 1$

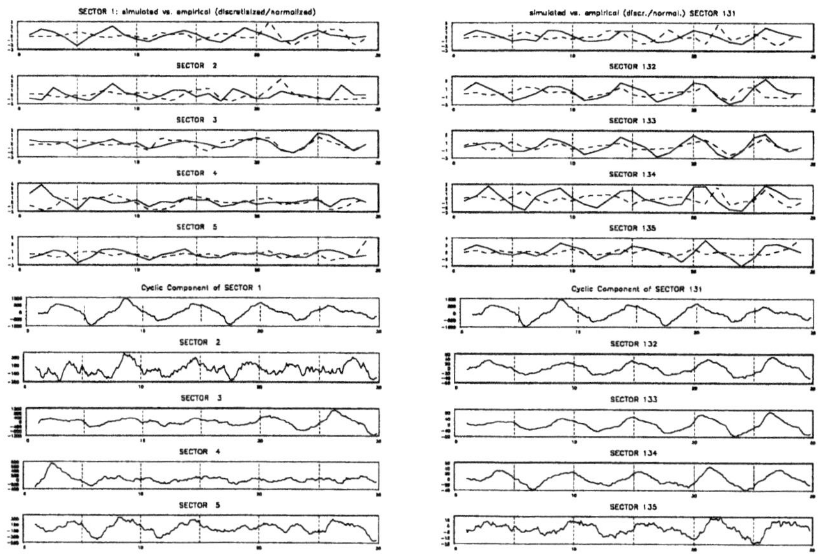

Note: Solid line: simulated, dashed line: empirical series;

1st column: 1st 5, 2nd column: last 5 top135 sectors;

1st row: simulated vs. empirical series (discretesized/normalized);

2nd row: simulated series (continuous)

Sector codes:

Sector 1	motor vehicles & car bodies	Sector 131	frozen fruits and veg.
Sector 2	petroleum refining	Sector 132	machine tool acc.
Sector 3	motor vehicle parts & acc.	Sector 133	gypsum products
Sector 4	blast furnaces & steel mills	Sector 134	canned specialities
Sector 5	paper mills	Sector 135	cereal breakfast food

(all displayed sectors are type I industries, except sector 134 and 135)

Fig. 8.4b. Aggregate dynamics for exemplary simulation run: $\gamma = 0.3$, $\vartheta = 1$

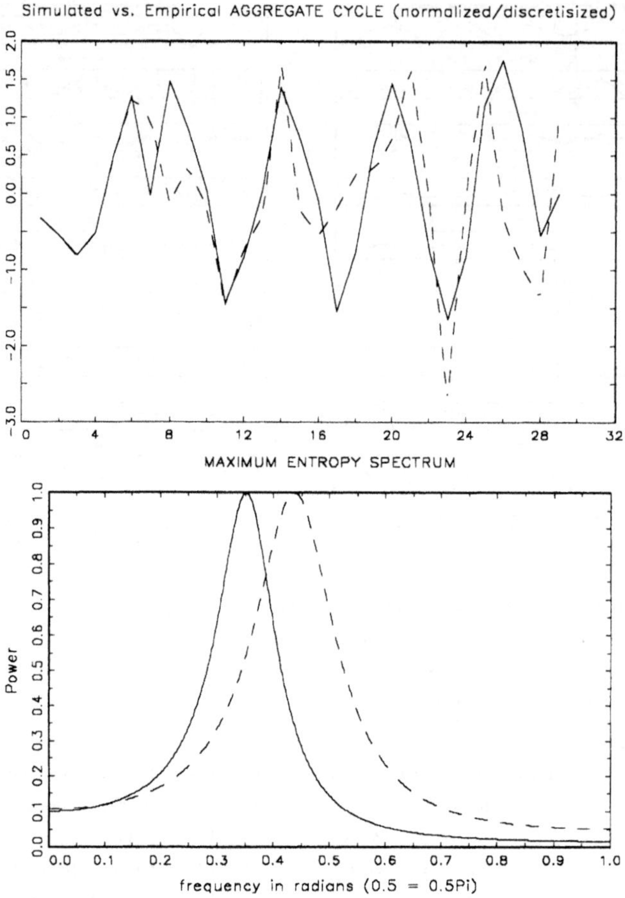

Note: Solid line: simulated, dashed line: empirical series/spectrum

Performance measures:	
Period length (years)	5.63 (4.55)[a]
mod	0.81 (0.75)[a]
RMSE	0.40
abs. std. dev. discrepancy	3.56 (0.001%)[b]

Note: Displayed in parantheses:

a) corresponding empirical results, b) share of actual std. dev.

Fig. 8.5a. Disaggregate dynamics - sample simulation run: $\gamma = 0.2$, $\vartheta = 1.1$

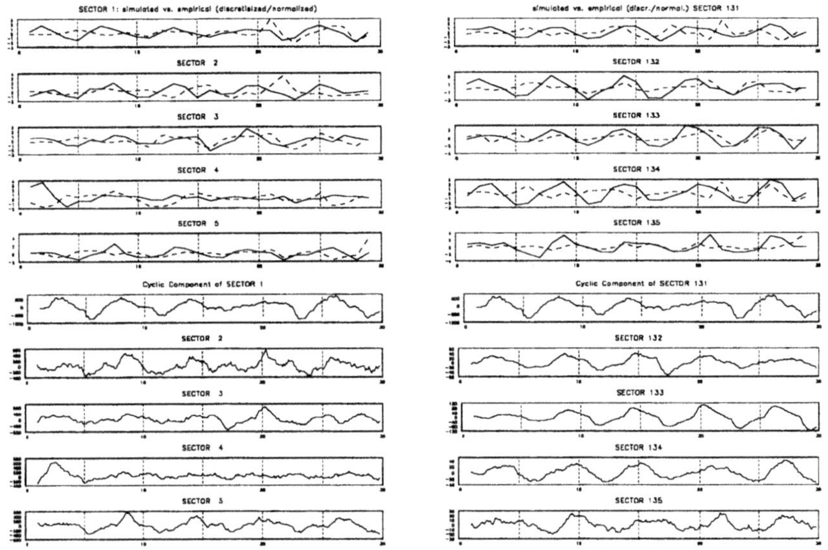

Note: Solid line: simulated, dashed line: empirical series;
1st column: 1st 5, 2nd column: last 5 top135 sectors;
1st row: simulated vs. empirical series (discretesized/normalized);
2nd row: simulated series (continuous)

Sector codes:

Sector 1	motor vehicles & car bodies	Sector 131	frozen fruits and veg.
Sector 2	petroleum refining	Sector 132	machine tool acc.
Sector 3	motor vehicle parts & acc.	Sector 133	gypsum products
Sector 4	blast furnaces & steel mills	Sector 134	canned specialities
Sector 5	paper mills	Sector 135	cereal breakfast food

(all displayed sectors are type I industries, except sector 134 and 135)

Fig. 8.5b. Aggregate dynamics for exemplary simulation run: $\gamma = 0.2$, $\vartheta = 1.1$

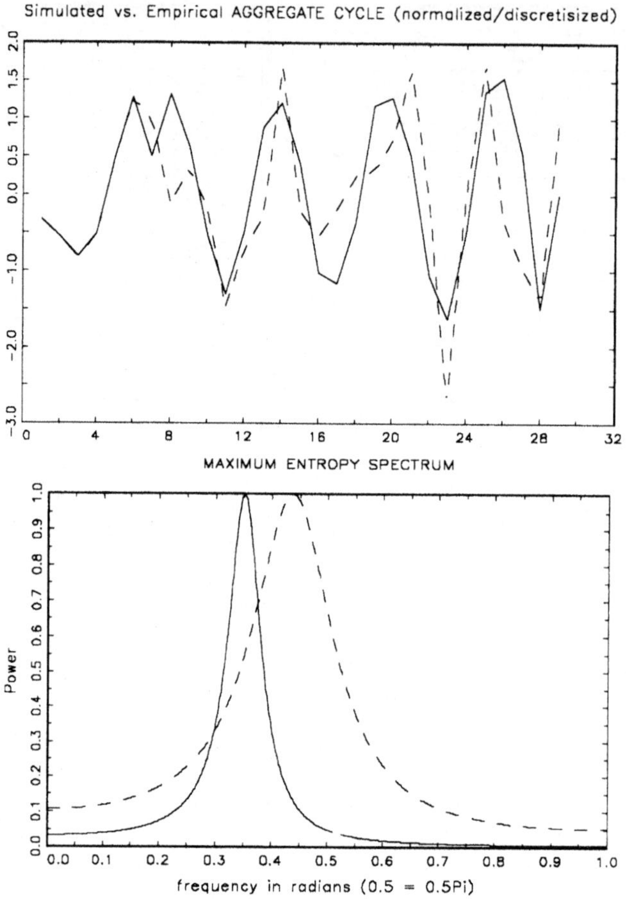

Note: Solid line: simulated, dashed line: empirical series/spectrum

Performance measures:	
Period length (years)	5.61 (4.55)[a]
mod	0.91 (0.75)[a]
RMSE	0.66
abs. std. dev. discrepancy	46.31 (0.01%)[b]

Note: Displayed in parantheses:

a) corresponding empirical results, b) share of actual std. dev.

Fig. 8.6a. Disaggregate dynamics - sample simulation run: $\gamma = 0.4$, $\vartheta = 0.8$

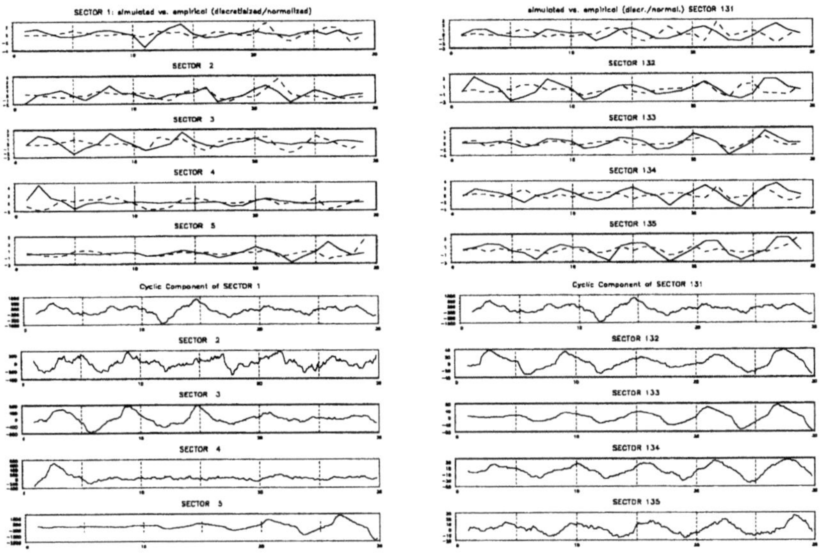

Note: Solid line: simulated, dashed line: empirical series;
st column: 1st 5, 2nd column: last 5 top135 sectors;
1st row: simulated vs. empirical series (discretesized/normalized);
2nd row: simulated series (continuous)

Sector codes:

Sector 1	motor vehicles & car bodies	Sector 131	frozen fruits and veg.
Sector 2	petroleum refining	Sector 132	machine tool acc.
Sector 3	motor vehicle parts & acc.	Sector 133	gypsum products
Sector 4	blast furnaces & steel mills	Sector 134	canned specialities
Sector 5	paper mills	Sector 135	cereal breakfast food

(all displayed sectors are type I industries, except sector 134 and 135)

Fig. 8.6b. Aggregate dynamics for exemplary simulation run: $\gamma = 0.4$, $\vartheta = 0.8$

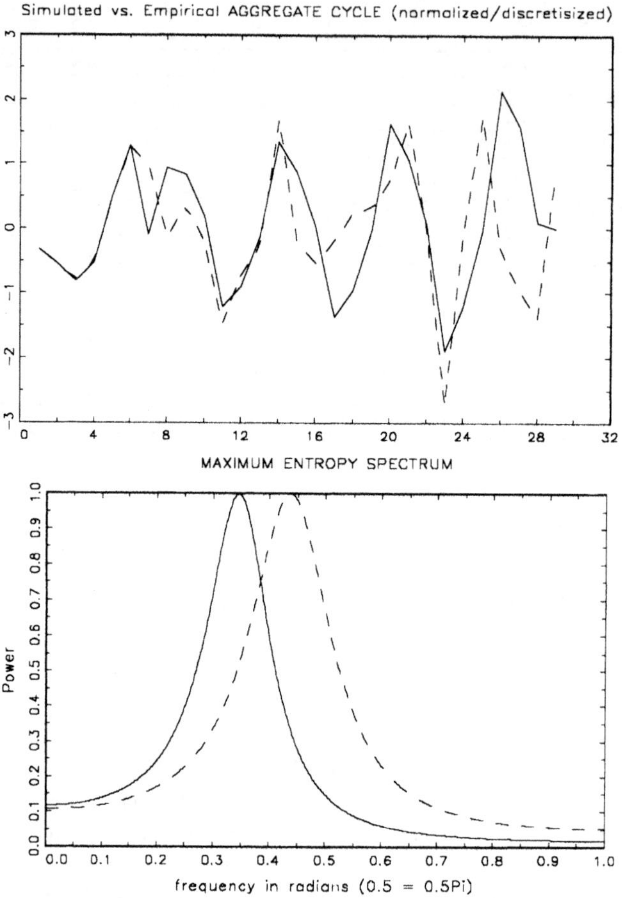

Note: Solid line: simulated, dashed line: empirical series/spectrum

Performance measures:	
Period length (years)	5.99 (4.55)[a]
mod	0.83 (0.75)[a]
RMSE	0.51
abs. std. dev. discrepancy	8.50 (0.002%)[b]

Note: Displayed in parantheses:

a) corresponding empirical results, b) share of actual std. dev.

9. Conclusion

The aim of the present study has been to outline and refine a coherent approach to identifying and modelling business cycles on various levels of aggregation. A further central task has been to demonstrate its potential and superiority to conventional methods and models by applying it to updated, as well as newly available sources of data. Three central and connected aspects, which are widely neglected issues, though of paramount importance,[1] in contemporary business cycle research, have been thoroughly investigated: Description, aggregation and comovement or synchronization of business cycles. Here I briefly summarize the major findings:

Chapter 2 and 3 outlined the methodology for the analysis of cyclical dynamics developed at SEMECON, especially in the latest contributions by C. Hillinger, U. Woitek and M. Reiter, which represent the direct precursors to the present study. I attempted to supplement and refine the existing methods, primarily in the following two respects: (i) definition and application of central volatility and contribution-to-variance measures and (ii) derivation of standard errors for estimated period lengths and moduli of found cyclicalities, based on the AR interpretation of ME spectral analysis. In chapter 3 this methodology was applied to a thorough analysis of the G7 and Euro15 national and supranational economies. A central finding was the revelation and evidence of classical business cycles with frequencies corresponding to about 2 to 4 and about 7 to 10 years period lengths. Both are reflected in the spectra of the G7 economies and the two supranational economies (G7 and Euro15). Central contributors to cyclic dynamic and volatility terms are the economies of Germany, Japan and the USA. Germany has been found to be predominated by a M/W-cyclical structure and mainly responsible for the secondary peak, corresponding to a classical short cycle, in the spectrum of the Euro15 supra-economy. An outstanding and robust finding was the identification of the US economy as an economy profoundly and exceptionally dominated by cyclic investment dynamics with an intermediary periodicity of about 5 to 6 years.

In chapter 5, I focussed on international business cycle comovement. First it was demonstrated that the recent model by Selover and Jensen (1997), as well as a surveyed literature on the synchronization of business cycles by

[1] As recently more frequently claimed in the literature.

means of nonlinear mode-locking mechanisms, are part of a more general class of mathematical models. This class of economic cycles' mode-lock modelling was elaborated, making parts of the findings by Selover and Jensen, based on simulations, obsolete. Furthermore, an endogenous mode-locking model of national business cycle synchronization, induced by the economic behavior of internationally and interactively operating firms in the presence of information externalities was derived, calibrated, enriched with exogenous shocks and simulated on the basis of empirical data and spectral analytic findings for six of the G7 countries and the Netherlands. It was shown that the simulations' outputs quite accurately fit the data and reflected the empirical synchronization process. It remains for future work to bring the results even closer to the findings of the strand of empirical literature on international business cycle comovement, see e.g. Imbs (1999). However, from a technical point of view, the simulation study of chapter 5 should be seen as prerequisite to the quite more sophisticated one conducted and outlined in chapter 8. Chapter 6 analyzed the generation of macroeconomic cycles from sectoral cycles on the basis of US investment data. 450 SIC 4-digit series, covering the period from 1958 to 1992, were tested for cyclicality and their central spectral features estimated. A first finding was that almost all of the disaggregated series, as well as the aggregate series, are strongly and significantly autoregressive. These series have complex roots that imply business cycles with traditional periods centered around five years. In this context alternative VAR specifications were tested. Their ability to explain the spectral features of constituent and aggregate series was examined in simulation experiments. Another central result was given by the fact that there is a substantial and statistically significant feedback effect from the aggregate activity on the sectoral series. In the VAR simulations this aggregate feedback was employed as a common shock impinging on the sectors. The residuals, which were interpreted as idiosyncratic shocks, are only weakly correlated among the sectors. In general, the VAR model was found to be able to describe the cyclical characteristics of the individual time series both accurately and parsimoniously. Nevertheless, the linear models were only partially successful in modelling the aggregation process. This pointed to the desirability of a nonlinear aggregation model. The analysis has been suggestive for the fact that business cycle transmission among different industries is not a direct linear impulse type of phenomenon. In summary, the findings of chapter 6 highlighted the limits of linear models, such as first generation RBC models, and gave grounds for nonlinear synchronization mechanisms in the form of resonant stimulation, phase- or mode-locking of industrial investment cycles with the aggregate activity.

In chapter 7, at first a set of clear cut definitions for different types of synchronization were developed in order to provide a basis for the quantification of synchronization phenomena over business cycles. This was done in accordance with the related strand of literature of the natural sciences, concerned with non-economic synchronization phenomena. Besides, the method suggested and applied for international business cycles by Selover and Jensen (1997) has been successfully applied to find indications for the synchronization of sectoral business cycles, too. In addition a new method, based on shifting a window with fixed length over the data and to estimate spectral measures position by position, has been developed and led to further evidence and more detailed information on the synchronization of business cycles in manufacturing investments on the fairly disaggregated 4-digit (SIC) industrial level.

Although chapter 8 maintained the structure of the Weser (1992) model in several main parts, it is innovative in at least the following respects: (i) providing a theoretical argumentation based on the recent literature on herding underpinning the model, (ii) calibration and simulation of the model based on actual data and estimations, whereby (iii) a natural rate of damping of observed sectoral investment cycles, as well as (iv) exogenous shocks have been taken into account. In addition (v) heterogeneous degrees of interaction between interacting industries have been considered. There is still room for improvement of the model. Nevertheless, it has become obvious that it is a successful and highly promising approach for explaining the synchronized pattern of business cycles, which is one of their most defining characteristics.

Abbreviations

Central introduced abbreviations and acronyms

CBC	Classic(al) business cycle
CON	Personal consumption expenditures (private consumption)
CTS	Contribution to standard deviation
GFCF	Gross fixed capital formation (fixed investment)
GOV	Government spending (consumption and gross investment)
II	Inventory investment (change in private inventories)
logD	Log first differences (approximating growth rates)
MBK	Modified Baxter-King filter, notation by Woitek (1998)
MFI	Manufacturing investment
ptf	Power transfer function
ps	Phase shift measure
R-squ.	R^2 goodness of fit measure
RTL	Relative trend level
sc	Squared coherency measure
SIC	Standard industrial classification (system)
SSD	Standardized standard deviation
TPI	Total private investment (gross private domestic investment)

Note: The list does not include abbreviations and acronyms that are widespread and commonly used in the literature.

All applied programs were written in the programming language of the *GAUSS*^{TM} (Aptech Systems, Inc.) mathematical and statistical system. They are available on request from the author. For the spectral estimations frequent use was made of the `VAR.SRC` procedure collection, kindly provided by U. Woitek.

References

Adelman, I. and F. Adelman (1959), "The Dynamic Properties of the Klein-Goldberger Model," *Econometrica*, Vol. 4, 596-625.

Arnol'd, V. I. (1983), "Remarks on the Perturbation Theory for Problems of Mathieu Type," *Russian Mathematical Surveys*, Vol. 38, No. 4, 215-233.

Artis, M. J. and W. Zhang (1999), "Further Evidence on the International Business Cycle and the ERM: Is there a European Business Cycle?," *Oxford Economic Papers*, Vol. 51, 120-132.

Asea, P. K. and P. J. Zak (1999), "Time-to-build and Cycles," *Journal of Economic Dynamics and Control*, Vol. 23, 596-625.

Bak, P., K. Chen, J. Scheinkman and M. Woodford (1993), "Aggregate Fluctuations from Independent Sectoral Shocks: Self-Organized Criticality in a Model of Production and Inventory Dynamics," *Ricerche Economiche*, Vol. 47, 3-30.

Banerjee, A. V. (1992), "A Simple Model of Herd Behavior," *Quarterly Journal of Economics*, Vol. 107, 797-817.

Banerjee, A., Dolado, J., Galbraith, J. and D. Hendry (1993), *Cointegration, Error-Correction and the Econometric Analysis of Non-Stationary Data*, Oxford University Press, Oxford.

Barker, T. and H. M. Pesaran (eds.) (1990), *Disaggregation in Econometric Modelling*, Routledge, London, New York.

Barro, R. J. (1993), *Macroeconomics*, 4th ed., John Wiley & Sons, New York.

Bartelsman, E. J. and W. B. Gray (1996), "NBER Manufacturing Productivity Database," *NBER Technical Working Paper*, No. 205.

Baxter, M. and R. G. King (1995), "Measuring Business Cycles: Approximate Band-Pass Filters for Economic Time Series," *NBER Working Paper*, No. 5022.

Bikchandani, S., D. Hirshleifer and I. Welch (1992), "A Theory of Fads, Fashion, Custom, and Cultural Change as Informational Cascades," *Journal of Political Economy*, Vol. 100, 992-1062.

Box, G. E. and G. M. Jenkins (1970), *Time Series Analysis: Forecasting and Control*, Holden-Day, San Francisco, Cambridge, London, Amsterdam.

Bradford de Long, J. and L. H. Summers (1992), "Equipment Investment and Economic Growth: How Strong is the Nexus?," *Brookings Papers on Economic Activity*, Vol. 2, 157-211.

Brenner, T., W. Weidlich and U. Witt (1998), " International Co-movements of Business Cycles in a 'Phase-Locking' Model," *Papers on Economics & Evolution - Max-Planck-Institute for Research into Economic Systems*, No. 9802.

Brockwell, P. J. and R. A. Davis (1991), *Time Series: Theory and Methods*, 2nd ed., Springer Series in Statistics, Springer, Berlin, Heidelberg, New York.

Burg, J. P. (1967), "Maximum Entropy Spectral Analysis," *Proceedings of the 37th Meeting of the Society of Exploration Geophysicists*; reprinted in D. G. Childers (ed.), *Modern Spectrum Analysis*, IEEE Press, New York, 1978, 34-41.

Burg, J. P. (1968), "A New Analysis Technique for Time Series Data," *NATO Advanced Study Institute on Signal Processing with Emphasis on Underwater Acoustics*; reprinted in D. G. Childers (ed.), *Modern Spectrum Analysis*, IEEE Press, New York, 1978, 42-48.

Burnside, A. C., M. S. Eichenbaum and S. T. Rebelo (1996), "Sectoral Solow Residuals," *European Economic Review*, Vol. 40, 861-869.

Canova, F. (1994), "Detrending and Turning Points," *European Economic Review*, Vol. 38, 614-623.

Canova, F. (1996), "Three Tests for the Existence of Cycles in Time Series," *Ricerche Economiche*, Vol. 50, 135-162.

Canova, F. (1998), "Detrending and Business Cycle Stylized Facts," *Journal of Monetary Economics*, Vol. 41, 475-512.

Caplin, A. and J. Leahy (1993), "Sectoral Shocks, Learning, and Aggregate Fluctuations," *Review of Economic Studies*, Vol. 60, 777-794.

Chamley, C. and D. Gale (1994), "Information Revelation and Strategic Delay in a Model of Investment," *Econometrica*, Vol. 62, 1065-1085.

Chalkley, M. and I. H. Lee (1998), "Learning and Asymmetric Business Cycles," *Review of Economic Dynamics*, Vol. 1, 623-645.

Christiano, L. J. (1988), "Why Does Inventory Investment Fluctuate So Much?," *Journal of Monetary Economics*, Vol. 21, 247-280.

Christiano, L. J. and T. J. Fitzgerald (1998), "The Business Cycle: It's Still a Puzzle," *Federal Reserve Bank of Chicago: Economic Perspectives*, 4th quarter, 56-83.

Cochrane, J. H. (1994), "Shocks," *NBER Working Paper*, No. 4698.

Collard, D. (1996), "Pigou and Modern Business Cycle Theory," *Economic Journal*, Vol. 106, 912-924.

Cont, R. and J.-P. Bouchaud (2000), "Herd Behavior and Aggregate Fluctuations in Financial Markets," *Journal of Macroeconomic Dynamics*, Vol. 4, 170-169.

Cooley, T. F. (1997), "Calibrated Models," *Oxford Review of Economic Policy*, Vol. 13, 55-69.

Cooper, R. and A. John (1988), "Coordinating Coordination Failures in Keynesian Models," *Quarterly Journal of Economics*, Vol. CIII, 441-463.

Courvisanos, J. (1996), *Investment Cycles in Capitalist Economies: A Kaleckian Behavioural Contribution*, New Directions in Modern Economics Series, Edward Elgar, Aldershot.

Courvisanos, J. (1998), "Dynamics in the Underground: Thought and Methodology in the Study of Investment Cycles," *University of Tasmania - School of Economics Discussion Paper*, No. 1998-07.

Croux, C., M. Forni and L. Reichlin (2001), "A Measure of Comovement for Economic Variables," *Review of Economics and Statistics*, Vol. 83, 232-241.

Den Haan, W. J. and S. Sumner (2001), "The Comovements between Real Activity and Prices in the G7," *NBER Working Paper*, No. 8195.

Diebold, F. X. and A. S. Senhadji (1996), "The Uncertain Unit Root in Real GNP: Comment," *American Economic Review*, Vol. 86, 1291-1298.

Doan, T., R. Litterman and C. A. Sims (1984), "Forecasting and Conditional Projections using Realistic Prior Distributions," *Econometric Reviews*, Vol. 3, 1-100.

Dueker, M. and K. Wesche (1999), "European Business Cycles: New Indices and Analysis of their Synchronization," *Federal Reserve Bank of St. Louis Working Paper*, No. 99-019.

Eisner, R. (1960), "A Distributed Lag Investment Function," *Econometrica*, Vol. 28, 1-29.

Fioretti, G. and B. Süssmuth (2001), "Business Cycle Dynamics in a Neural Net Framework," *International Journal of Computer Research*, Vol. 2, Special Issue on Neural Networks: Past, Present and Future, prepared to commemorate the retirement of Prof. Teuvo Kohonen, 171-192.

Fitzgerald, T. J. (1997), "Inventories and the Business Cycle: An Overview," *Economic Review of the Federal Reserve Bank of Cleveland*, 11-22.

Focardi, S. and M. Marchesi (2000), "Self-Organization in Global Stochastic Models of Production and Inventory Dynamics," in D. Delli Gatti, M. Gallegati and A. P. Kirman (eds.), *Interaction and Market Structure: Essays on Heterogeneity in Economics*, Lecture Notes in Economics and Mathematical Systems, Springer, Berlin, Heidelberg, New York, 167-183.

Forni, M., M. Hallin, M. Lippi and L. Reichlin (2001), "The Generalized Factor Model: Identification and Estimation," forthcoming in *Review of Economics and Statistics*.

Forni, M., M. Hallin, M. Lippi and L. Reichlin (2001), "Coincident and Leading Indicators for the EURO Area," *Economic Journal*, Vol. 111, C61-C85.

Forni, M. and M. Lippi (1997), *Aggregation and the Microfoundations of Dynamic Macroeconomics*, Clarendon Press, Oxford.

Forni, M. and L. Reichlin (1998), "Let's Get Real: A Factor Analytic Approach to Disaggregated Business Cycle Dynamics," *Review of Economic Studies*, Vol. 65, 453-473.

Forni, M. and L. Reichlin (1999), "Federal Policies and Local Economies: Europe and the US," forthcoming in *European Economic Review*.

Forrester, J. W. (1977), "Growth Cycles," *De Economist*, Vol. 125, 525-543.

Gale, D. (1996a), "What Have We Learned from Social Learning?," *European Economic Review*, Vol. 40, 617-628.

Gale, D. (1996b), "Delay and Cycles," *Review of Economic Studies*, Vol. 63, 169-198.

Gallegati, M. and M. Gallegati (2000), "Business Cycle Fluctuations in Europe (1960-1998)," mimeo, University of Ancona and University of Teramo.

Gandolfo, G. (1981), *Qualitative Analysis and Econometric Estimation of Continuous Time Dynamic Models*, North-Holland, Amsterdam.

Goodwin, R. M. (1984), "Disaggregating Models of Fluctuating Growth," International Symposium, University of Siena; reprinted in R. M. Goodwin, M. Krüger and A. Vercelli (eds.), *Nonlinear Models of Fluctuating Growth, Lecture Notes in Economics and Mathematical Systems 228*, Springer, Berlin, Heidelberg, New York, 67-72.

Gordon, R. J. and J. M. Veitch (1986), "Fixed Investment in the American Business Cycle," in R. J. Gordon (ed.), *The American Business Cycle: Continuity and Change*, University of Chicago Press, Chicago, 267-357.

Granger, C. W. J. (1966), "The Typical Spectral Shape of an Economic Variable," *Econometrica*, Vol. 34, 150-161.

Granger, C. W. J. and P. Newbold (1986), *Forecasting Economic Time Series*, 2nd ed., Academic Press, Orlando.

Greenwood, J., Z. Hercowitz and P. Krussel (1998), "The Role of Investment-Specific Technological Change in the Business Cycle," *Rochester Center for Economic Research Working Paper*, No. 449.

Gregory, A. W. and G. W. Smith (1991), "Calibration as Testing: Inference in Simulated Macroeconomic Models," *Journal of Business and Economic Statistics*, Vol. 9, 297-303.

Gregory, A. W. and G. W. Smith (1995), "Business Cycle Theory and Econometrics," *Economic Journal*, Vol. 105, 1597-1608.

Guay, A. and P. St-Amant (1997), "Do the Hodrick-Prescott and Baxter-King Filters Provide a Good Approximation of Business Cycles?," *CREFE Working Paper (Cahier de Recherche) - Université du Québec à Montréal*, No. 53.

Gul, F. and R. Lundholm (1995), "Endogenous Timing and the Clustering of Agents' Decisions," *Journal of Political Economy*, Vol. 103, 1039-1066.

Hall, T. E. (1990), *Business Cycles: The Nature and Causes of Economic Fluctuations*, Praeger, New York.

Hamilton, D. (1994), *Time Series Analysis*, Princeton University Press, Princeton, New Jersey.

Hansen, L. P. and J. J. Heckman (1996), "The Empirical Foundations of Calibration," *Journal of Economic Perspectives*, Vol. 10, 87-104.

Hartley, J. E., K. D. Hoover and K. D. Salyer (1997), "The Limits of Business Cycle Research: Assessing the Real Business Cycle Model," *Oxford Review of Economic Policy*, Vol. 13, 34-54.

Harvey, A. C. and A. Jaeger (1993), "Detrending, Stylized Facts and the Business Cycle," *Journal of Applied Econometrics*, Vol. 8, 231-247.

Haxholdt, C., C. Kampmann, E. Mosekilde and J. D. Sterman (1995), "Mode-Locking and Entrainment of Endogenous Economic Cycles," *System Dynamics Review*, Vol. 11, 177-198.

Heintel, M. (1998), "A Note on a Bayesian Order Determination Procedure for Vector Autoregressive Processes," *Statistical Papers*, Vol. 39, 213-221.

Hillinger, C. (1992), "Paradigm Change and Scientific Method in the Study of Economic Fluctuations," in C. Hillinger (ed.), *Cyclical Growth in Market and Planned Economies*, Clarendon Press, Oxford, 5-46.

Hillinger, C., M. Reiter and T. Weser (1992), "Micro Foundations of the Second-Order Accelerator and of Cyclical Behaviour," in C. Hillinger (ed.), *Cyclical Growth in Market and Planned Economies*, Clarendon Press, Oxford, 167-180.

Hillinger, C. and M. Sebold-Bender (1992), "The Stylized Facts of Macroeconomic Fluctuations," in C. Hillinger (ed.), *Cyclical Growth in Market and Planned Economies*, Clarendon Press, Oxford, 63-110.

Hillinger, C. and T. Weser (1988a), "The Aggregation Problem in Business Cycle Theory," *Journal of Economic Dynamics and Control*, Vol. 12, 37-40.

Hillinger, C. and T. Weser (1988b), "Aggregation and Parametric Resonance in Business Cycle Theory," in A. Chikan and M. C. Lovell (eds.), *The Economics of Inventory Management - Studies in Production and Engineering Economics 7*, Elsevier, North-Holland, Amsterdam, 169-182.

Hodrick, R. J. and E. C. Prescott (1997), "Postwar US Business Cycles: An Empirical Investigation," *Journal of Money, Credit, and Banking*, Vol. 29, 1-16.

Hornstein, A. and J. Praschnik (1997), "Intermediate Inputs and Sectoral Comovement in the Business Cycle," *Journal of Monetary Economics*, Vol. 40, 573-595.

Hors, I. and F. Lordon (1997), "About Some Formalism of Interaction: Phase Transition Models in Economics?," *Journal of Evolutionary Economics*, Vol. 7, 355-373.

Horvath, M. (1998a), "Cyclicality and Sectoral Linkages: Aggregate Fluctuations from Independent Sectoral Shocks," *Review of Economic Dynamics*, Vol. 1, 781-808.

Horvath, M. (1998b), "Sectoral Shocks and Aggregate Fluctuations," forthcoming in *Journal of Monetary Economics*.

Howrey, P. E. (1980), "The Role of Time Series Analysis in Econometric Model Evaluation," in J. Kmenta and J. B. Ramsey (eds.), *Evaluation of Econometric Models*, Academic Press, New York, London, 275-307.

Imbs, J. (1999), "Co-Fluctuations," *CEPR Discussion Paper*, No. 2267.

Iwanga, S. and A. Namatame (2000), "Nonlinear Dynamics between Micro-Motives and Macro-Behavior," mimeo, National Defense Academy, Yokosuka; paper presented at the 7th Viennese Workshop on Nonlinear Dynamics and Dynamic Games, Vienna.

Judd, K. L. (1998), *Numerical Methods in Economics*, MIT Press, Cambridge, Massachusetts, London.

Juglar, C. (1889), *Des Crises Commerciales et de leur Retour Periodique en France, en Angleterre et aux Etats-Unis*, 2nd ed., Guillaumin, Paris.

Kampmannn C., C. Haxholdt, E. Mosekilde and J. D. Sterman (1994), "Entrainment in a Disaggregated Economic Long-Wave Model," in L. Leyersdorff and P. van den Besselaar (eds.), *Evolutionary Economics and Chaos Theory*, Pinter Publishers, London, 109-124.

Kiefer, D. (1996), "Searching for Endogenous Business Cycles in the U.S. Postwar Economy," *Metroeconomica*, Vol. 47, 34-56.

Kydland, F. E. (1995), "Business Cycles and Aggregate Labor Market Fluctuations," in T. F. Cooley (ed.), *Frontiers of Business Cycle Research*, Princeton University Press, Princeton, New Jersey, 128-156.

Kiyotaki, N. and K. D. West (1996), "Business Fixed Investment and the Recent Business Cycle in Japan," in B. S. Bernanke and J. J. Rotemberg (eds.), *NBER Macroeconomics Annual 1996*, MIT Press, Cambridge, London, 277-323.

Koopmans, L. H. (1995), *The Spectral Analysis of Time Series*, 2nd ed., Academic Press, San Diego.

Krugman, P. (1996), *The Self-Organizing Economy*, Blackwell Publishers, Massachusetts.

Kuramoto, Y. and I. Nishikawa (1987), "Statistical Macrodynamics of Large Dynamical Systems: Case of a Phase Transition in Oscillator Communities," *Journal of Statistical Physics*, Vol. 49, 569-605.

Long, J. B. and C. I. Plosser (1983), "Real Business Cycles," *Journal of Political Economic*, Vol. 91, 39-69.

Long, J. B. and C. I. Plosser (1987), "Sectoral vs. Aggregate Shocks in the Business Cycle," *American Economic Review*, Vol. 77, 333-336.

Larsen, E. R., J. D. W. Morecroft, J. S. Thomsen and E. Mosekilde (1992), "Devil's Staircase and Chaos from Macroeconomic Mode Interaction," *Journal of Economic Dynamics and Control*, Vol. 17, 759-769.

Lucas, R. E. (1977), "Understanding Business Cycles," in K. Brunner and A. Metzler (eds.), *Stabilization of the Domestic and International Economy, Carnegie-Rochester Series on Public Policy*, Vol. 5; reprinted in R. E. Lucas (1981), *Studies in Business-Cycle Theory*, Basil Blackwell, Oxford, 215-239.

Lütkepohl, H. (1991), *Introduction to Multiple Time Series Analysis*, Springer, Berlin, Heidelberg, New York.

Maddala, G. S. and I.-M. Kim (1998), *Unit Roots, Cointegration, and Structural Change*, Cambridge University Press, Cambridge.

Mankiw, G. N. (1989), "Real Business Cycles: A New Keynesian Perspective," *Journal of Economic Perspectives*, Vol. 3, 79-90; reprinted in B. Snowdon and H. R. Vane (eds.), *A Macroeconomics Reader*, Routledge, London, 1997, 425-436.

Mariano, R., T. Schuermann and M. J. Weeks (eds.) (2000), *Simulation-Based Inference in Econometrics: Methods and Applications*, Cambridge University Press, Cambridge.

Marple, L. S. Jr. (1987), *Digital Spectral Analysis with Applications*, Prentice Hall, Englewood Cliffs, New Jersey.

Mass, N. J. (1975), *Economic Cycles: An Analysis of Underlying Causes*, Wright-Allen Press, Cambridge, Massachusetts.

Matsumoto, A. (1997), "A Non-Linear Macro Model of Endogenous Inventory Oscillations," *Research in Economics*, Vol. 51, 101-129.

McKenzie, M. D. (1999), "The Impact of Exchange Rate Volatility on International Trade Flows," *Journal of Economic Surveys*, Vol. 13, 71-106.

Metzler, L. (1946), "Business Cycles and the Modern Theory of Employment," *American Economic Review*, Vol. 36, 278-291.

Mosekilde, E., E. R. Larsen, J. D. Sterman and J. S. Thomsen (1992), "Nonlinear Mode-Interaction in the Macroeconomy," *Annals of Operations Research*, Vol. 37, 185-215.

Mosekilde, E., E. R. Larsen, J. D. Sterman and J. S. Thomsen (1993), "Mode-Locking and Nonlinear Entrainment of Macroeconomic Cycles," in R. H. Day and P. Chen (eds.), *Nonlinear Dynamics and Evolutionary Economics*, Oxford University Press, Oxford, 58-83.

Muellbauer, J. (1997), "The Assessment: Business Cycles," *Oxford Review of Economic Policy*, Vol. 13, 1-18.

Néda, Z., E. Ravasz, T. Vicsek, Y. Brechet and A. L. Barabási (2000a), "Physics of the Rhythmic Applause," *Physical Review E*, Vol. 61, 6987-6994.

Néda, Z., E. Ravasz, T. Vicsek, Y. Brechet and A. L. Barabási (2000b), "Self-Organization in the Concert Hall: The Dynamics of Rhythmic Applause," *Nature*, Vol. 403, 849-853.

Norris, J. W. (1993), "The Closing of Arnol'd Tongues for a Periodically Forced Limit Cycle," *Nonlinearity*, Vol. 6, 1093-1114.

Oliner, S. D., G. D. Rudebusch and D. E. Sichel (1999), "New and Old Models of Investment: A Comparison of Forecasting Performance," in F. X. Diebold and G. D. Rudebusch (eds.), *Business Cycles - Durations, Dynamics and Forecasting*, Princeton University Press, Princeton, 361-386.

Perlo, V. (1974), *The Unstable Economy: Booms and Recessions in the U.S. since 1945*, 2nd ed., International Publishers, New York.

Plosser, C. I. (1991), "Real Business Cycles under Test: A Comment," *European Economic Review*, Vol. 35, 961-965.

Prescott, E. C. (1986), "Theory Ahead of Business Cycle Measurement," *Federal Reserve Bank of Minneapolis Quarterly Review*, 9-22; reprinted in B. Snowdon and H. R. Vane (eds.), *A Macroeconomics Reader*, Routledge, London, 1997, 366-388.

Press, W. H., Teukolsky, S. A., Vetterling, W. T. and B. P. Flannery (1992), *Numerical Recipes in C*, Cambridge University Press, Cambridge.

Quah, D. T. (1994), "Business Cycle and Trends: New Empirical Approaches - One Business Cycle from (Many,) Many Disaggregates," *European Economic Review*, Vol. 38, 605-613.

Quah, D. T. (1995), "Business Cycle Empirics: Calibration and Estimation," *Economic Journal*, Vol. 105, 1594-1596.

Radzicki, M. J. and J. D. Sterman (1994), "Evolutionary Economics and System Dynamics," in R. W. England (ed.), *Evolutionary Concepts in Contemporary Economics*, University of Michigan Press, Ann Arbor, 61-89.

Reeves, J. J., C. A. Blyth, C. M. Triggs and J. P. Small (1996), "The Hodrick Prescott Filter, a Generalisation, and a New Procedure for Extracting an Empirical Cycle from a Series," *University of Auckland - Department of Economics Working Paper*, No. 160.

Reichlin, L. (1991), "Real Business Cycles under Test: A Comment," *European Economic Review*, Vol. 35, 966-969.

Reichlin, L. (2000), "Extracting Business Cycle Indexes from Large Data Sets: Aggregation, Estimation, Identification," mimeo, University of Brussels; paper presented at the World Congress of the Econometric Society, Seattle.

Reiter, M. (1995), *The Dynamics of Business Cycles: Stylized Facts, Economic Theory, Econometric Methodology and Applications*, Physica (Springer), Heidelberg.

Reiter, M. and U. Woitek (1999), "Are There Classical Business Cycles?," *University of Glasgow - Discussion Papers in Economics*, No. 9905.

Ritschl, A. and U. Woitek (2000), "Did Monetary Forces Cause the Great Depression? A Bayesian VAR Analysis for the U.S. Economy," *CEPR Discussion Paper*, No. 2547.

Rosser, J. B. Jr. (1996), "On the Complexity of Complex Economic Dynamics," *Journal of Economic Perspectives*, Vol 13, 169-192.

Samuelson, P. A. (1961), *Economics: An Introductory Analysis*, 5th ed., McGraw Hill, New York, Toronto, London.

Sargent, T. J. (1987), *Macroeconomic Theory*, 2nd ed., Academic Press, San Diego.

Scharfstein, D. S. and J. C. Stein (1990), "Herd Behavior and Investment," *American Economic Review*, Vol. 80, 465-479.

Schenk-Hoppé, K. R. (2000), "Economic Growth and Business Cycles: A Critical Comment on Detrending Time Series," *Institute for Empirical Research in Economics, University of Zürich, Working Paper*, No. 54.

Schlicht, E. (1985), *Isolation and Aggregation in Economics*, Springer, Berlin, Heidelberg, New York.

Schumpeter, J. (1939), *Business Cycles*, McGraw Hill, New York.

Selover, D. D. (1997), "Business Cycle Transmission between the United States and Japan: A Vector Error Correction Approach," *Japan and the World Economy*, Vol. 9, 385-411.

Selover, D. D. and R. V. Jensen (1999), "'Mode-Locking' and International Business Cycle Transmission," *Journal of Economic Dynamics and Control*, Vol. 23, 591-618.

Sgroi, D. (1999), "Endogenous Timing and Information Revelation in Herding Models," mimeo, Nuffield College, Oxford; paper presented at the Young Economist Meeting, Amsterdam.

Sgroi, D. (2000), "The Right Choice at the Right Time: A Herding Experiment in Endogenous Time," *Nuffield College Discussion Papers in Economics*, W15.

Sims, C. A. (1996), "Macroeconomics and Methodology," *Journal of Economic Perspectives*, Vol. 10, 105-120.

Slutzky, E. (1937), "The Summation of Random Causes as the Source of Cyclic Processes," *Econometrica*, Vol. 5, 19-60.

Smylie, D. E., G. K. C. Clarke and T. J. Ulrych (1973), "Analysis of Irregularities in the Earth's Rotation," *Methods in Computational Physics*, Vol. 13, 391-430.

Snowdon, B. and H. R. Vane (1995), "New Keynesian Economics Today: The Empire Strikes Back," *American Economist*, Vol. 39, 48-65; reprinted in B. Snowdon and H. R. Vane (eds.), *A Macroeconomics Reader*, Routledge, London, 1997, 452-477.

Söderlind, P. (1994), "Cyclical Properties of a Real Business Cycle Model," *Journal of Applied Econometrics*, Vol. 9, S113-S122.

Sosnovtseva, O. V., A. G. Balanov, T. E. Vadivasova and E. Mosekilde (1999), "Loss of Lag Synchronization in Coupled Chaotic Systems," *Physical Review E*, Vol. 60, 6560-6565.

Stadler, G. W. (1994), "Real Business Cycles," *Journal of Economics Literature*, Vol. XXXII, 1750-1783.

Sterman, J. D. (1989), "Modelling Managerial Behavior: Misperceptions of Feedback in a Dynamic Decision Making Experiment," *Management Science*, Vol. 35, 321-339.

Sterman, J. D. and E. Mosekilde (1994), "Business Cycles and Long Waves: A Behavioral Disequilibrium Perspective," in W. Semmler (ed.), *Business Cycles: Theory and Empirical Methods*, Kluwer Academic Publishers, Massachusetts, 13-51.

Stock, J. H. and M. W. Watson (1998), "Business Cycle Fluctuations in U.S. Macroeconomic Time Series," *NBER Working Paper*, No. 6528.

Summers, L. H. (1986), "Some Skeptical Observations on Real Business Cycle Theory," *Federal Reserve Bank of Minneapolis Quarterly Review*, 23-27; reprinted in B. Snowdon and H. R. Vane (eds.), *A Macroeconomics Reader*, Routledge, London, 1997, 389-395.

Süssmuth, B. (2002a), "Can Herding Explain Cyclic Comovement?," *International Game Theory Review*, Vol. 4, No. 1, 33-51.

Süssmuth, B. (2002b), "To be or not to be of Maxentropic Type? An Appraisal of Parametric Spectral Analysis in Econometrics," mimeo, University of Modena.

Süssmuth, B. (2002c), "National and Supranational Business Cycles (1960-2000): A multivariate description of central G7 and EURO15 NIPA aggregates," forthcoming in *CESifo Studies* (*ifo-Studien: Zeitschrift für empirische Wirtschaftsforschung*).

Theil, H. (1965), *Linear Aggregation of Economic Relations*, North-Holland, Amsterdam.

Tinbergen, J. (1931), "Ein Schiffbauzyklus?," *Weltwirtschaftliches Archiv*, Vol. 34.

Tvede, L. (1997), *Business Cycles: From John Law to Chaos Theory*, Harwood Academic Publishers, Amsterdam.

Uhlig, H. (1994), "What Macroeconomists should know about Unit Roots: A Bayesian Perspective," *Econometric Theory*, Vol. 10, 645-671.

Uhlig, H. (1996), "A Law of Large Numbers for Large Economies," *Economic Theory*, Vol. 8, 41-50.

Ulrych, T. J. and T. N. Bishop (1975), "Maximum Entropy Analysis and Autoregressive Decomposition," *Review of Geophysics and Space Physics*, Vol. 13, 183-200; reprinted in D. G. Childers (ed.), *Modern Spectrum Analysis*, IEEE Press, New York, 1978, 54-71.

Vallés, J. (1997), "Aggregate Investment in a Business Cycle Model with Adjustment Costs," *Journal of Economic Dynamics and Control*, Vol. 21, 1181-1198.

Van Daal, J. and A. H. Q. M. Merkies (1984), *Aggregation in Economic Research*, D. Reidel Publishing, Dordrecht.

Van den Bos, A. (1971), "Alternative Interpretation of Maximum Spectral Analysis," *IEEE Transactions on Information Theory*, Vol. 17, 493-494.

Watson, M. W. (1993), "Measures of Fit for Calibrated Models," *Journal of Political Economy*, Vol. 101, 1011-1041.

Wecker, W. E. and C. F. Ansley (1983), "The Signal Extraction Approach to Nonlinear Regression and Spline Smoothing," *Journal of the American Statistical Association*, Vol. 78, 81-89.

Weidlich, W. and G. Haag (1983), *Concepts and Models of a Quantitative Sociology*, Springer, Heidelberg, New York, Tokyo.

Wen, Y. (1998), "Investment Cycles," *Journal of Economic Dynamics and Control*, Vol. 22, 1139-1165.

Weser, T. (1992), The Aggregation Problem for Economic Cycles," in C. Hillinger (ed.), *Cyclical Growth in Market and Planned Economies*, Clarendon Press, Oxford, 181-200.

Woitek, U. (1996), "The G7 Countries: A Multivariate Description of the Business Cycle Stylized Facts," in W. A. Barnett, G. Gandolfo and C. Hillinger (eds.), *Dynamic Disequilibrium Modelling*, Cambridge University Press, Cambridge, 283-309.

Woitek, U. (1997), *Business Cycles: An International Comparison of Stylized Facts in a Historical Perspective*, Physica (Springer), Heidelberg.

Woitek, U. (1998), "A Note on the Baxter-King Filter," *University of Glasgow - Discussion Papers in Economics*, No. 9813.

Wymer, C. R. (1993), "Continuous-time Models in Macroeconomics: Specification and Estimation," in G. Gandolfo (ed.), *Continuous Time Econometrics - Theory and Applications*, Chapman and Hall, London, 35-79.

Yoshikawa, H. (1995), *Macroeconomics and the Japanese Economy*, Oxford University Press, Oxford.

Zarnowitz, V. (1985), "Recent Work on Business Cycles in a Historical Perspective: A Review of Theory and Evidence," *Journal of Economic Literature*, Vol. 23, 523-580.

Zarnowitz, V. (1996), *Business Cycles: Theory, History, Indicators, and Forecasting*, University of Chicago Press, Chicago.

Zeira, J. (1994), "Informational Cycles," *Review of Economic Studies*, Vol. 61, 31-44.

Cited articles from daily press:

Wall Street Journal Europe, May 7, 2001, article: "Rx for the Economy - Let's not blame U.S. policy makers for the downturn just yet. But we might need to soon," by K. Hassett.

Wall Street Journal Europe, July 5, 2001, article: "Memory-Chip Prices Near Lows Amid Inventory Glut, Weak Demand - Some manufacturers are taking a loss with every processor they ship," by T. Uimonen.

Wall Street Journal Europe, July 6-7, 2001, article: "In this Economy, Chicken Little Might be Right - Global Contagion seen possibly severe," by M. R. Sesit.

Druck und Bindung: Strauss Offsetdruck GmbH

Contributions to Economics

Nikolaus Thumm
Intellectual Property Rights
2000. ISBN 3-7908-1329-X

Max Keilbach
Spatial Knowledge Spillovers and the Dynamics of Agglomeration and Regional Growth
2000. ISBN 3-7908-1321-4

Alexander Karmann (Ed.)
Financial Structure and Stability
2000. ISBN 3-7908-1332-X

Joos P. A. van Vugt/Jan M. Peet (Eds.)
Social Security and Solidarity in the European Union
2000. ISBN 3-7908-1334-6

Johannes Bröcker/Hayo Herrmann (Eds.)
Spatial Change and Interregional Flows in the Integrating Europe
2001. ISBN 3-7908-1344-3

Kirstin Hubrich
Cointegration Analysis in a German Monetary System
2001. ISBN 3-7908-1352-4

Nico Heerink et al. (Eds.)
Economic Policy and Sustainable Land Use
2001. ISBN 3-7908-1351-6

Friedel Bolle/Michael Carlberg (Eds.)
Advances in Behavioral Economics
2001. ISBN 3-7908-1358-3

Volker Grossmann
Inequality, Economic Growth, and Technological Change
2001. ISBN 3-7908-1364-8

Thomas Riechmann
Learning in Economics
2001. ISBN 3-7908-1384-2

Miriam Beblo
Bargaining over Time Allocation
2001. ISBN 3-7908-1391-5

Peter Meusburger/Heike Jöns (Eds.)
Transformations in Hungary
2001. ISBN 3-7908-1412-1

Claus Brand
Money Stock Control and Inflation Targeting in Germany
2001. ISBN 3-7908-1393-1

Erik Lüth
Private Intergenerational Transfers and Population Aging
2001. ISBN 3-7908-1402-4

Nicole Pohl
Mobility in Space and Time
2001. ISBN 3-7908-1380-X

Pablo Coto-Millán (Ed.)
Essays on Microeconomics and Industrial Organisation
2002. ISBN 3-7908-1390-7

Mario A. Maggioni
Clustering Dynamics and the Locations of High-Tech-Firms
2002. ISBN 3-7908-1431-8

Ludwig Schätzl/Javier Revilla Diez (Eds.)
Technological Change and Regional Development in Europe
2002. ISBN 3-7908-1460-1

Alberto Quadrio Curzio/Marco Fortis (Eds.)
Complexity and Industrial Clusters
2002. ISBN 3-7908-1471-7

Friedel Bolle/Marco Lehmann-Waffenschmidt (Eds.)
Surveys in Experimental Economics
2002. ISBN 3-7908-1472-5

Pablo Coto-Millán
General Equilibrium and Welfare
2002. ISBN 7908-1491-1

Wojciech W. Charemza/Krystyna Strzala (Eds.)
East European Transition and EU Enlargement
2002. ISBN 3-7908-1501-2

Natalja von Westernhagen
Systemic Transformation, Trade and Economic Growth
2002. ISBN 3-7908-1521-7

Josef Falkinger
A Theory of Employment in Firms
2002. ISBN 3-7908-1520-9

Engelbert Plassmann
Econometric Modelling of European Money Demand
2003. ISBN 3-7908-1522-5

Reginald Loyen/Erik Buyst/Greta Devos (Eds.)
Struggeling for Leadership: Antwerp-Rotterdam Port Competition between 1870–2000
2003. ISBN 3-7908-1524-1

Pablo Coto-Millán
Utility and Production, Second Edition
2003. ISBN 3-7908-1423-7

9 783790 815320

GPSR Compliance

The European Union's (EU) General Product Safety Regulation (GPSR) is a set of rules that requires consumer products to be safe and our obligations to ensure this.

If you have any concerns about our products, you can contact us on ProductSafety@springernature.com

In case Publisher is established outside the EU, the EU authorized representative is:

Springer Nature Customer Service Center GmbH
Europaplatz 3
69115 Heidelberg, Germany

Batch number: 10725973

Printed by Printforce, the Netherlands